TIME LIFE ® BOOKS

*This volume is one of a series that explains and demonstrates
how to prepare various types of food, and that offers in each
book an international anthology of great recipes.*

Salads

BY
THE EDITORS OF TIME-LIFE BOOKS

TIME-LIFE BOOKS/ALEXANDRIA, VIRGINIA

Cover: An assortment of crisp leaves—Boston, Bibb and buttercrunch lettuces, along with escarole—forms the basis of this classic green salad. Red and purple basil leaves provide extra color, as do bright sections of peeled tomato. Just before serving, the salad will be tossed with a mustard-flavored vinaigrette *(recipe, page 167).*

Time-Life Books Inc.
is a wholly owned subsidiary of
TIME INCORPORATED

Founder: Henry R. Luce 1898-1967

Editor-in-Chief: Henry Anatole Grunwald
President: J. Richard Munro
Chairman of the Board: Ralph P. Davidson
Executive Vice President: Clifford J. Grum
Chairman, Executive Committee: James R. Shepley
Editorial Director: Ralph Graves
Group Vice President, Books: Joan D. Manley
Vice Chairman: Arthur Temple

TIME-LIFE BOOKS INC.

Managing Editor: Jerry Korn. *Text Director:* George Constable. *Board of Editors:* Dale M. Brown, George G. Daniels, Thomas H. Flaherty Jr., Martin Mann, Philip W. Payne, Gerry Schremp, Gerald Simons. *Planning Director:* Edward Brash. *Art Director:* Tom Suzuki; *Assistant:* Arnold C. Holeywell. *Director of Administration:* David L. Harrison. *Director of Operations:* Gennaro C. Esposito. *Director of Research:* Carolyn L. Sackett; *Assistant:* Phyllis K. Wise. *Director of Photography:* Dolores A. Littles. *Production Director:* Feliciano Madrid; *Assistants:* Peter A. Inchauteguiz, Karen A. Meyerson. *Copy Processing:* Gordon E. Buck. *Quality Control Director:* Robert L. Young; *Assistant:* James J. Cox; *Associates:* Daniel J. McSweeney, Michael G. Wight. *Art Coordinator:* Anne B. Landry. *Copy Room Director:* Susan B. Galloway; *Assistants:* Celia Beattie, Ricki Tarlow

Chairman: John D. McSweeney. *President:* Carl G. Jaeger. *Executive Vice Presidents:* John Steven Maxwell, David J. Walsh. *Vice Presidents:* George Artandi, Stephen L. Bair, Peter G. Barnes, Nicholas Benton, John L. Canova, Beatrice T. Dobie, Carol Flaumenhaft, James L. Mercer, Herbert Sorkin, Paul R. Stewart

THE GOOD COOK

The original version of this book was created in London for Time-Life International (Nederland) B.V.
European Editor: Kit van Tulleken; *Design Director:* Louis Klein; *Photography Director:* Pamela Marke; *Planning Director:* Alan Lothian; *Chief of Research:* Vanessa Kramer; *Chief Sub-Editor:* Ilse Gray; *Production Editor:* Ellen Brush; *Quality Control:* Douglas Whitworth

Staff for *Salads:* *Series Coordinator:* Liz Timothy; *Head Designer:* Rick Bowring; *Text Editor:* Norman Kolpas; *Anthology Editor:* Liz Clasen; *Staff Writers:* Gillian Boucher, Jay Ferguson, Mary Harron, Thom Henvey; *Designer:* Derek Copsey; *Researchers:* Suad McCoy, Mary-Claire Hailey, Margaret Hall; *Sub-Editor:* Katie Lloyd; *Assistant Designer:* Mary Staples; *Design Assistant:* Cherry Doyle; *Editorial Department:* Anetha Besidonne, Pat Boag, Debra Dick, Philip Garner, Brian Sambrook, Molly Sutherland, Julia West, Helen Whitehorn

U.S. Staff for *Salads:* *Series Editor:* Gerry Schremp; *Designer:* Ellen Robling; *Chief Researcher:* Juanita Wilson; *Picture Editor:* Adrian Allen; *Text Editors:* Robert Menaker, Ellen Phillips; *Staff Writers:* Carol Dana, Malachy Duffy, Bonnie Kreitler; *Researchers:* Christine Schuyler (principal), Mariana Tait, Reiko Uyeshima, Maria Zacharias; *Assistant Designer:* Peg Schreiber; *Copy Coordinators:* Allan Fallow, Tonna Gibert; *Art Assistants:* Robert Herndon, Cynthia Richardson; *Picture Coordinator:* Alvin Ferrell; *Editorial Assistants:* Audrey Keir, Patricia Kim

CHIEF SERIES CONSULTANT

Richard Olney, an American, has lived and worked for some three decades in France, where he is highly regarded as an authority on food and wine. Author of *The French Menu Cookbook* and of the award-winning *Simple French Food,* he has also contributed to numerous gastronomic magazines in France and the United States, including the influential journals *Cuisine et Vins de France* and *La Revue du Vin de France.* He is a member of several distinguished gastronomic societies, including L'Académie Internationale du Vin, La Confrérie des Chevaliers du Tastevin and La Commanderie du Bontemps de Médoc et des Graves. Working in London with the series editorial staff, he has been basically responsible for the planning of this volume, and has supervised the final selection of recipes submitted by other consultants. The United States edition of The Good Cook has been revised by the Editors of Time-Life Books to bring it into complete accord with American customs and usage.

CHIEF AMERICAN CONSULTANT
Carol Cutler is the author of a number of cookbooks, including the award-winning *The Six-Minute Soufflé and Other Culinary Delights.* During the 12 years she lived in France, she studied at the Cordon Bleu and the École des Trois Gourmandes, and with private chefs. She is a member of the Cercle des Gourmettes, a long-established French food society limited to just 50 members, and is also a charter member of Les Dames d'Escoffier, Washington Chapter.

SPECIAL CONSULTANT
Jeremiah Tower is an eminent American restaurateur who lived for many years in Europe, and is a member of La Commanderie du Bontemps de Médoc et des Graves and La Jurade de Saint-Émilion. He has been largely responsible for the step-by-step photographic sequences in this volume.

PHOTOGRAPHERS
Aldo Tutino has worked in Milan, New York City and Washington, D.C. He has received a number of awards for his photographs from the New York Advertising Club.
Tom Belshaw specializes in food and still-life photography, undertaking both editorial and advertising assignments.
Alan Duns studied at the Ealing School of Photography. He specializes in food, and has contributed to major British publications.

INTERNATIONAL CONSULTANTS
GREAT BRITAIN: *Jane Grigson* has written a number of books about food and has been a cookery correspondent for the London *Observer* since 1968. *Alan Davidson* is the author of several cookbooks and the founder of Prospect Books, which specializes in scholarly publications about food and cookery. *Jean Reynolds,* who prepared many of the dishes for the photographs in this volume, is from San Francisco. She trained as a cook in the kitchens of several of France's great restaurants. FRANCE: *Michel Lemonnier,* the cofounder and vice president of Les Amitiés Gastronomiques Internationales, is a frequent lecturer on wine and vineyards. GERMANY: *Jochen Kuchenbecker* trained as a chef, but worked for 10 years as a food photographer in several European countries before opening his own restaurant in Hamburg. *Anne Brakemeier* is the co-author of a number of cookbooks. ITALY: *Massimo Alberini* is a well-known food writer and journalist, with a particular interest in culinary history. His many books include *Storia del Pranzo all'Italiana, 4000 Anni a Tavola* and *100 Ricette Storiche.* THE NETHERLANDS: *Hugh Jans* has published cookbooks and his recipes have appeared in a number of Dutch magazines. THE UNITED STATES: *Julie Dannenbaum,* the director of a cooking school in Philadelphia, Pennsylvania, also conducts cooking classes at the Gritti Palace in Venice, Italy, and at The Greenbrier in White Sulphur Springs, West Virginia. She is the author of several cookbooks and numerous magazine articles. *Judith Olney,* author of *Comforting Food* and *Summer Food,* received her culinary training in England and France. In addition to conducting cooking classes, she regularly writes articles for gastronomic magazines.

Correspondents: Elisabeth Kraemer (Bonn); Margot Hapgood, Dorothy Bacon, Lesley Coleman (London); Susan Jonas, Lucy T. Voulgaris (New York); Maria Vincenza Aloisi, Josephine du Brusle (Paris); Ann Natanson (Rome).
Valuable assistance was also provided by: Jeanne Buys (Amsterdam); Hans-Heinrich Wellmann, Gertraud Bellon (Hamburg); Judy Aspinall, Karin B. Pearce (London); Diane Asselin (Los Angeles); Bona Schmid, Maria Teresa Marenco (Milan); Carolyn T. Chubet, Miriam Hsia, Christina Lieberman (New York); Michele le Baube (Paris); Mimi Murphy (Rome).

For information about any Time-Life book, please write:
Reader Information, Time-Life Books
541 North Fairbanks Court, Chicago, Illinois 60611

Library of Congress CIP data, page 176.

CONTENTS

A Serendipitous Course

More than any other part of the menu, a salad invites the play of artful imagination. Meant to refresh, it may be served at the beginning of a meal to tempt the appetite, as a side course to provide relief from heavier dishes, or after the main course to cleanse the palate. In hot weather a salad may be the entire meal. Depending on its function, the dish may be as casual as a bowl of lettuces not half an hour from the earth, or as structured as medallions of salmon encased in a shimmering aspic; salads may, in fact, include almost any food known to cookery, in a near-infinitude of guises and arrays.

The introductory section of this book explains some of the most important elements of salad making. On pages 8-11, there are guides to the greens—lettuces, cabbages and other leaves from field and garden—that form the foundation or the substance of the majority of salads. Pages 12-15 discuss the oils and vinegars—including the best vinegars of all, which are made at home—that can be used to anoint a salad. Pages 16-17 describe how to make other basic dressings—mayonnaises and creams.

The remainder of the first half of the book consists of a series of chapters dealing with the ways salads are created from various types of foods, beginning with the simplest—salads made from raw vegetables and fruits. Later chapters demonstrate the techniques of producing cooked vegetable, meat, fish and shellfish salads. A final chapter explains how to combine these different foods with one another and with ingredients as diverse as noodles, rice and cheese to make those elaborate collations known as composed salads.

The second half of the book explores the realm of salad making in a complementary way. It consists of an anthology of more than 200 salad recipes, both old and new, that have been gathered from the cookbooks of more than 30 countries.

A brief history

The word "salad" comes from the Latin *herba salata*—salted greens. Its derivation suggests what the earliest salads must have been: freshly picked leaves, seasoned with salt to enhance their taste and eaten raw. By the time of imperial Rome, true dressings had appeared. The Romans garnished raw or cooked vegetables with fresh and dried herbs, then filmed the whole with liquid ingredients that included vinegar and oil—the staples of our modern dressings.

Salads of fresh vegetables, of course, have never lost their importance. Most people, in fact, think of a salad as a bit of the garden brought to the table. In the days before mass vegetable production, the salad was an edible symbol of summer, the an-

tithesis of the dried vegetables and salted meat that were winter fare. *The English House-wife,* a 17th Century cookbook published by Gervase Markham, included a recipe for a simple salad that is almost a paean to nature's fecundity: "First, the young Buds and Knots of all manner of wholesome Herbs at their first springings; as red Sage, Mint, Lettice, Violets, Marigolds, Spinage, and many other mixed together, and then served up to the Table with Vinegar, Sallet-Oyl and Sugar." Minus the sugar, this sort of impromptu amalgam of summer's offerings comes to the table today in the form of leafy salads or, more simply, in a plate of sun-ripened August tomatoes, garnished with nothing more than salt, oil, vinegar and perhaps a little basil.

An opposite impulse, toward formality and elaboration, began to appear in 18th Century cookbooks. An early example of the trend was the Salamongundy recommended by Hannah Glasse in *The Art of Cookery, Made Plain and Easy,* published in 1747: First, a dish was lined with lettuce. Then a mixture of sliced cold chicken, anchovies, egg yolks, chopped parsley and boiled small white onions was placed on the lettuce. Next, a vinaigrette dressing was poured over all, and finally the dish was adorned with grapes, beans or flowers *(recipe, page 135).*

Among the endless salads of this type that followed, perhaps the most luxurious is that described by the great French chef, Auguste Escoffier, in 1913. It was called *Salade des Fines Gueules*—salad for those with fine palates—and it included celery, partridge breasts, fresh truffles and crayfish tails. Its dressing was "the finest virgin olive oil of Provence and the delicious mustard of Dijon."

Escoffier's mannered arrangement would seem as far removed as possible from the sweet disorder of *The English House-wife's* "wholesome herbs," yet the same principles govern both extremes—and every salad in between. Various ingredients are combined to produce a subtle interplay of tastes and textures, then are dressed in a way that gives them a pleasing unity. Provided these principles are honored, a cook can invent successful salads from almost any materials that come to hand.

The makings of a salad

It should go without saying that in all salads, simple or elaborate, the first consideration is the quality of the ingredients. Dubious quality can be masked in many cooked dishes. Elderly vegetables, for example, still can render their flavor to stocks and stews. A salad, though, exists to display its ingredients at their almost unvarnished best.

In every case, then, a salad should be inspired by whatever

is freshest in the market on a particular day. For many vegetable salads, this means locally grown produce bought in season. Tomatoes may be readily available all year, but there is little point in making a salad from the pallid, cottony specimens sold in winter. Instead, choose a winter vegetable—Belgian endive or such roots as celeriac. Or make the salad from vegetables unaffected by the season—leeks, for instance *(pages 38-39)*.

When it comes to fashioning alliances of salad ingredients—whether meat, vegetables, fish, shellfish or grains—one general rule should be kept in mind: The more assertively flavored the food, the smaller its place in the salad should be. Strong tastes overpower mild ones. Similarly, too many strong accents cancel one another out. Careful orchestration is the goal, as exemplified by the mixed green salad demonstrated on pages 20-21. The main theme of this salad is sounded by mild-flavored lettuces such as ruby and oakleaf, but a range of minor notes—bitter, tart and sweet—are provided by small amounts of strongly flavored escarole and rocket as well as herbs and flowers *(box, below)*.

The tie that binds the various components of a salad into a coherent whole is the dressing—the sauce that coats each element and is common to all. In most cases, the dressing is nothing more than a vinaigrette, a temporary emulsion composed of oil—often olive oil—and an acid such as vinegar or lemon juice. The oil serves as a vehicle for the sharp-flavored acid, while contributing its own subtle taste; the acid's astringency intensifies the tastes of the components of the salad. The nature of the oil and its proportion to acid are variables. For a green salad of very delicate leaves, a mild golden olive oil such as the French *extra-vièrge* described on page 12 is in order, and the amount of acid should be small; strong-flavored leaves can support the more dominant flavor of green olive oil, and a more generous use of sharp-flavored vinegar.

Whether the dressing is a thin vinaigrette or a silky, thick mayonnaise or cream, it may be augmented in ways that reinforce its unifying role. In the lobster salad demonstrated on pages 70-71, for example, the greens used as a bed for the lobster meat are an integral part of the salad and should be treated as such. This is accomplished by making a sauce with the juices from the lobster itself, along with its coral (roe) and tomalley (liver), and adding some of it to the mild vinaigrette that is tossed with the leaves, thereby extending the lobster's essence to every element on the platter. Similarly, the tart cream sauce for the fruit salad demonstrated on pages 28-29 is brightened by the addition of orange juice from the fruit used in the salad.

Presentation

The success of a salad depends as much on the eye as on the palate. A salad should be a garden of bright images that prepares the diner for pleasures to come. To this end, salad ingredients may be seen as the materials of a painting: A tomato slice is a scarlet circle, an avocado slice a green crescent, a piece of cheese a golden cube. The various ingredients may be arranged in formal patterns that by careful juxtaposition of color and shape enhance the qualities of each element. Pale slices of chicken breast, for example, are unprepossessing in themselves; however, arranged in a pinwheel around a bouquet of dark green watercress and wreathed in a crimson tomato vinaigrette

A Salad Maker's Repertoire of Herbs and Flowers

Any salad—even a meat salad—ought to contain echoes of the garden, and some of the most vivid of such allusions are herbs and edible flowers. The herbs should be fresh, which usually means they must be grown at home, either in the garden or in pots in sunny windows. Flowers, too, are best if home-grown—insurance against chemically sprayed blooms. Flowers, like herbs, should be picked just before you plan to use them.

In winter, it may be necessary to forego the use of flowers and to season salads with dried herbs—steeped beforehand in the vinegar or lemon juice of the dressing to refresh their flavor. Herbs will have the finest flavor if they are dried at home; to dry them, cut the herbs just as they begin to flower, leaving their stems long, and tie them in loose bundles with string. Then hang the herbs in an airy dark place to dry for two or three weeks. After the leaves are dry, they can be plucked off and stored in sealed jars.

The choice of herbs and flowers for a salad is a matter of both taste and culinary logic. The following list should provide inspiration for experiment.

Basil leaves and flowers: Sweet and clovelike, basil's green or purple leaves and white or lavender flowers are natural complements to almost any vegetable, particularly tomatoes. While basil does not combine well with dill, it has affinities for oregano, thyme, tarragon and strong salad greens.

Borage leaves and flowers: Reminiscent of the flavor of cucumber, borage complements fish, shellfish and almost all vegetables.

Burnet leaves: The delicate hint of cucumber in this herb is best set off by mild lettuces.

Calendula (pot marigold) flowers: A little bitter in flavor, these flowers add interest to rice and pasta salads.

Chervil leaves: The anise-like taste of chervil suits any mild salad; it blends well with parsley, tarragon or chives.

Chive stems and flowers: These mild relatives of the onion make a distinctive accompaniment to any vegetable.

Coriander leaves: This assertive herb, which is also called Chinese parsley or cilantro, can be used sparingly with any robust salad.

Day-lily flowers: A natural complement to mild-flavored greens, day lilies taste like sweetened chestnuts. The only edible blossoms come from the orange *Hemerocallis fulva* and yellow *Hemerocallis flava* varieties; both these flow-

(pages 60-61), the pale meat acquires visual distinction. Similarly, a noodle salad ceases to be an amorphous jumble when the mound of noodles is framed by concentric circles of red tomatoes and green basil leaves (page 72).

If the salad is to be an informal medley of greens, it will depend less on the shapes of the ingredients than on colors—the varying greens of the different leaves and the darker accents of the herbs and flowers used to season the salad. For salads of this type, the presentation should be a performance. Modern-day Romans say that it takes four people to make the salad properly—a miser to put in the vinegar, a spendthrift to add the oil, a wise man to season the salad and a madman to toss it. All these characters, of course, reside in the person of the host or hostess, and properly done, the mixing of the salad with its dressing—which must be done at the last minute to prevent the dressing from wilting the leaves—can be one of the happiest rituals of the dining room. "Tossing" is something of a misnomer. In reality, the ingredients are turned gently from top to bottom and from side to side until all are shining with dressing.

The choice of platters, bowls and utensils is another important facet of presentation. For formal salads, ceramic or glass serving platters are the best choice. Salad bowls for tossing should be roomy to allow easy turning of the ingredients. Glass, ceramic and clear, hard plastic are the best materials for bowls because they are easy to clean. Wooden bowls, especially those carved from olive wood, are beautiful objects prized by many salad lovers, but the wood, being porous, is difficult to clean, and in time it may take on the taste of rancid oil.

Blunt wooden or clear plastic salad servers are useful implements for tossing most salads without damaging their elements. But the surest way to avoid bruising delicate ingredients such as fresh green leaves is to turn the salad with your hands.

Wine with salad

As is well known, sharply acid tastes such as those of a vinaigrette or even of a lemon-and-cream dressing conflict with wine. Wine is therefore not usually served with the highly flavored vegetable or leaf salads that follow the main course of a meal. However, if the salad begins the meal (or is the meal) and the dressing's acidity is moderated, a rosé or a simple young red wine—a Beaujolais or a fruity California Zinfandel, for example—can provide a friendly competition of tastes. Fine, subtly flavored wines would be wasted in this situation.

When salads include meat, poultry, fish and eggs or cheese, and the dressing is mild, the choice of beverages broadens. The potato and bacon salad demonstrated on page 41, for example, might well be served with beer or a plain hearty wine such as a Côtes du Rhône or an Italian Dolcetto. A *vitello tonnato (pages 54-55)* —slices of poached veal swathed in tuna-flavored mayonnaise—would not overwhelm a finer wine such as a Meursault or a California Chardonnay, although an Italian would serve this dish with a simpler Frascati. If the salad is cold duck or other poultry, a dry rosé or a Sauvignon Blanc from California could be a perfect, light accompaniment.

In general, the beverage should reflect the approach to the salads themselves. More than any other dish, a salad is a creative improvisation; by the same token, the beverage that complements a salad best may well be selected by an inspired guess.

---

ers should be eaten the day they bloom.

Dill leaves and seeds: This herb's tart-flavored leaves are particularly attractive with fish and shellfish; among vegetables, cucumber and potato are dill's great allies. Dill seeds are strong in fragrance and good in potato salads.

Fennel leaves: Another herb for fish, common fennel has an anise flavor that also goes well with spinach. The leaves of the sweet, or Florence, fennel grown as a vegetable have little flavor.

Hyssop leaves and flowers: The refreshing bitterness of this herb's flowers allies nicely with salads that include fresh greens and hard-boiled eggs.

Lovage leaves and seeds: A taste that is reminiscent of both celery and parsley distinguishes this herb, which complements both vegetables and seafood.

Marjoram leaves and flowers: Fragrant and mild, sweet and pot marjoram are best paired with delicate greens.

Mint leaves: A favorite in the Middle East, mint is good with cucumber and adds lightness to salads based on carrots, grains and all kinds of fruit.

Nasturtium leaves and flowers: The pepperiness of this plant sets off fruits and lettuces.

Oregano leaves and flowers: A mildly peppery herb traditional as a garnish for tomatoes, oregano blends well with basil, thyme or savory.

Parsley leaves: For fragrance, choose flat-leafed—also called Italian—parsley; it blends well with almost any salad, and has a special affinity for garlic.

Rose flowers: Sweet in flavor, rose petals complement any fruit or green salad. For the most pronounced flavors, choose the most fragrant roses.

Rosemary leaves: A good partner for meats, rosemary may be used with restraint on cold poultry or lamb; it is sometimes sprinkled on salads that contain oranges.

Savory leaves and flowers: This robust herb is a good choice for bean salads. Summer savory is sweeter than its peppery relative, winter savory.

Tarragon leaves: A classic element of the fines herbes mixture described on page 20, tarragon has a strong anise flavor. It should be used sparingly—alone or with basil, burnet or thyme.

Thyme leaves and flowers: Common thyme's light bitterness enhances most vegetables; lemon thyme gives salads a delightful fragrance.

Violet leaves and flowers: The delicate flavor of these petals and leaves blends well with fruits and mild greens.

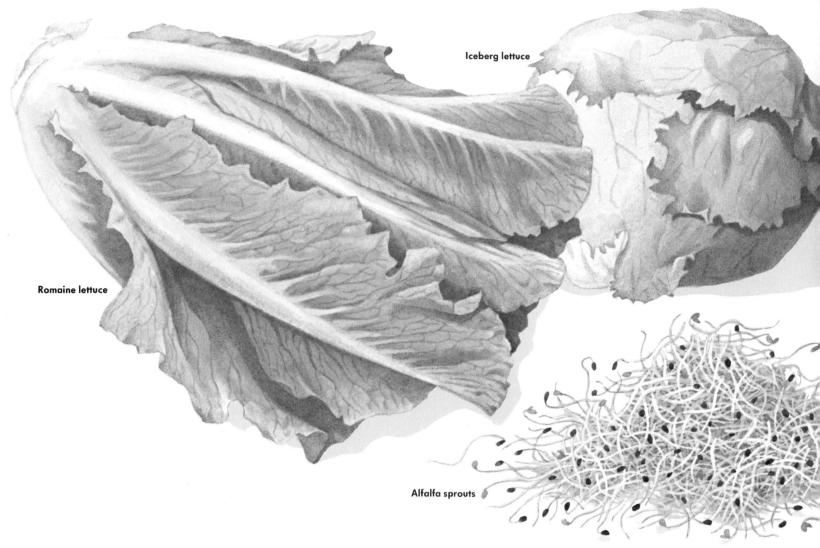

Iceberg lettuce

Romaine lettuce

Alfalfa sprouts

The Basic Resource: Mild-flavored Greens

Lettuces and other greens, the fundamentals of salad making, range from mild-flavored varieties, many of which are shown here, to the more assertive types described on pages 10-11.

Iceberg, the most common mild lettuce, has exceptionally crisp, circular, tightly furled leaves. It suffers, however, from an almost total lack of flavor. Romaine lettuce, on the other hand, has loosely packed, oblong leaves that are crisp and mildly pungent. Loosely furled butterhead lettuces—including Boston and the smaller Bibb—have soft textures and subtly sweet flavors. Like iceberg, romaine and butterhead lettuces are available year round. Loose-leafed lettuces such as notched oakleaf and red-

edged ruby also are sweet and rather soft. Delicate oakleaf is found mainly in local markets in the spring and summer; ruby lettuce is available all year.

Among the other mild greens, spinach, with its faintly musky flavor and coarse texture, is available all year. Corn salad—so called because it springs up in cornfields—is a perishable green found in local markets in fall; its leaves are sweet. Sprouts run the gamut from the delicate seedlings of alfalfa *(above)* to the coarse shoots of mung beans; all contribute crispness and a faintly nutty tang. They are sold year round in health-food stores and some supermarkets.

When buying greens, avoid leaves that are yellow, spotted, oversized or limp; these are generally past their prime.

Sprouts should be crisp and free of the brown spots that signal decay.

Greens lose flavor quickly; store them in the refrigerator for no longer than two days. To allow air circulation, wrap them in perforated plastic bags.

Before use, sprouts should be washed in a strainer under cold running water. Other greens require a more thorough cleansing to remove grit. Separate the leaves, drop them into a bowl of cold water and plunge them down several times. Transfer them to a second bowl of water and repeat the process. Then lift out the leaves a few at a time (pouring the whole batch into a colander to drain would trap grit in them) and dry them carefully, as shown on page 20.

Spinach

Boston lettuce

Bibb lettuce

Corn salad

Oakleaf lettuce

Ruby lettuce

9

Assertive Leaves for Tangy Effects

The leaves shown on these pages share a pleasant sharpness that can add a tingle to the salad bowl. Some are less widely cultivated than the milder leaves described on the previous pages, but their lively tastes make any extra shopping worth the effort.

Members of the chicory family, shown below and at right, are in peak supply from late summer through the winter. These leaves have an attractive bitterness—and a confusion of names. Satiny Belgian endive—also called witloof chicory—is the mildest; red Verona chicory is a little stronger. Chicory (or curly-leafed endive) and escarole (or broad-leafed endive) are so sharp-tasting that they are commonly used only as accents.

Cabbage *(far right)* is readily available year round. The crinkly-leafed Savoy is slightly milder than the smooth-leafed green and red cabbages.

Tart rocket *(center),* faintly lemony sorrel, piquant purslane and pungent dandelion are spring and summer leaves; peppery watercress can be found all year. Rocket is usually sold in Italian markets as *arugula* or *rugula;* the other small leaves may be purchased from a well-stocked greengrocer or grown from seed.

Since all of these leaves deteriorate with age, choose young, brightly colored plants. Refrigerate them in perforated plastic bags and try to use them the day you buy them; even cabbage will not keep much more than a week. Most leaves are separated, washed and dried as described on page 8. Cabbage, however, needs only rinsing, trimming and coring *(page 24).* Belgian endive must be cored.

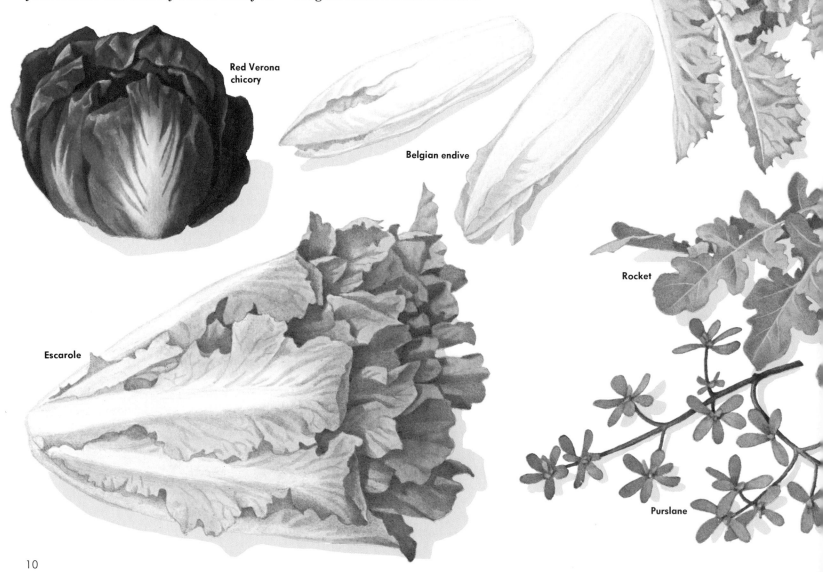

Chicory

Red Verona chicory

Belgian endive

Rocket

Escarole

Purslane

Red cabbage

Savoy cabbage

Green cabbage

Sorrel

Watercress

Dandelion

A Spectrum of Vinegars and Oils

Red wine vinegar

Chinese rice vinegar

Sherry vinegar

Aceto balsamico

White wine vinegar

The character and quality of almost any salad dressing depends on its basic ingredients—vinegar and oil. Each is available in enough different versions to suit every type of salad.

Among the vinegars, for example, the best types for dressing salads are those made by fermenting red or white wine into vinegar in wood barrels. This method of vinegar making, known as the Orleans process after the French city where it has been practiced since the 17th Century, produces a vinegar with a faintly nutty undertaste and a fruity aroma. It is richer than vinegars made from grains or cider, and it has more character than wine vinegars that are created by artificially accelerated fermentation. Both France and California make vinegars by the Orleans process; they also can be made at home *(pages 14-15)*.

Robust red wine vinegar is the better complement to meat salads or assertive leaves. More delicate white wine vinegar is well suited to sweet lettuce salads. Both types may be infused with berries or herbs *(box, opposite; recipe, page 167)*.

Several imported vinegars available at specialty stores and ethnic markets give an exotic note to a dressing. Italian *aceto balsamico* (aromatic vinegar), for example, has a high acid content, kept in balance by the use of a sweet wine as its basis and by long aging, which mellows flavor. Spanish sherry vinegar has a rich body and sweet aftertaste that complements fruit and cheese salads. Chinese and Japanese rice vinegars are excellent with delicate salads of fish, seafood and cooked vegetables; the Chinese version has a sharp, clean acidic taste; the Japanese is milder and sweeter.

Vinegars are not the only acidic ele-

ments used in salads. In dressings for the most delicate green leaves, light, fruity lemon or lime juice may provide all or part of the acid.

The oils suited to salads vary as much as the acids, and the preeminent salad oil—olive—comes in several forms. To extract their oils, olives are crushed and then pressed. Successive pressings produce increasingly inferior oil, because they require the addition of hot water or chemical solvents that alter its flavor and texture. Oil labeled "first pressing virgin," "cold-pressing virgin" or *"extra-vièrge"* is the best choice for salads, fruity and soft on the palate. If extracted from ripe olives, it will be sweet in taste and golden in color. When made from partially ripe olives—the kind of oil preferred in Italy—it will have a slightly sharper taste and a greenish hue.

12

Golden olive oil

Green olive oil

Walnut oil

Peanut oil

Second pressings produce the less expensive, more harshly flavored oil labeled "fine" or "extra fine." Its flavor may be improved by the addition of garlic or herbs *(box, opposite)*. When the olives are pressed a third time, the result is labeled merely "pure olive oil" and is too bland and greasy for salad dressings.

Walnuts or hazelnuts as well may be pressed to extract oil. Possessing a distinctive, nutty flavor, their oils give a delicate balance to bitter leaves such as chicory. Unlike olive oil, which will last at least six months if tightly closed and kept in a cool, dark place, walnut or hazelnut oil turns rancid after a few weeks.

Chemically refined peanut, corn and safflower oils keep even better than olive oil and are much less expensive. Most lack character, however: They may be used for dressings such as mayonnaise, where blandness is sometimes desirable.

Fruit-flavored Vinegar

Straining the berries. In an enameled or stainless-steel pan, bring 1 quart [1 liter] of wine vinegar and 2 cups [½ liter] of berries — here, raspberries — to a simmer. Pour into a crock or jar, cover, and steep for 10 to 20 days. Strain through muslin into bottles.

Herb-infused Oil

Combining the ingredients. Half-fill a bottle with fresh herb leaves — in this case basil. Then fill the bottle almost to its rim with olive oil. Cover, steep for at least a week, then strain, pressing the herb leaves lightly to extract the flavors. Store in a snugly covered container.

Producing Your Own Wine Vinegar

The way to obtain the best possible vinegar for use in salad dressings is to make it at home. Because you control the quality of the ingredients, the product will be far superior to almost any vinegar you can buy, more than repaying your investment in time and materials.

Vinegar (from the French *vin aigre,* or sour wine) forms when an alcoholic liquid is exposed to bacteria of the Acetobacter group. The bacteria gradually convert the alcohol in the liquid to acetic acid, turning the liquid into vinegar. To achieve this metamorphosis, you will need a proper vessel, a bacteria culture and, for the finest flavored vinegar, wine —red, white or fortified.

The ideal vinegar-making vessel allows ventilation: The bacteria require oxygen to change alcohol to acid. The container also should have an opening for pouring in wine and a spigot for drawing off vinegar. If you cannot find a vinegar barrel, a wine keg, available from wine-making suppliers or kitchen-equipment shops, can be adapted to your purposes *(box, opposite).* The 2-gallon [8-liter] keg shown is more than sufficient for the needs of an average family. Chestnut or oak kegs are the best; the tannic acid in these woods imparts a mellow, nutty flavor to the vinegar.

Acetobacter bacteria are present in the air, along with other, less beneficial micro-organisms that may also act on the wine. To give Acetobacter a competitive advantage, the vinegar-making process usually begins with a starter culture that is put into the keg. A bottle of unpasteur-

Flavoring homemade vinegar. Put the flavorings — here, clockwise from the top, rosemary, sage, oregano, bay leaves, garlic and thyme — into an earthenware or enameled pot. Fill the pot with vinegar drawn from the keg and heated just to simmering. Cover, and steep until the flavor is to your taste. Meanwhile, refill the keg with leftover wines that have been stored in tightly corked bottles, and fill the bottles with more leftover wine — shown in the carafe.

zed vinegar, available at specialty food stores, contains enough living bacteria to perform this function. Alternatively, anyone who makes vinegar can give you either a piece of the culture visible on the surface as a white veil or part of the more concentrated culture called the "mother," which is visible just below the surface as a gelatinous mass. If you use a veil or mother as a culture, add it after filling the keg with wine.

The next addition to the keg is the wine. Since the vinegar will mirror its character, the wine should be of good quality, dry rather than sweet. A young Beaujolais or Chenin Blanc from California makes a light vinegar; a mature Bordeaux will yield vinegar with a more robust, complex flavor. For economy's sake, you can use bottle ends and unfinished glasses of red and white wine, mixed if you like. Fortified wines such as sherry must be diluted by half with water, then fermented separately. Store leftovers in corked bottles until you are ready to make the vinegar; by excluding air, you shut out undesirable bacteria that might adversely affect the flavor of the wines.

When you first pour in the wine, fill the keg to just beneath the ventilation hole, then leave it undisturbed at a temperature of 75° to 80° F. [about 25° C.]. After about a month—as soon as the liquid tastes more of vinegar than of wine—you can draw off liquid if you wish. The vinegar will not reach its full strength, however, for another month or two. To avoid unnecessarily disturbing the fermentation process, always draw off a large amount of vinegar at a time and replace it with an equal amount of wine.

You can use the vinegar straight from the keg or flavor it with herbs (left). Let herbs steep from 10 days to a month, depending on how pronounced a flavor you like. Then strain the vinegar through cheesecloth (page 13).

Store the vinegar in full, tightly corked bottles laid on their sides in a cool, dark place. Shutting out air arrests the acetic reaction so that the vinegar will keep indefinitely. As you use it, the vinegar in a partially full bottle may develop a culture again; the white veil is harmless and can be strained out.

A Wine Keg Modified for Vinegar

Before you adapt a new keg for vinegar making, soak it to swell the wood and prevent leakage. Remove the wooden plug from the bunghole at the top, immerse the keg in water and leave it for two or three days.

After the keg has been drained, prepare a ventilation hole (Steps 1 and 2) that will guarantee the constant circulation of air necessary to promote the growth of the acetic culture. Then drive the spigot into place with a mallet. Finally, you must provide a means of adding wine without submerging the culture. Two items are needed: a bunghole cork and a plastic or glass funnel with a neck long enough to extend below the spigot level (Step 3). The cork is available where kegs are sold, the funnel from laboratory suppliers.

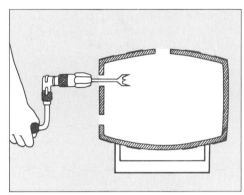

1 Providing ventilation. Using a brace and bit or an electric drill with a spade bit, drill a hole 1 inch [2½ cm.] in diameter through the face of the keg above the spigot hole and as close as possible to the keg's upper rim.

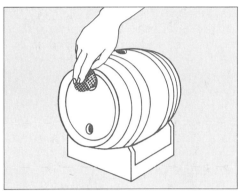

2 Covering the hole. Using heavy scissors, cut a circle about 2 inches [5 cm.] across out of fine plastic screen. Secure the screen over the ventilation hole with tacks. Insert the spigot into its hole and tap it gently but firmly with a mallet to seat it tightly.

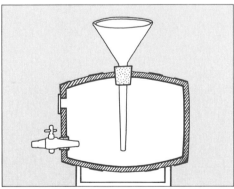

3 Inserting the funnel. Set the bunghole cork in a vise to hold it steady. Drill a hole just wide enough to hold the neck of a long funnel through the center. Slide the funnel into the cork and push the cork firmly into the bunghole.

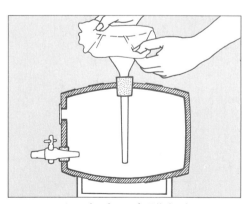

4 Covering the funnel. Fill the keg with a bottle of unpasteurized vinegar and enough wine to come to just below the ventilation hole. Cover the funnel with plastic film or a clean cloth to keep dust and dirt out of the liquid.

The Primary Dressings — Avenues to Improvisation

The traditional dressings for salads are vinaigrettes, thickened creams and the egg-and-oil emulsions that are known as mayonnaises. Each type is the foundation for dozens of variations.

Basic vinaigrette, for example, is a mixture of vinegar or lemon juice, oil, and salt and pepper—usually blended at the last minute. Vinaigrette often is enhanced by garlic, mustard or chopped fresh herbs *(recipe, page 167)*; other possible additions include puréed tomato, juice from broiled peppers or chopped hard-boiled egg.

Unlike vinaigrette, the cream and the egg dressings must be prepared in advance. The lemon-and-cream dressing in the demonstration at right *(recipe, page 165)* is made by whipping heavy cream —very gradually, to prevent curdling— into lemon juice. Ground mustard, ginger or cayenne will lend a touch of fire. Covered and refrigerated, the dressing will keep for two or three hours.

Another variation on thickened cream is the dressing demonstrated below *(recipe, page 166)*, which starts with tart cream, an Americanized *crème fraîche*. To make it, heavy cream is fermented by the addition of an agent containing the requisite bacteria: fresh commercial sour cream or the cultured buttermilk used here. Fermentation thickens the cream, which will keep, refrigerated, for a week.

(If the cream becomes too thick to be pourable, it can be thinned with milk.) After citrus juice is whisked into the cream, the dressing should be used within a few hours. With this dressing, the choices for extra flavoring range from fresh herbs to broiled, chopped peppers.

The making of mayonnaise, an equally rich and versatile dressing, is a simple matter of whisking together egg yolks and oil. The ingredients will emulsify naturally *(demonstration, opposite; recipe, page 166)*. Only two precautions need be observed. To ensure that an emulsion forms, ingredients and utensils must be at room temperature. And, most important, the oil must be whisked gradually into the beaten yolks so that the yolks have time to absorb it. Adding too much oil too fast will cause the emulsion to break, or liquefy. Fortunately, this mishap is easy to rectify: Beat a fresh yolk in a separate bowl and gradually whisk in the broken mayonnaise.

A food processor or blender produces mayonnaise quickly. To achieve proper consistency, however, the dressing must include the white of the egg *(recipe, page 166)*, which diminishes its richness.

Either type of mayonnaise can be flavored with herbs, chopped gherkins or spices, but the most famous variation probably is aioli, made by mixing the egg with garlic before adding the oil.

Lemony Whipped Cream

Making the dressing. Whisk salt, pepper and lemon juice together until the salt dissolves. Whisking constantly, pour heavy cream —2 cups [½ liter] to the juice of two large lemons —into the bowl in a thin stream *(top)*. Continue whisking until the dressing is just thick enough to fall from the whisk as a thin, soft ribbon *(bottom)*.

Tart Cultured Cream

1 **Heating the cream.** In an enameled pan, stir the buttermilk and cream over low heat until the mixture reaches 85° F. [30° C.]. Check the temperature with a meat thermometer.

2 **Incubating.** Pour the cream into a jar or a crock. Cover, and leave it at room temperature (60° to 85° F. [15° to 30° C.]) for six to eight hours; the lower the temperature, the longer the incubation.

3 **Checking the consistency.** When a spoonful of cream dropped on the surface forms a ring, the cream is ready. To turn it into a dressing, whisk in lime or lemon juice, salt and pepper.

Mayonnaise: A Rich Emulsion of Egg Yolks and Oil

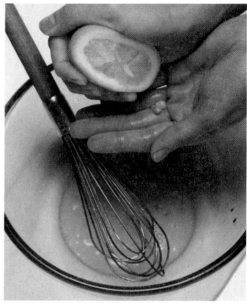

1 **Separating the eggs.** Crack each eggshell on the side of a small bowl. Empty the egg onto the closed fingers of one hand *(above)* and let the white slip through your fingers into the bowl. Put the yolk into a larger mixing bowl.

2 **Whisking the yolks.** To steady the bowl, set it on a damp, folded towel. Add salt to the yolks. Beat the yolks with a whisk for a few minutes, until they are smooth in texture and pale in color.

3 **Adding lemon juice.** To add a hint of sharpness and make the dressing more stable, add a little vinegar or, as here, lemon juice, squeezing the lemon over your fingers to hold back seeds. Whisk to combine yolks and juice.

4 **Adding the oil.** For easy pouring, put the oil in a bottle that enables you to control the flow by keeping your thumb over the mouth. Dribble in the oil *(above, left),* whisking continuously. When the mixture starts to thicken, whisk in the oil in a thin stream *(center).* When more than half of the oil has been added, increase the flow to a thicker stream *(right).*

5 **Finishing the dressing.** Add oil until the mayonnaise forms soft peaks *(above).* Add more lemon juice or seasoning if desired. Refrigerated, the dressing will keep for three days or so.

1
Vegetables and Fruits
The Delights of Freshness

Perhaps the best-known salads are those that bring the garden to the table—salads composed of leaves or vegetables or fruits, changed as little as possible from their natural states and united in a dish by the subtlest of dressings. Making these salads is the work of an instant: The best are improvisations for which there are no recipes. But successful improvisation depends on an educated eye and palate. The cook must learn to choose only the finest, ripest ingredients—their quality, after all, cannot be disguised—and these ingredients must be combined in ways that take full advantage of tastes, textures and colors.

Lettuce salads, perhaps the archetypes of the genre, suggest the range of possibilities. A lettuce salad may be nothing more than leaves from a tender head of Bibb, their sweet taste emphasized by the thinnest coating of oil and lemon juice. For an elaboration on this basic theme, the soft leaves may be accented by tart, crisp greens such as chicory or escarole. And other ingredients may be added to lettuces in small quantities, so as not to dominate the greens: Salads of this kind may include nuts, the grated cheese, croutons and anchovies of a Caesar salad (*pages 22-23*), or the flowers and herbs shown in the riotous display at left. Most lettuce salads are best dressed with a vinaigrette; a heavy sauce would overwhelm the fragile leaves.

Denser vegetables and fruits, from carrots to pineapples, offer a wider range of tastes and textures than leaves, hence a broader basis for creativity. Slices of ripe tomatoes, still warm from the sun and served with just a sprinkling of salt, are supremely pleasurable fare, but their sweet flavor will be thrown into relief by onion slices, and their texture will be emphasized if they are combined with cucumbers made crisp by layering them with ice cubes (*page 26*). Contrast is not always the rule, however. In some salads—such as the tropical fruit assemblage shown on pages 30-31—the goal is smoothness and blended flavors.

Vegetables and fruits may be bathed in a vinaigrette, of course, but they have enough body to support such heavier dressings as mayonnaise and tart cream (*pages 16-17*). And in certain cases, these rich dressings have a practical function: When vegetables, including leaves, are sliced into ribbon-like strips, the dressing—unlike a vinaigrette—serves to bind the disparate elements into a coherent whole (*pages 24-25*).

A garnish of edible blossoms — including petals of yellow and orange nasturtiums, roses, tiny purple thyme and gold day lilies — transforms a salad of mixed greens into a colorful centerpiece. Crossed salad implements separate the leaves from a vinaigrette dressing in the bottom of the bowl — thus preventing wilted leaves — until the salad is ready to be tossed and served.

Variations on a Green Theme

A perfect green salad is a model of simplicity. It consists of nothing but fresh lettuce leaves or other greens, sprinkled with herbs and glossed with a light dressing—vinaigrette is the classic choice—designed to accent the flavor of the leaves while adding just the slightest sting.

Such a salad may contain only one type of green, in which case it is best made with mild, sweet lettuces such as Bibb (*top row, right*). If you combine greens, aim for contrasts of color, flavor and texture. For example, the salad demonstrated at bottom is based on sweet buttercrunch and oakleaf lettuces, but includes tangy escarole and rocket, added in small quantities to prevent them from being overpowering. Ruby lettuce contributes color, as do edible flower petals.

The leaves for a green salad must be washed (*page 8*) to eliminate grit. They should be dried with towels (*top*) or in a salad spinner (*bottom*); any moisture would dilute the dressing. Washing and drying are best done just before a salad is made; however, prepared leaves will keep for as long as two or three days if they are interlayered with paper towels and refrigerated in plastic bags.

Small leaves may be tumbled whole into the salad bowl, but large leaves are easiest to manage if they are torn up. Other flavorings are added at the same time in small amounts. For an aromatic bouquet, try the fines herbes of French cookery: chopped parsley, chervil, tarragon and chives. Stronger flavorings, such as garlic, should be used sparingly.

Dressings for green salads should be kept to the bare essentials: oil, vinegar or lemon juice, and salt and pepper. For mild leaves, allow four to five parts oil to one part vinegar or lemon juice. Assertive greens benefit from robust dressings with an oil-to-vinegar ratio of 3 to 1.

Use only enough dressing to give the leaves a thin coat (about ½ cup [125 ml.] for each quart [1 liter] of greens). To prevent wilting, mix the dressing with the greens at the moment of serving. However, you can make dressing up to half an hour in advance; one technique is to blend the dressing in the salad bowl and then add the leaves, separating them from the liquid with salad spoons (*Step 3, bottom*) until tossing.

An Exercise in Simplicity

1 Preparing fines herbes. Stem and wash fresh parsley, chervil and tarragon, rinse chives, and dry all of the herbs on paper towels. Gather them into a compact bunch. With a large, sharp knife, cut the leaves into thin slices. Steady the blade with your free hand and rock it over the herbs to chop them.

2 Preparing the lettuce. Separate and wash the lettuce leaves—Bibb lettuce is used here. Place the leaves between two kitchen or paper towels and roll them up gently to dry them. Pile the leaves in a salad bowl and sprinkle them with the fines herbes.

A Bouquet of Leaves and Flowers

1 Washing the greens. Separate the leaves of head lettuces by pulling them one by one from the stalks. Twist off the stalk tips of loose-leafed lettuces (*above*); the leaves will fall away. After discarding bruised or wilted leaves, wash the greens in a bowl of cold water.

2 Drying the greens. Transfer the washed leaves to an empty bowl so that you can sort through them, discarding tough stems and tearing the leaves to a uniform size. Put the greens in a salad spinner. Spin the leaves. Remove the cover of the spinner, fluff up the leaves with your hands, then spin them again.

3 **Mixing a vinaigrette.** Put salt and pepper and vinegar in a serving spoon. Hold the spoon over the salad and stir with a fork to dissolve the salt *(above, left)*. Empty the spoon over the salad, then pour in oil *(above, right)*. Empty the spoon and refill it three or four times. Turn the leaves to coat them *(right)*.

3 **Making dressing.** Mash garlic with salt and pepper in a bowl. Add vinegar and stir to dissolve the salt, then add oil. Cross salad spoons over the dressing and place the leaves on top. Garnish with herbs and edible petals — here, parsley, chives, burnet, tarragon, basil, lovage, day lilies, nasturtiums and roses.

Expanding the Bounds of Taste and Texture

A salad composed primarily of greens may be amplified in myriad ways by adding small amounts of other ingredients: croutons, sliced vegetables, nuts, grated cheese, and slivers of meat, fish or bacon. As with an all-leaf green salad, a vinaigrette is the most appropriate dressing, but it may be enriched with hard-boiled egg yolks or a whole, barely cooked egg.

One classic salad of this type—named for a Tijuana chef who invented it in the early 1920s—is the Caesar salad demonstrated here (recipe, page 95). Only one type of green is used: flavorful romaine lettuce hearts, their crunchy leaves left whole because the salad is traditionally eaten with the fingers. Parmesan cheese, anchovies and garlic-flavored croutons give the salad pleasing tastes and textures, and its lemon vinaigrette dressing is thickened with a coddled egg.

The juiciest and tastiest anchovies are whole ones preserved in salt; these are available in cans or by weight at markets that carry imported Mediterranean foods. They must be filleted and soaked in water to remove their salt and soften them (box, right). Lacking salt anchovies, you can use oil-packed flat fillets. They do not require boning or soaking in water, but the briny oil that covers them must be carefully rinsed off. Before chopping anchovies of either sort, steep them in some oil to flavor it for the dressing.

While the anchovies marinate, prepare the other ingredients. Besides crisping lettuce (Step 1, top row), squeezing lemon juice and grating cheese, you must sauté bread cubes, either with garlic and oil, as here, or in oil in which peeled garlic cloves have steeped overnight.

The final preliminary is coddling the egg that thickens the vinaigrette. Bring an egg to room temperature, immerse it in boiling water, cover the pan, remove it from the heat, and let the egg cook just one minute—long enough to barely set it. Crack the egg into a small dish.

For the presentation (part of the pleasure this salad offers), all of the prepared ingredients should be arranged within easy reach of the bowl of leaves. Assembling the salad is a simple matter of rolling the leaves gently together with the other ingredients as they are added in succession (Steps 4 and 5, opposite).

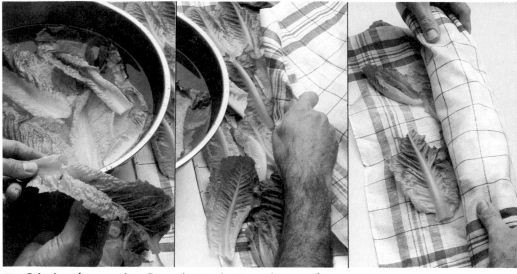

1 **Crisping the romaine.** Rinse the tender, inner leaves of romaine in cold water and break off the tough bottom end of each leaf (left). Place the leaves on a towel and pat them dry (center), working the towel into the creases of the leaves to remove all the water. After the leaves have been dried, gently roll up the towel (right) and place the roll in the refrigerator to crisp the romaine.

Dealing with Salt Anchovies

1 **Filleting anchovies.** Rinse the fish in cold water. With your nail, split open the belly of each anchovy; pull it apart into two fillets, leaving the bones on one. Place the boneless fillet in cold water. Slide your thumb under the backbone that runs down the center of the other fillet and peel away the backbone and ribs. Add the fillet to the water.

2 **Marinating the fillets.** Soak the fillets in the water until they are soft and do not taste oversalty. (Thirty minutes' soaking is usually enough.) Dry the fillets on paper towels, then marinate them one hour in olive oil to flavor the oil. Drain the fillets before use, reserving the marinade for the salad dressing.

2 **Preparing the croutons.** Remove the crusts from firm-textured white bread and cut the bread into ½-inch [1-cm.] cubes. In a shallow pan over medium heat, cook peeled garlic cloves in a thin layer of olive oil until they begin to color. Add enough bread cubes to cover the bottom of the pan.

3 **Sautéing the croutons.** Jerk the pan back and forth to turn the cubes. As soon as they have browned, transfer the croutons to paper towels to drain. Sauté the remaining bread cubes in small batches, adding more oil if necessary. If the garlic begins to burn, pick out the cloves with a fork.

4 **Assembling.** Place the lettuce in a salad bowl. Pour in a little olive oil and gently roll the leaves to coat them; season with pepper and salt. Then chop and add anchovies, a spoonful of the anchovy-enriched oil *(box, opposite)* and lemon juice. Roll the leaves again.

5 **Finishing.** Add the coddled egg and the grated Parmesan and roll them with the leaves. Then garnish the salad with the croutons, rolling it a final time. To prevent wilting, serve the salad immediately on chilled plates. Add a final pinch of salt and pepper to each salad to bring out flavors.

Cutting Vegetables Down to Size

Shredding is a quick and easy way to transform many firm-textured vegetables into valuable salad ingredients. For example, raw cabbage leaves—difficult to separate and ordinarily too thick to eat whole—acquire instant usability when they are shredded into easily managed strips. Tough root vegetables such as carrots and celeriac become supple slivers when shredded. Nor is the treatment reserved for tougher vegetables. Tender greens such as lettuce or spinach may be shredded simply as an attractive alternative to serving the leaves whole.

Shredding can be done with a knife, a grater, a rotary shredder or a food processor, depending on the form and firmness of the vegetable. In the classic coleslaw shown here *(recipe, page 91)*, a green cabbage is halved, cored and sliced thin so that its leaves fall in shreds. The carrots that form its major accompaniment could also be cut with a knife, but a box grater or rotary shredder *(Step 3)* produces the finest of shreds.

Other kinds of raw vegetables may call for different shredding techniques *(box, opposite)*. The loosely packed leaves of lettuce and other salad greens, for example, are separated, stacked and sliced to the desired thickness; these strips, known as a chiffonade, are either dressed and served on their own or used as a bed on which molded and mayonnaise-bound salads can be presented.

Celeriac is a special case. Not only is it tough, but it discolors rapidly when cut. Raw celeriac may be shredded with a grater, a rotary shredder, or the food processor used here. To keep the celeriac shreds from turning brown, dress them immediately with a sauce that has been made in advance—a lemon-and-cream dressing *(page 16; recipe, page 165)* flavored with a little mustard, perhaps, or the coleslaw dressing that is demonstrated on these pages.

When shredding is applied to cooked vegetables such as baked beets, boiled carrots or broiled peppers, gentler tactics are in order. The flesh has been softened by the cooking and should be cut into strips with a well-sharpened knife.

1 **Coring the cabbage.** Discard any blemished outer leaves from the cabbage. With a sturdy knife, cut the cabbage in half. Cut out the solid, wedge-shaped core from each half.

2 **Cutting the shreds.** Place the cored cabbage flat side down. Starting at the end opposite the core, slice across the cabbage to make thin shreds, guiding the knife with your knuckles *(above)*. Pile the shreds in a mixing bowl.

6 **Serving the coleslaw.** Serve the coleslaw at once or, if you prefer, cover and refrigerate it for one hour so that the acids in the dressing soften the vegetables and the seasonings permeate the cabbage and carrots. Garnish with finely chopped parsley.

3 **Shredding the carrots.** Wash and peel the carrots. Cut the carrots into 2-inch [5-cm.] sections and pass them through a rotary shredder, using a julienne disk (above). Add the shredded carrots to the bowl.

4 **Mixing the dressing.** First prepare mayonnaise (page 17). Then, for a sharper flavor, add Dijon mustard and freshly squeezed lemon juice (above). Stir the mixture well, taste the mayonnaise and correct its seasoning.

5 **Tossing the coleslaw.** Pour the dressing over the shredded vegetables. Toss the coleslaw with your hands or two large spoons until all of the shreds are well coated with the dressing. Transfer the salad to a serving dish.

Shredding Techniques for Special Cases

Slicing a chiffonade. Separate the lettuce leaves — in this case, Boston — and wash and dry them. Stack several leaves at a time and slice them into strips of the desired width. If the leaves are thin, you can slice them easily by rolling them up into a cylinder after stacking, and then slicing the cylinder crosswise.

Cutting beet sticks. Wash the beets but do not trim or peel them. Coat them with oil and bake at 325° F. [160° C.] for one and a half to four hours, depending on their size and age. When they feel tender, remove and cool them, then peel them. Cut the beets into slices of the desired thickness, then cut each slice into sticks.

Shredding celeriac. Prepare a thick, lemony mayonnaise or cream dressing. Carefully peel off the skin of the gnarled celeriac. Quarter the vegetable and cut out any spongy core (above). If necessary, cut the quarters into smaller pieces, then shred them in a food processor. Toss the shreds immediately with the dressing.

Altering Texture with Salt or Ice

To serve various salad-making purposes, the textures of raw vegetables may be altered by two straightforward techniques. Salting softens a vegetable by drawing out its excess liquid; icing crisps the vegetable by restoring the water it has lost since picking.

Salting is a necessity for ripe tomatoes that will be accompanied by a creamy dressing, such as the one in this demonstration; if left unsalted, the vegetables would exude enough juice to dilute the dressing. Slices of cucumber, zucchini and yellow squash also may be salted to give them an unexpected suppleness.

The details of salting may vary slightly with the type of vegetable. Tomatoes, for example, should be peeled, seeded and sliced thin so that a sprinkling of salt can draw moisture from the greatest possible surface area. The slices are placed in one or two layers on a flat drum sieve or kitchen towel. As they drain, their flesh will become fragile, and they must be handled very gently when added to the salad assembly.

Cucumber and zucchini are sturdier and can be salted in many layers in a bowl. If the vegetables are small and tender, the skin may be left on for color. Older vegetables that have tougher skins should be peeled. In either case, the vegetables should be sliced thin before they are salted. After 30 minutes to an hour, they are squeezed lightly between towels to rid them of excess, salty liquid.

Icing is for firm vegetables only: fennel, cucumber, carrot, summer squashes or radishes. The procedure makes these vegetables extremely crunchy, a quality that shows to advantage beside the soft texture of a salted vegetable, as in this demonstration, where salted tomatoes are presented with chilled cucumbers.

The vegetables should be sliced thin for efficient cooling. Older, larger cucumbers have watery centers and large seeds that are best removed before slicing. One method is to peel the cucumber, halve it lengthwise and then scoop out the seeds with your finger tip, a teaspoon or a grapefruit knife. Or, to produce ring-shaped slices, you can seed cucumbers with an apple corer, as demonstrated here, before chilling the slices between layers of ice cubes.

1 **Loosening the skin.** Cut a small cone from the stem of each tomato to remove the core. To loosen their skins, immerse the tomatoes in boiling water for about 10 seconds. Lift out each tomato with a perforated spoon *(above)*.

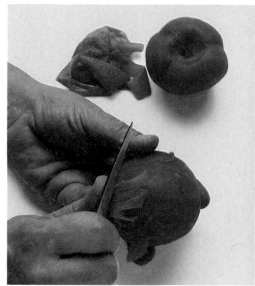

2 **Peeling the tomatoes.** Begin peeling each tomato at its bottom end, where the skin is less firmly attached. Lightly slit the skin with a small knife; grip a flap of skin between your thumb and the flat of the blade, and peel the skin toward the stem end. Then peel the rest of the tomato and discard the skin.

6 **Preparing the cucumbers.** Trim off the bitter-flavored ends and scrape off the peel. Cut each cucumber into sections no longer than the blade of an apple corer. Push the corer through each section and rotate it to remove the seeds *(above)*. Slice each cored section into thin rings.

7 **Chilling cucumber rings.** Cover the bottom of a bowl with ice cubes. Spread the cucumber rings on top. Cover the rings with more ice and leave them for at least 10 minutes — until they are very crisp. Meanwhile, prepare a lemon-and-cream dressing *(page 16)*.

3 **Seeding the tomatoes.** Cut each tomato in half crosswise to expose the seed pockets. Hold each half and, with your finger tip *(above)* or a teaspoon, scoop out the seeds and juice from each seed pocket.

4 **Slicing the tomatoes.** Place the tomato halves flat sides down on a cutting surface. Steady each tomato half with your finger tips and cut it horizontally into slices *(above)*.

5 **Salting the tomato slices.** Lightly salt one side of the tomato slices and place them salted sides down on the mesh of a drum sieve set over a plate. Sprinkle more salt over the slices. Let the slices drain for 15 to 20 minutes.

8 **Drying the vegetables.** Prepare fines herbes *(page 20)* and reserve them as a garnish. Spread the dressing on a serving dish. Carefully lift the tomato slices from the sieve onto a kitchen towel; put the cucumber rings alongside *(above)*. Cover the vegetables with a towel and pat them dry.

9 **Presenting the salad.** Sprinkle half of the fines herbes over the cream dressing on the serving dish. Arrange the cucumber rings and tomato slices on top of the dressing and garnish them with the remaining herbs. Serve at once on chilled plates.

Adroit Balancing Acts with Fruits

Most often considered a dessert ingredient, fresh fruit also produces particularly interesting salads, provided the cook introduces a foil for the fruit's natural sweetness. When assembled, a fruit salad should be a savory dish that will not dull the appetite for courses that follow.

The simplest way of achieving this is to include tart fruits—combined, perhaps, with vegetables—and dress the salad with a light sauce that underscores the tartness. You could, for example, pair tangy grapefruit with mild-flavored avocado and bathe the mixture in a lemony vinaigrette sauce. More complex blends of sweet, tart and savory tastes are characteristic of many Mediterranean salads: A typical assembly might include pungent onions, salty black olives and sweet oranges, all dressed with oil *(recipe, page 106)* or with a mixture of oil and orange and lemon juice.

If the salad is made with sweet or bland fruits or vegetables, however, the dressing alone must provide a balancing tartness, as exemplified by the salad demonstrated here. Oranges and pineapples constitute the foundation of this salad; mild-tasting tomatoes contribute color. To unify flavors, lettuces that form a bed for the salad are lightly dressed with a vinaigrette spiked with pineapple juice. And to balance the sweetness, the fruits are served with a tart cream dressing *(page 16)* flavored with orange juice.

Some salad fruits—apples and pears, for instance—require special treatment to prevent discoloration after they are peeled: Tannins in their flesh turn the fruit brown when it is exposed to air. Cover these peeled fruits with acidulated water—a mixture of lemon or lime juice and water. The ascorbic acid in the citrus juice slows the chemical reaction that causes browning, and the liquid keeps air away from the exposed flesh. Delicate fruits—peaches and nectarines, for example—also discolor when they are exposed to air, but acidulated water may soften their flesh. Protect these fruits with a coat of lemon or lime juice and sugar *(box, opposite)*.

1 **Seeding the tomatoes.** Peel three tomatoes *(Steps 1 and 2, page 26)* and cut each into wedges. Scoop the seeds out of each section with your finger, working over a bowl for neatness. Place the seeded sections in a bowl and sprinkle them lightly with sugar.

2 **Preparing the oranges.** Peel three oranges, cutting deep enough to remove the bitter, white membrane under the peel. Separate the segments by cutting down to the core on either side of each. Work over a bowl to catch juice; place the segments in the bowl.

5 **Assembling the salad.** Wash and dry lettuce leaves *(page 8)* — romaine and ruby lettuces are used here. Drain the pineapple and mix a little of the juice with light olive oil, using one part of juice to three parts of oil. Toss the lettuce leaves in this dressing and place them on a platter. Arrange the tomato and pineapple wedges with the orange segments on the lettuce. Garnish the salad with lime slices and fresh mint leaves, if you like; just before serving, spoon on the flavored cream dressing *(above)*.

3 **Preparing the pineapples.** Select two pineapples. To trim each one, cut off the top and bottom, then stand the pineapple on end and slice off the skin *(left)*. Use the knife point to dig out the tough brownish "eyes" *(right)*. Quarter the pineapple lengthwise, then lay each quarter on its side and cut off the pale section of the core. Slice each quarter into wedges, place the wedges in a large mixing bowl and sprinkle them with lemon juice.

4 **Flavoring the dressing.** Drain the orange segments, reserving the juice. Stir the juice a little at a time into tart cream dressing *(page 16)*. Continue pouring in juice until the dressing reaches a pourable consistency.

Tricks for Trimming and Shaping

Coring apples. Halve a lemon and squeeze its juice into about a quart [1 liter] of water; float the lemon halves in the water, if you like. Insert the tip of the blade of an apple corer into the stem end of a peeled apple. Push the blade halfway through the apple and twist the corer in a complete circle. Repeat from the other end, then push the corer through to press out the core. Immerse the apple in the water.

Peeling soft-fleshed fruits. Bring a pot of water to a boil, then take it off the heat. Spearing one fruit at a time with a fork, immerse peaches, nectarines and plums first in the hot water for a few seconds, then immediately in ice water. With a small, sharp knife, slit and peel off the loosened skins. To prevent discoloring, roll the fruits in sugar mixed with lemon or lime juice *(above)*.

Preparing melon balls. Halve watermelons; halve honeydew melons and canteloupe and scoop out the seeds and fiber. Twist a melon baller into the flesh of each melon to form balls. Be careful to work around the seeds of a watermelon; if they become trapped in a ball, remove them with the tip of a knife.

Evoking a Natural Harmony

Although fruit salads invariably juxtapose tart and sweet tastes, they need not be built entirely around contrast. In fact, the use of only one fruit, or of fruits that are similar in at least one respect, gives a salad satisfying unity. Salads may be made with fruits of the same color, or texture may provide the unifying thread.

The salad demonstrated here is a case in point. Mangoes, papayas and avocados are combined to make a dish almost uniformly smooth in texture, although there are, of course, color and flavor contrasts.

Whereas avocados are readily available all year, papayas and mangoes are most plentiful in the summer months. Because these tropical fruits are often picked green and shipped long distances, they may not be fully ripe when sold. All three types, however, will ripen in two or three days at room temperature. A papaya changes from green to yellow as it matures; mangoes become yellow-orange with a reddish blush; avocados turn to darker green, brown or purple, depending on the variety. When fully ripe, each of these fruits will yield to light pressure on its skin. If necessary, the fruits can be kept refrigerated for two or three days after they reach ripeness.

Because avocados and mangoes are especially soft and easily mashed, they must be peeled and sliced with care. Mango flesh clings both to the skin and to the pit; for smooth pieces, peel off the skin a section at a time and remove the flesh in wedges *(Step 2)*. A ripe avocado is so soft that it is easily misshapen by peeling; instead, you can ease the flesh out of the skin intact, using a spoon *(Step 4)*. Avocados should be brushed with lemon or lime juice to prevent browning after they are peeled.

Tropical fruits like these are so creamy and rich they require a light, tart dressing to prevent them from being cloying. The fruits can be dressed with nothing but lime juice. The more elaborate lime-based vinaigrette used here is another good choice. It is made with walnut oil, which enhances the nutty taste of the avocado; a garnish of chopped walnut meat echoes the flavor.

1 **Preparing the papaya.** Slice off the ends of each papaya, then peel it with a knife, removing the skin in narrow, lengthwise strips. Pare off any uneven slice marks so that the fruit's surface will be smooth and rounded. Cut the fruit in half lengthwise. Scoop out the seeds from each half with a spoon.

2 **Preparing the mango.** To minimize handling the slippery flesh, score each mango lengthwise to outline one quarter. Peel away the skin of the quarter, then cut lengthwise slices through to the pit and pry out each slice. Peel and slice the second and third quarters. For the fourth quarter, hold the pit to avoid mashing the flesh.

6 **Transferring the fruit.** Slip a spatula under the sliced avocado half and, steadying the fruit with your hand to keep the slices together, transfer the avocado to an individual serving plate. Use your finger to gently push the fruit off the spatula onto the plate.

7 **Arranging the avocado.** Hold the flat side of a knife blade along the outer edge of the avocado half to keep the slices aligned while you press the top of the fruit with your finger and slide the slices toward yourself. This will cause the slices to fall back like dominoes in an overlapping row.

3 **Pitting the avocado.** To halve each avocado, insert the knife in the narrow top of the fruit and slice down one side to the base, then up the other side, cutting all the way to the pit. Gently twist the halves in opposite directions to separate them. Jab the blade into the pit and remove it.

4 **Removing the skin.** Slip a large spoon just inside the skin at the broad base of each avocado half. Working close to the skin, slide the spoon down and around the flesh until it cradles the fruit. Gently lift the spoon to remove the half in one piece. Squeeze lime or lemon juice over the peeled halves.

5 **Slicing the avocado.** For each serving, place an avocado half, cut side down, on a cutting board. With a sharp knife, cut the fruit into narrow, slightly angled crosswise slices. Discard the slice from the broad end.

3 **Completing the salad.** Slice a papaya half, transfer it to the plate and make overlapping slices as you did for the avocado. If you like, exchange adjacent avocado and papaya slices for decorative effect. Surround the fruits with angular mango pieces created by cutting slices into thirds diagonally. Garnish with chopped walnuts and dress with walnut oil and lime juice.

Fruit Set in Wine Jelly

One way to counterbalance the sweetness of fresh fruits is to suspend them in a tart jelly. The jelly, a simple combination of liquid and gelatin, can be based on fruit juice or, for a more unusual salad, it can be made with wine *(recipes, pages 157-158)*. The best choice of wine for this sort of jelly is a not-too-dry white or a delicate rosé, used in this demonstration. A robust red wine would mask the color and flavor of the fruit.

Commercial gelatin is obtainable in powdered or—less commonly—in leaf form. As a general rule, use 1 tablespoon [15 ml.] of powdered or 4 sheets [2 grams] of leaf gelatin for each 2 cups [½ liter] of liquid. To ensure even blending, soften either type of gelatin in cold water before making the jelly. Then dissolve the gelatin either by warming this water-and-gelatin mixture (to which wine is subsequently added) or by adding the mixture to wine that has been heated to the boiling point. The latter method, shown here, has a secondary purpose; heating the wine evaporates much of its alcohol and subdues its acidic overtones.

Almost any fresh fruit may be suspended in jelly. The exceptions are figs, kiwi fruit, papayas and pineapples: An enzyme they contain prevents jelling.

To center fruit in its sparkling casing, you must set the gelatin mixture in successive layers *(Steps 3 and 4)*. A shallow layer in the bottom of the mold provides a base for the fruit. If you are using dense fruits such as peaches, oranges or grapes, which do not float, you can place them on the base layer after it sets, then fill the mold with the remaining liquid jelly and chill it. Floating fruits—apples, bananas, pears or the strawberries used here—should be laid on top of the base, then only partly covered with more liquid jelly. When this layer has set, trapping the fruits, fill the mold with the rest of the jelly.

The best way to unmold the completed jelly is to wrap it briefly in a hot towel *(Step 5)* to soften the surface of the jelly slightly so that it slides easily from the mold. The jelly may be served with a garnish of lettuce or watercress and dressed with a vinaigrette flavored with wine. For a more elaborate effect, garnish the jelly with creamy dressing—tart cream *(page 16)* or the mayonnaise and sour cream chosen here.

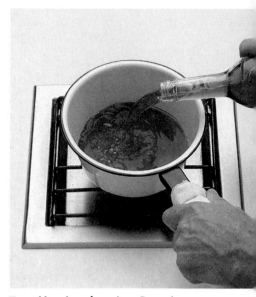

1 Heating the wine. Pour the wine into an enameled or stainless-steel pan; aluminum would interact with the wine, changing its flavor. Warm the wine over medium heat just until it reaches the boiling point. Turn off the heat immediately: Any further cooking would concentrate the flavor of the wine and darken its color.

5 Unmolding the jelly. Invert each mold over a chilled plate. Cover the mold for five seconds *(left)* with a hot, damp towel. Dampen the towel again, then briefly apply it only to the sides of the mold *(center left)*. Lift the mold; if the jelly does not slip out easily, insert a knife along one edge of the mold *(center right)* to let in air, filling any vacuum. Then unmold the jelly onto the plate *(right)*.

2 **Dissolving the gelatin.** Soften powdered gelatin in cold water. Stir in a little hot wine, then stir the mixture into the remaining hot wine. Skim off foam; set the pan in ice. Meanwhile, marinate strawberries and mint leaves in wine.

3 **Adding fruit.** Set small molds in ice. Pour gelatin mixture into each to a depth of ½ inch [1 cm.]. Refrigerate for 15 minutes to set the jelly. Arrange mint leaves on the jelly and center a strawberry, base down, on the leaves.

4 **Setting the fruit.** Ladle more gelatin mixture into each mold to half-submerge the strawberry. Refrigerate the molds for 20 minutes to set the second jelly layer. Fill each mold with jelly and refrigerate again until firm.

6 **Dressing the salad.** Flavor a vinaigrette with a bit of wine, then use this to dress the greens — in this case, watercress. Arrange the greens around the jellies. Spoon mayonnaise, thinned with sour cream and flavored with lime peel, onto each jelly.

2
Cooked Vegetables
A Generous Range of Effects

Three ways to wilt leaves
Bundling leeks and asparagus
The potato's varied possibilities
Peeling and seeding peppers
Cooking in flavored liquids

Separately cooked chick-peas, red kidney beans and black beans — delineated by strips of sieved, hard-boiled egg yolks and dressed with a garlicky vinaigrette — make up a hearty three-bean salad *(page 43)*. Lovage leaves, red onion rings and broiled pepper strips garnish the triad, and a ring of chopped scallions encircles the array. The components will be amalgamated at table.

Almost any vegetable that is cooked and served hot can be cooked and served cold as a salad. Not all cooking methods produce good cold dishes, of course, but the choices are varied enough to provide a broad scope for improvisation.

If the salad is simply a cold presentation of a single type of vegetable, cooking should be kept to a minimum so that the vegetable's essential character is altered as little as possible. Tough-textured leaves — those of cabbage, for instance — are frequently softened, or wilted, by techniques that hardly qualify as cooking at all *(pages 36-37)*. Most other vegetables to be served on their own benefit from brief boiling in large quantities of water: They emerge tender, bright in color and still in full possession of their own flavors. The classic salad of this type consists of asparagus, served with nothing more complicated than a mild vinaigrette dressing *(page 39)*. Leeks can be treated the same way *(pages 38-39)*, as can broccoli, Swiss chard or Belgian endive. Other boiled vegetables, by contrast, are complemented by aromatic garnishes. Fresh peas, for example, blend especially well with watercress or mint leaves, and boiled potatoes lend themselves to innumerable kinds of garnishes and dressings *(pages 40-41)*.

If a salad is to include several different types of vegetables, the range of cooking options broadens. The vegetables may be boiled separately and then combined, their diversity unified by a dressing, as in the three-bean salad at left, or — for a particularly glittering effect — by a translucent casing of jelly *(pages 44-45)*. Alternatively, the vegetables can be cooked together to create a more complex mingling of flavors. One classic version of this approach is to simmer the vegetables briefly in court bouillon — a seasoned cooking liquid. After absorbing the different vegetable tastes, the court bouillon is reduced to serve first as a marinade for the vegetables and then as their dressing *(pages 46-47)*. For a salad with more thoroughly blended tastes and more tender textures, vegetables can be stewed and then chilled in a thick tomato sauce *(pages 46-47)*. Vegetables for a salad may even be sautéed in oil — briefly, so that they are softened rather than browned — then chilled. The oil, fragrant with the essences of the different vegetables, becomes the basis for the lemony vinaigrette that dresses the finished salad.

Tenderizing Tough Leaves

A method unique to salad making, and not strictly classifiable as cooking, is wilting leaves. Wilting can be done by layering leaves in salt, by soaking them in boiling water or parboiling them briefly, or even by drenching them with a hot, vinegary dressing. The object in all cases is to break down the fiber of coarse-textured leaves such as cabbage, dandelion, rocket or chicory, and thereby give them a welcome suppleness.

Sturdy cabbage leaves require fairly drastic wilting methods. Salting *(demonstration, top right)* will draw juices from the leaves, rendering them limp—and also flavoring them somewhat. Alternatively, an immersion in hot water *(demonstration, bottom)* cooks the cabbage just enough to soften it, and does not alter its flavor.

After either method of wilting, the cabbage can be drained and dressed with a vinaigrette *(recipe, page 167)*; take care not to overseason cabbage that has been salted. For a striking contrast in texture and flavor, crunchy sautéed bacon or salt pork and its hot fat often are added to salads still warm from wilting with boiling water; the fat would congeal if it were poured onto chilled leaves.

Leaves more fragile than cabbage—dandelion or chicory, for example—can be wilted with a hot dressing alone. If sautéed salt pork or bacon is included to garnish the salad, as in the demonstration at far right, you can pour vinegar into the pan in which the bacon was cooked—thus deglazing the pan of savory bacon fragments at the same time that you heat the dressing. To prevent the bacon fat from congealing, dress and serve the salad in a hot bowl.

Red Cabbage Softened with Salt

1 **Salting the cabbage.** Shred the leaves fine—in this case, red cabbage leaves—and put a layer of shreds in a large bowl; salt the shreds lightly. Add the rest of the shreds in salted layers, ending with a sprinkling of salt. Cover the bowl and leave it at room temperature for about four hours.

2 **Drying the cabbage.** A chemical interaction during salting will turn the shreds a deep bluish purple. Lift the wilted shreds from the bowl and squeeze out excess water. Place the shreds in a kitchen towel *(above)* and pat them dry. Taste a shred; if it is too salty, rinse the cabbage in cold water and dry it again.

Green Cabbage Steeped in Boiling Water

1 **Soaking the cabbage.** Shred the leaves—green cabbage is shown here. Pack the shreds into a large bowl and barely cover them with boiling water *(above)*. Place a pan lid or heavy plate, slightly smaller than the diameter of the bowl, on top to keep the cabbage submerged. Leave to soak.

2 **Draining the cabbage.** After about 10 minutes of soaking, empty the warm cabbage into a colander and drain it for a few minutes. Then press it down with your hands *(above)* to squeeze out any water that remains.

3 **Dressing the cabbage.** Transfer the cabbage to a salad bowl. Prepare a vinaigrette, season it according to the saltiness of the shreds, and pour it over them. The acidity of the vinegar will restore most of the cabbage's original reddish purple color.

4 **Tossing the salad.** Toss the salad thoroughly by hand or with two large spoons. The flavor will improve if the cabbage marinates in the vinaigrette for a few hours before it is served.

1 **Pouring on hot dressing.** Place washed, dried leaves — dandelion, here — in a warmed bowl. Add bacon pieces and the olive oil in which they crisped. Deglaze the sauté pan with vinegar; pour the liquid on the salad.

3 **Adding sautéed bacon.** Sauté small cubes of slab bacon in a little oil until they are just crisp. Empty the wilted cabbage into a large, warmed salad bowl. Season with salt and pepper. Before dressing the salad, add the pieces of sautéed bacon together with their hot fat *(above)*.

4 **Tossing the salad.** Immediately dress the salad with a vinaigrette made, because of the presence of bacon fat, with a minimum of oil: Two parts of oil to each part of vinegar is about the right ratio. Garnish the salad with chopped parsley, toss it well and serve it warm.

2 **Tossing the salad.** Using salad servers, turn over the leaves and bacon quickly in the dressing, so that the leaves are wilted thoroughly by the heat. Serve at once on warmed plates.

A Pair of Kindred Classics

Leeks Served with Vinaigrette and Egg

The simplest way to soften almost any vegetable destined for a salad is to boil it briefly in a large quantity of water. Boiling, unlike salting, alters a vegetable's natural taste very little, preserving the essences of even such delicate vegetables as the asparagus and leeks shown here.

Both vegetables are prepared for boiling in the same way: To protect the fragile asparagus tips and the leek's scrolled leaves, the stalks are tied into bundles. Only the trimming and cleaning differ. Leeks should be slit and washed to rid them of grit *(Steps 1 and 2, right)*; asparagus stalks have tough skins that must be carefully pared away to make them edible *(Step 1, opposite, below)*.

Leeks and asparagus are best appreciated when served at room temperature with minimum adornment. A mild vinaigrette *(recipe, page 167)* will highlight their flavors, as will simple garnishes— a soupçon of parsley or chives, say, or some chopped hard-boiled egg *(below)*.

1 Slitting the leeks. Trim the root from each leek and cut off the fibrous leaf tops. Peel off any blemished leaves. Pierce the leek where the green part joins the white; draw the knife through the green to the top. Then slit the leek lengthwise at a right angle to the first cut *(above)*. Immerse the leeks in cold water.

2 Washing out the grit. Shake the leeks vigorously under the water to wash out all the grit held within their tightly packed leaves. Change the water and repeat the process until the water is clear. Rinse the leeks under cold running water.

6 Dressing the salad. Add chopped fresh parsley to a vinaigrette. Halve hard-boiled eggs; chop the yolks and cut the whites into strips *(above)*. Gently stir the eggs into the vinaigrette. Just before serving, ladle the dressing over the leeks *(right)*.

3 **Tying the bundles.** Gather together a fist-sized bunch of leeks. Wind kitchen string around the bundle several times, up and down its length *(above)*. Tie the string in a secure knot.

4 **Cooking the leeks.** Bring a pot of salted water to a boil. Immerse the leeks; when the water returns to a boil, reduce the heat. Simmer the leeks, uncovered, until the whites offer only slight resistance when pierced with a knife — about 10 minutes. To lift the bundles, slip the tine of a fork through the strings.

5 **Draining the leeks.** Place the bundles of leeks on a kitchen towel. Cut the strings, spread out the leeks and cover them with another towel. Let them drain on the towel while they cool. Arrange the leeks on a serving platter.

Asparagus with Its Dressing Mixed on the Spot

1 **Peeling the asparagus.** Rinse asparagus stalks. Snap or cut off the tough bottom ends. Beginning at the base of each stalk, peel off the thick skin with a sharp knife. Pare less deeply as you near the thin-skinned tip. Bundle the stalks, boil them for seven or eight minutes and drain them *(Steps 3-5, above)*.

2 **Serving the asparagus.** Present the asparagus with salt, pepper, vinegar and olive oil, so that each diner can mix a vinaigrette on his or her own plate. Tilt the plate by placing a spoon or knife beneath its far side: The dressing will form a pool at the near side. Eat each stalk by hand, dipping it into the dressing.

The Potato: An Adaptable Partner

The flavor of boiled potatoes marries well with a range of dressings and accompanying ingredients *(recipes, pages 119-121)*. A simple potato salad *(right, top)* can be completed with just a vinaigrette, some fresh herbs and chopped shallots. A more elaborate salad *(right, bottom)* may include chopped egg and, for contrast, crisp or strongly flavored vegetables, all lightly bound with mayonnaise. Or you can serve a hot potato salad *(opposite, far right)*, garnished with onion and bacon, ham or sausage.

For salads, choose waxy-fleshed boiling potatoes, which, unlike mealy baking potatoes, remain firm when cooked so that they can be cut up and tossed without crumbling apart.

Although some recipes call for the potatoes to be peeled in advance, it is better to cook them unpeeled; their skins hold in flavor and nutrients that would otherwise be drawn out into the cooking water. Once the potatoes have been cooked, you can remove their skins easily.

Because the flesh of hot potatoes absorbs liquid readily, you can give the salad extra flavor, if you like, by cutting the freshly peeled potatoes directly into dry white wine and letting them steep until cool before dressing them. If the potatoes are destined for a mayonnaise-bound salad, they must be cooled in any case, lest their heat make the dressing separate. Alternatively, you can toss hot potatoes in a vinaigrette and serve the salad immediately or cool it to room temperature.

Slices Bathed in Wine and Enlivened with Herbs

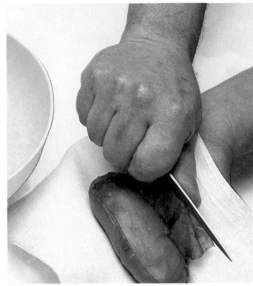

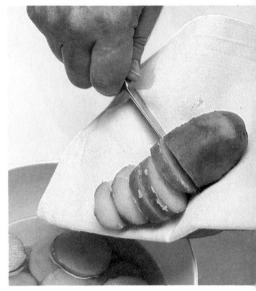

1 **Peeling the potatoes.** Add unpeeled potatoes to boiling water and cook them 15 to 20 minutes, until they can easily be pierced with a knife. Drain. Holding each hot potato in a towel, make a lengthwise slit in its skin with the knife tip. Grip each flap of skin between the flat of the blade and your thumb and pull off the skin.

2 **Marinating the potatoes.** Slice the peeled potatoes into a bowl containing dry white wine *(above)*. If the knife sticks as you slice the potatoes, dip the blade in cold water. Turn the slices about in the wine to coat them, cover the bowl and let them soak for about 15 minutes. Drain off excess wine: You can reserve it for cooking.

An Aromatic Alliance Dressed with Mayonnaise

1 **Dicing the potatoes.** Boil the potatoes and let them cool. Peel them. Halve each potato lengthwise, place each half cut side down and cut it into thick horizontal slices. Stack the slices and cut them lengthwise into sticks, then crosswise into cubes *(above)*.

2 **Mixing the dry ingredients.** Put the cubed potatoes in a mixing bowl with the other diced or chopped ingredients — in this case, hard-boiled egg, onion, celery and parsley. Season with salt and pepper. With your hands, toss the ingredients together.

A Hot Bacon Vinaigrette

3 **Mixing the vinaigrette.** Put salt and pepper in the salad serving dish. Add vinegar and stir with your finger — an easy way to tell when the salt has dissolved. Add chopped shallots and olive oil in the desired proportions; mix the dressing well with your finger *(above)*. Taste and correct the seasoning.

4 **Tossing the salad.** Add the potato slices to the vinaigrette. Sprinkle on chopped fresh herbs — parsley, chervil and tarragon are used here. To coat the potato slices with the dressing without breaking them up, turn the salad gently with your hands *(above)*.

1 **Mixing the dressing.** Cut bacon slices into small pieces, sauté them lightly and drain them. In a bowl, prepare a vinaigrette and add the bacon and finely chopped onion *(above)*.

2 **Heating the dressing.** Discard the bacon fat and pour the dressing into the sauté pan. Bring to a boil, then simmer, stirring from time to time, until the onion softens, about three minutes.

3 **Adding mayonnaise.** Prepare mayonnaise *(page 17)*. Spoon it onto the potato salad *(above)*, adding just enough to bind the ingredients — about 1 cup [¼ liter] to every 2 pounds [1 kg.] or 6 cups [1½ liters] of potatoes.

4 **Tossing the salad.** With your hands, gently mix the mayonnaise into the salad until the ingredients are evenly coated. Serve the salad directly from the mixing bowl, or present it on a platter — garnished, if you like, with black olives and hard-boiled eggs.

3 **Presenting the salad.** Peel freshly boiled, still-hot potatoes and slice them onto a heated serving dish. Pour the hot dressing over the slices *(above)* and serve the salad immediately.

How to Bring Out Peppers' Sweet Essence

Unlike most salad vegetables, peppers benefit from broiling. The intense dry heat loosens the papery skin so that it may be easily peeled off. At the same time, the peppers' pungently sweet flesh cooks to softness and releases fragrant juices that can be used in the dressing.

To ensure that the skin chars and blisters evenly, the peppers should be cooked whole—either under a broiler or over an open flame—and repeatedly turned. Depending on ripeness, it will take anywhere from four to 10 minutes of cooking to loosen the skin from the flesh; during that time, juices will collect within the pepper. After peeling, the pepper is seeded and deribbed.

The prepared peppers are at their best when dressed with a mild vinaigrette that is enhanced, as in this demonstration, with garlic, fines herbes and the peppers' own juices. Other appropriate flavorings are basil or oregano; the traditional garnishes include olives, capers, anchovies or chopped, hard-boiled eggs.

1 Peeling the peppers. Broil whole peppers for four to 10 minutes about 2 inches [5 cm.] from the heat, either under a broiler or — spearing each pepper with a fork — over an open flame. To broil them evenly, turn the peppers as their skins blister. When the peppers are cool enough to handle, peel away the skins, holding the peppers over a plate to catch any juices.

2 Removing the seeds. Slit each pepper along its length and open it flat on a plate. Pull off the stem and the cluster of seeds attached to it. Scrape out the ribs and any remaining seeds with a spoon. Reserve the pepper juices that collect in the plate.

3 Mixing the dressing. Using a mortar and pestle, mash a peeled garlic clove with salt and pepper. Stir in a large spoonful of vinegar, then add four or five spoonfuls of olive oil, the reserved pepper juices and chopped fresh herbs. Stir thoroughly.

4 Dressing the peppers. Lay the peppers, peeled sides up, in overlapping rows on a large platter. Ladle the dressing evenly over them. Serve the salad immediately or marinate the peppers at room temperature for several hours before serving.

The Challenge of Pulses

Once they are cooked, dried beans, peas and lentils lend themselves to as many garnishes and dressings as potatoes do (pages 40-41). But pulses—as these leguminous seeds are collectively called—require a bit more preparation.

Dried beans and chick-peas must first be softened: either soaked overnight or boiled for two minutes and steeped for an hour. Tiny lentils need no soaking.

After these preliminaries, the pulses are simmered—not boiled, which would burst their skins—to tenderness; cooking times vary from 20 minutes for lentils to two hours for chick-peas (recipes, pages 123-124). Flavors can be enhanced if the cooking liquid is meat stock (recipe, page 164), and if aromatic vegetables are added to the liquid, which may be reduced and used to enrich the dressing.

The cooked, drained pulses should be tossed immediately with dressing: Like potatoes, the pulses are absorbent when warm. A garlic-flavored dressing—used for the three-bean salad shown here (recipe, page 123)—complements all pulses.

1 Preparing the pulses. Wash the pulses—dried red kidney beans, chick-peas and black beans are shown—and pick out any broken beans or debris. Place the pulses in separate bowls and add enough cold water to cover them by 2 inches [5 cm.]. Let them soak overnight, then drain them.

2 Cooking. Place the pulses in separate pots and cover them with cold stock, as above, or water. Bring the liquid to a boil, skimming off any scum. To each pot, add a bouquet garni, carrots, onions and celery. Reduce the heat and simmer the pulses, keeping them covered with water, until tender.

3 Dressing the salad. Drain the pulses, put them in separate bowls and moisten them with vinaigrette (above, left). To remove skins, rub chick-peas between your fingers (above, right). Cool, then spoon the pulses—divided here by cardboard—into a serving dish (right); remove the cardboard, and garnish (pages 34-35).

A Gleaming Medley of Vegetables

For the most festive of presentations, an assortment of cooked vegetables may be suspended together in a mold of sparkling aspic. Choose whatever vegetables are freshest and most abundant: This demonstration includes carrots, scallions and asparagus *(recipe, page 157)*; other possibilities are whole boiling onions, peas and snow peas, turnips, broccoli, zucchini and green beans. Limit your selection, however, to three or four different vegetables; otherwise their individual characters will be lost in the medley. Boil each vegetable separately so that all will be perfectly done—cooked through, but still crisp. To conserve flavor, cook them one after another in the same water *(Step 1, right)*.

The aspic that encases the vegetables may be a gelatinous chicken or veal stock *(recipe, page 164)* that will set of its own accord when chilled. Or you could use a nongelatinous clarified chicken stock, augmenting it with commercial gelatin, as explained on page 32, to set the salad.

1 **Cooking the vegetables.** Peel and slice the vegetables — carrots, scallions and asparagus are shown. Boil the carrots in lightly salted water for two or three minutes until they are barely tender. Lift them out with a mesh skimmer*(above, left)* and set them aside to drain. In the same water, boil the scallions for one minute; lift them out and drain them *(center)*. Then boil the asparagus for one minute and drain it *(right)*. Cool all of the vegetables.

4 **Adding the remaining vegetable layers.** On top of the carrots, spread the slices of scallion, creating a second level layer that completely covers the first. Finally, add the asparagus, packing it gently but firmly and filling the mold almost to the top.

5 **Filling the mold with aspic.** Ladle the remaining liquid aspic over the vegetables until the mold is filled to its rim. Leave the mold in the coldest part of the refrigerator for a minimum of three hours, until the aspic jelly has set firmly.

2 **Lining the base of the mold.** Melt jellied stock over low heat, or combine hot chicken stock with gelatin. Flavor this aspic, if you like, with a little dry sherry or Madeira. Ladle the liquid aspic into a chilled mold or soufflé dish to a depth of about ½ inch [1 cm.]. Put a sprig of flat-leafed parsley or chervil in the center.

3 **Forming the first vegetable layer.** Put the mold in the refrigerator until the aspic is set — about 15 minutes. Carefully place cooled, drained carrot slices one by one on top of the aspic to cover it in a single, neat layer. Ladle in more liquid aspic and chill the mold again until set. Add the rest of the carrots, spreading them out in a level layer to the sides of the mold.

6 **Serving the salad.** Put a chilled serving dish upside down on top of the mold and invert them together. To loosen the aspic, wrap the mold briefly in a hot towel, as demonstrated on page 32, Step 5. Lift the mold from the aspic and garnish the salad with parsley, tarragon or chervil. If you like, accompany the salad with a mayonnaise mixed with fines herbes.

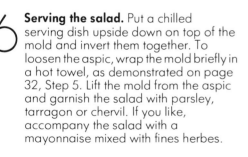

Simmering and Marinating to Unite Flavors

When a mélange of firm vegetables is first simmered and then marinated in an aromatic liquid, the result is a salad distinguished by subtle contrasts of flavors and textures. Zucchini, peppers, mushrooms, artichoke bottoms, fennel, cauliflower, celery and leeks in any mixture are all firm enough for such treatment.

The liquid may be no more complicated than a court bouillon flavored with wine, olive oil and lemon juice. For a more emphatic taste, the court bouillon may be laced with herbs and garlic to produce the salad commonly described as Greek-style, or *à la grecque (top right; recipe, page 125)*. For a thicker coating, the liquid may be a tomato sauce—a variation once deemed exotic enough to deserve the appellation *orientale (recipe, page 126)*.

When the base is court bouillon, the slow-cooking vegetables are added to it before the rest, so that all the vegetables remain slightly crisp. With the sauce base, all the vegetables are put in together and simmered longer, yielding a more thorough mingling of flavors.

Cooking in a Simple Court Bouillon

1 **Flavoring court bouillon.** Bring white wine, water, olive oil and lemon juice to a boil. Add a bouquet garni, fennel leaves, coriander, garlic and salt. Put in slow-cooking vegetables — in this case, whole onions plus quartered fennel and artichoke bottoms, made by trimming whole artichokes down to the pale hearts and scraping out the chokes.

2 **Adding tender vegetables.** Bring the court bouillon to a boil over medium heat. Reduce the heat to low, cover the pan and simmer for about 10 minutes. Add cauliflower florets, cover and simmer for about five more minutes. Then add whole mushrooms *(above)*.

Stewing in a Tomato-based Sauce

1 **Making the tomato sauce.** Sauté chopped onion in olive oil until it softens. Stir in sliced garlic and add raisins that have been soaked in tepid water for about one hour to make them plump. Add peeled, seeded and chopped tomatoes. Season with salt, cayenne pepper and a little sugar.

2 **Assembling.** Simmer the sauce for 10 minutes. Add the vegetables — in this case, mushrooms, onions, celery, leek whites and quartered artichoke bottoms. Cover, simmer for five minutes, then add dry white wine and lemon juice — squeezed through your fingers to strain out the seeds *(above)*.

3 **Straining the liquid.** Cover the pan and cook the vegetables over low heat for 30 minutes longer. To strain the juices, pour the contents of the pan into a colander set over another saucepan. Return the vegetables to the pan in which they were cooked.

3 **Straining the liquid.** Cover the pan and simmer the vegetables for five minutes, or until barely tender. To strain the liquid, pour the mixture into a colander set over a saucepan *(above)*. Discard the bouquet garni and the garlic cloves. Boil the strained liquid to reduce it by about half.

4 **Dressing the vegetables.** Arrange the vegetables in a shallow dish and dress them with the reduced liquid *(above)*. Let the vegetables cool, then refrigerate the salad for at least four hours, but let it warm to room temperature again before serving it.

4 **Binding the vegetables.** Boil the strained liquid until it is reduced to about half of its original volume and reaches the consistency of a light syrup. Pour the reduced liquid over the vegetables *(above)*, and simmer them uncovered for 15 minutes: The resulting mixture will be thickly bound by the tomato sauce.

5 **Finishing the dish.** Transfer the vegetables in their sauce to a serving dish and let them stand until cool. Serve the salad at room temperature, garnished with chopped fresh parsley, chervil or — as in this instance — coriander leaves.

Sautéing Tailored to the Demands of Salads

An assortment of vegetables sautéed together makes an exceptionally aromatic salad—a prime example being the classic Middle Eastern combination shown here *(recipe, page 115)*. This heady mixture with the colorful name (it is called *imam bayildi*—"the priest swooned") depends for success on principles that apply to any sautéed vegetable salad.

Cooking must be just long enough to soften the vegetables without altering their essential character. For example, in *imam bayildi*, aromatic onions begin cooking first, quicker-cooking strips of green pepper are added to the pan next, and fragile eggplant cubes are added last. (If zucchini or summer squash were included in a sautéed salad, they would be put in a few minutes after the eggplant, as would mushrooms.) Tomatoes are not sautéed with the other ingredients of this salad, because their rendered juices would turn the mixture into a stew; instead, the tomatoes are added raw to the cooked vegetable mixture.

The cooking medium should be oil, not butter, which will brown too quickly and harden into unappetizing granules as the salad cools. During sautéing, oil absorbs the vegetable essences, forming a richly flavored base for the salad dressing.

Vegetables sautéed together present a jumbled appearance less attractive in cold dishes than in hot ones. To contain the kaleidoscope of colors, *imam bayildi* is traditionally served in a hollowed-out eggplant half. In this demonstration, the eggplant halves are used uncooked so that their skins remain firm and shiny. The eggplant may, however, be parboiled to tenderize it. Other good natural containers include hollowed peppers, tomatoes, cucumbers or zucchini. Garnishes should be light and very crisp to provide a contrast to the softened vegetables. Here, sautéed pine nuts accompany the salad; a garnish of toasted sesame or sunflower seeds could be used instead.

1 **Preparing shells.** Halve each eggplant and loosen its flesh: Run a knife blade around the edge inside the skin and make a deep cut down the center. Using a curved grapefruit knife, pry out the flesh. Rub the cut surfaces of the shells with lemon juice, invert them on paper towels and refrigerate.

2 **Cubing the pulp.** Slice the eggplant pulp into ½-inch [1-cm.] cubes and drop them into a bowl. Immediately squeeze lemon juice over the cubes and toss them to coat each cut surface. Cover the bowl with plastic wrap and set the eggplant cubes aside.

6 **Completing the filling.** Peel, seed and chop tomatoes. Stir them into the sautéed vegetables. Then stir in lemon juice and olive oil. Add salt and pepper, overseasoning slightly: The flavors will fade when the filling is chilled. Cover the bowl and refrigerate the mixture for a minimum of four hours.

7 **Sautéing the garnish.** Lightly coat the bottom of a sauté pan with olive oil—tangy green Italian oil is used here—and set the pan over medium heat for a moment to warm the oil. Add a handful of pine nuts and slide the pan back and forth over the heat for two or three minutes to toss the nuts and brown them. When the nuts are golden brown, drain them on paper towels.

3 **Preparing aromatics.** Chop garlic into fine bits. Cut onions into thin slices. Halve green peppers lengthwise, remove the seeds and trim the inner ribs. Then slice the peppers into thin strips.

4 **Sautéing the filling.** Over low heat, sauté the onions and garlic in a little olive oil — in this case flavored with basil leaves — for about five minutes, until the onions are wilted but not brown. Add the green peppers and cook until they are limp; the skin should remain green and unwrinkled.

5 **Cooking the eggplant.** Stir in the eggplant and sauté briefly, adding olive oil if the cubes stick. Cover, and cook for seven or eight minutes, until the eggplant is tender. Add chopped fresh basil and oregano, cover again and cook for two minutes. Transfer the mixture to a bowl to cool slightly.

8 **Assembling the salad.** Bring the vegetables to room temperature before spooning them into the eggplant shells *(left)*. Arrange the shells on a platter and garnish them if you like, with basil leaves and lemon wedges. Sprinkle the sautéed pine nuts around the inner edge of each shell *(above)*.

3
Meats and Poultry
Imaginative Approaches to Flesh and Fowl

When cold meat is the featured attraction, a salad becomes a main course. Almost any bird or any sizable cut of beef, veal, lamb or pork—including such unexpected treats as brains, tongue or sweetbreads—can be served up as salad. Depending on the size and shape of the cut, the meat may be carved into symmetrical slices for display on a platter *(opposite)* or divided into bite-sized pieces and heaped in a bowl. The meat can be dressed with a vinaigrette or mayonnaise, either of which may be enriched with vegetable purée. And, as a further source of variation, practically any raw or cooked vegetable—from onions to beets—may be sliced, diced or shredded to complement the taste of the meat and stretch the number of portions a cut will provide.

When the salad has yesterday's roasted or poached meat as its starting point, the cook's job is simple. A roast duck or leg of lamb, for example, often needs only to be trimmed, cut up and combined with dressing. If the cut has been roasted to dryness or boiled to blandness, it can be revived by marinating it for about an hour beforehand.

Leftovers, however, tend to be skimpy and often represent the less-than-prime parts of a cut or bird. To ensure ample portions in appealing arrangements, meat must be cooked to order. For a perfect chicken salad, the bird should be roasted *à point*—to the exact degree of succulence desired—by removing the quickly finished breast as soon as it is tender and returning the legs to the oven to cook them through *(pages 60-61)*. Poaching is the key to producing economic yet elegant meat salads from such gelatinous cuts as round, brisket or shoulder; the slow application of moist heat tenderizes the meat without harming its texture *(pages 54-55)*. Both cooking methods yield a dividend: The roasting juices from the chicken may be degreased, or the poaching stock from the meat boiled down, and this rich liquid can be used to augment the dressing.

Innards destined for salads also are poached. Popularly esteemed in the Victorian era, these meats have fallen from cooks' favor since then, perhaps because of the soaking, salting, peeling and other preparations they require. But the extra handling is a modest price to pay for such distinctive results: Poached brains prove to be delicate in flavor and satiny in texture *(pages 58-59)*, while tongue has robust-tasting, fine-grained meat splendidly suited to a salad format *(pages 56-57)*.

inely cut chives are strewn over oiled-beef salad *(pages 52-53)*, already ecked with a sharply flavored ressing and rings of red onion. The eftover meat was first marinated in a inaigrette, then topped with a sauce ased on *tapenade* — an assertive urée of black olives, capers and nchovies *(recipe, page 163)*.

Making the Most of Leftovers

Leftover meat—beef, veal, lamb or pork —can be the starting point for hearty and handsome salads. How you prepare them depends on how the meat was originally cooked and on the quantity.

Poached meat, for example, is tender, but some of its flavor and moisture has been lost to its cooking liquid. To compensate, you can marinate boiled beef or other poached meat in a vinaigrette and serve it with a lively dressing such as *tapenade (right)*.

Braised cuts and meats roasted long enough to lose all traces of pink also profit from marinating. Roasts and broiled meats that are still pink and juicy can be simply dressed with mayonnaise, seasoned—if you wish—with fresh herbs and garlic *(opposite, bottom)*.

If you have large pieces of leftover meat, you can make the salad with fair-sized slices or strips. Small pieces lend themselves best to dicing. Either way, adding vegetables yields extra servings *(below)*. To complement the meat's flavor and soft texture, choose assertive, crisp vegetables, such as fennel or cucumber.

A Counterpoint to Boiled Beef

1 **Slicing the meat.** Trim the meat — beef brisket and short ribs are shown — of all bones, fat and gristle. If necessary, separate the meat into muscle layers. Cut the meat across the grain into uniform slices ¼ inch [6 mm.] thick. Make a vinaigrette and marinate the meat in it with thin rings of onion.

2 **Preparing the dressing.** In a mixing bowl, combine white wine vinegar, pepper and a pinch of salt; sti until the salt dissolves. Add ½ cup [125 ml.] of *tapenade (recipe, page 163)* for each ¼ cup [50 ml.] of vinegar. Stir i olive oil bit by bit until the dressing is smooth and just thin enough to pour.

Extending a Limited Quantity of Meat

1 **Dicing the meat.** Trim poached meat — in this case, blade roast and shank — of all fat. Cut the meat first into slices about ½ inch [1 cm.] thick, then into strips of the same dimension. Cut across the strips to make dice.

2 **Tossing the salad.** Prepare a vinaigrette, using less vinegar than usual if you are adding pickles to the salad. Add the meat, and vegetables and herbs — here, sliced scallions, sliced sour gherkins and chopped fresh parsley. Toss the salad with your hands or two large spoons.

3 **Serving.** Cover the bowl, then leave the salad at room temperature so that th ingredients can marinate in the vinaigrette for at least one hour. Transfe the salad to a serving dish and garnish it with coarsely chopped parsle or chives before serving it.

3 **Arranging the slices.** After the meat slices have marinated at room temperature for at least one hour, lift them singly from the vinaigrette. Without draining or drying the slices, arrange them on a serving platter in a neat pattern, such as the sunburst design shown above. Reserve the onion rings.

4 **Dressing the beef.** Stir the *tapenade* dressing to make sure that it is still smooth. Spoon a generous amount of the dressing along the length of each meat slice. Then strew the reserved onion rings over the salad.

5 **Serving the beef.** Sprinkle finely cut fresh chives, as here, or chopped fresh parsley, chervil or coriander over the meat. Serve a few slices of meat to each diner, lifting them from the platter with a spoon and fork *(above)*.

A Garlic-flavored Filigree for Lamb

1 **Slicing the meat.** Cut any fat or gristle from the roast — in this case, a leg of lamb. Cut off the meat from one end of the bone to make a handle by which you can hold the leg and steady it for carving. With a long, sharp knife, cut roughly parallel to the bone to carve the meat into thin slices.

2 **Making the dressing.** Prepare mayonnaise *(page 17)*. In a mortar, pound to a paste a chopped garlic clove, salt, pepper and a handful of chopped fresh herbs — parsley, tarragon and chives are used here. Add the mayonnaise, sliced scallions and more chopped herbs. Stir with the pestle.

3 **Presenting the meat.** Arrange the lamb slices on a large platter, overlapping them slightly. To distribute the dressing evenly and attractively, use a spoon to dribble it along the edges of each slice. Serve the remaining dressing in a bowl.

The Sumptuous Rewards of Poaching

Slow cooking of meat in liquid that is kept at the barest bubble transforms even the humblest of cuts into a succulent basis for a salad, and meat flavor that escapes into the liquid can be retrieved by using the liquid to enrich the dressing. Strong-flavored beef and pork take on new dimensions with this treatment. So, too, does mild veal. One of the most esteemed of cold meat presentations, in fact, is the Italian *vitello tonnato* shown at right; it consists of poached veal slices anointed with a creamy mayonnaise that includes puréed tuna, anchovies and capers *(recipe, page 130)*.

Although *vitello tonnato* may be produced with veal rump or round, its flavor is heightened by substituting more gelatinous (and less costly) veal cuts such as breast or—as here—shoulder. Similarly, the best beef candidates for the poaching pot are the muscular round or brisket; the best cuts of pork are Boston shoulder and blade.

Boning the cut ahead of time, then rolling and tying it into a compact cylinder ensures that the meat cooks evenly and carves tidily. The poaching medium may be stock, a mixture of water and wine, or, as in this demonstration, water alone. In all cases, aromatics and a bouquet garni provide a welcome addition of flavor both to the meat and to the dressing that subsequently incorporates some of the cooking liquid *(Step 3)*.

However gentle the poaching is, the meat must be tested repeatedly for doneness toward the end of its cooking time: Overcooking robs the meat of flavor and draws out so much of its gelatin that it becomes stringy. Insert a skewer, fork or knife tip; when the meat is fully done, it will offer only slight resistance.

For easy carving into the neat shapes favored for salads, the meat must be allowed to rest and firm up after poaching. The slices should be at room temperature when combined with their marinade or dressing in order to absorb its flavor.

Poaching. In a pot just large enough to hold it easily, immerse the veal in water. Bring the liquid to a simmer, removing scum as it rises. When the liquid is clear, add aromatic vegetables and a bouquet garni. Cover the pot, setting the lid ajar, and simmer for about 30 minutes a pound [½ kg.]. Cool the veal in the liquid.

Arranging the platter. Cut the cooled veal into thin slices. Spoon a layer of dressing onto a platter *(left)* and overlap the slices on it *(center)*. Mask the slices with more dressing *(right)*, seal the platter with plastic wrap and refrigerate it for at least 24 hours. Cover and refrigerate the remaining dressing.

2 **Puréeing the flavorings.** Place drained, canned tuna in a food processor or blender and add lemon juice, squeezing the lemon over your fingers to catch the seeds. Then add anchovies *(page 22)* and capers, and purée the mixture. With the appliance running, dribble in olive oil to bind the ingredients.

3 **Mixing the dressing.** Transfer the veal to a cutting board. Strain its poaching broth. Turn on the processor or blender again and dribble broth into the tuna purée until the mixture is smooth. Whisk the purée into twice its volume of mayonnaise. If needed, add oil or lemon juice to give the dressing the consistency of cream.

5 **Serving the salad.** Coat the veal with more dressing *(above)* and garnish it with lemon slices, pitted olives, capers and fresh parsley. Lift the slices to beds of buttercrunch lettuce leaves on individual plates. Add dressing from the platter to each serving *(right)*.

Tactics for Dealing with Tongue

Prized in Europe, beef tongue too often is neglected by American cooks unfamiliar with its potential—particularly for salads. Tongue's hearty flavor, which is more akin to that of beef than to that of other organ meat, marries well with vinaigrette or with highly seasoned cream dressings *(pages 16-17)*. And the smooth-textured flesh is easy to slice or dice neatly into salad-sized pieces.

Beef tongue or the less common veal tongue may be found at most markets in fresh, smoked or corned forms. Of these, fresh tongue, as shown at right, has the mildest flavor.

All tongue benefits from advance preparation. Smoked or corned tongue must be soaked in water for an hour, brought to a simmer in fresh water and blanched for 15 minutes to attenuate the strong salty taste. Fresh tongue, by contrast, may be cooked as is, but will be more tender and flavorful if it is first packed in salt for 24 hours. For salting, choose coarsely grained sea salt, kosher salt or pickling salt. (Table salt is processed so that it does not absorb moisture readily; thus it will not cling to the meat.)

Because tongue is composed chiefly of muscle fiber, it must be softened by gentle cooking. After soaking or salting, it should be poached for about one hour per pound [½ kg.]. Do not try to speed the process by increasing the heat: Boiling will toughen the meat.

Before being cut up for serving, the tongue has to be peeled *(Steps 3 and 4)*. This operation is most easily performed while the meat is still warm.

1 **Salting tongue.** Line a deep dish with coarse salt, set the tongue on top and pack more salt around the meat. Cover, and refrigerate the tongue overnight. Then rinse the salt from the tongue *(above)*. Place the tongue in a casserole just big enough to hold it.

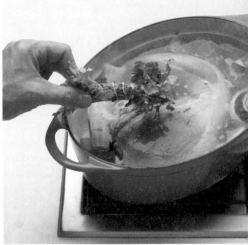

2 **Poaching the tongue.** Cover the tongue with cold water. Bring the water to a bare simmer, skimming off scum as it surfaces. When no more scum rises add carrots, celery, onions and a bouquet garni. With the lid ajar, poach the tongue for three hours, or until a skewer easily pierces the tip.

6 **Slicing the tongue.** With the knife, score the side of the tongue at regular intervals to mark off slices *(above)*. Then, starting at the tip of the tongue, use a sawing motion to cut the first few slices diagonally. Gradually reduce the angle of each successive slice until you are cutting across the grain at a right angle where the tongue widens.

7 **Marinating the tongue.** Dip each slice in the dressing and lay the slices in the prepared dish. Trim off the fat from the reserved wedge of meat. Removing gristle or small bones as you work, slice the wedge and cut it into julienne *(above)*. Toss the julienne with the remaining dressing and add the mixture to the dish. Cover, and marinate the tongue for up to two hours.

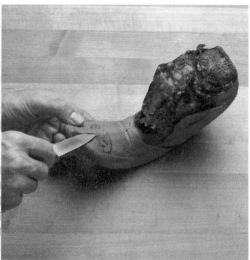

3 **Peeling the underside.** Let the meat steep in its poaching liquid until it cools enough to handle. Set the tongue on a board, with the underside up. Slit the skin lengthwise by sliding the point of a knife underneath it from the tip to the base of the tongue. Peel the skin from the slit toward each edge.

4 **Peeling the top skin.** Just above the base, slit the skin on top of the tongue crosswise from edge to edge. Peel the skin from the slit toward the tip. Then slide the knife between the skin and meat to ease the skin away from the base.

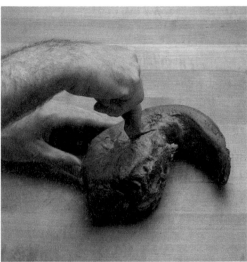

5 **Trimming the tongue.** Make a semicircular cut to remove the underside of the base in a wedge. Reserve the wedge. Mix the dressing — in this case, a mustard vinaigrette laced with a little of the cooled tongue stock, some chopped shallots and parsley — and pour about half of it into a shallow dish.

8 **Assembling the salad.** Drain the marinade into a serving bowl, add the julienne and toss it with the garnish — in this case, warm, wilted cabbage *(above)*. Arrange the tongue slices over the julienne mixture and sprinkle them with more garnishes; cubed beets, chopped pickles, hard-boiled egg quarters and fresh chervil are used here. Toss gently *(right)* and serve.

Brains: A Versatile Delicacy

Those who venture to sample calf's or lamb's brains generally are delighted by their mild flavor and firm, creamy texture. Poached in a basic court bouillon *(recipe, page 165),* then cooled and served with a lemon-and-cream dressing, a tangy mayonnaise or a vinaigrette *(recipe, page 167),* brains constitute a salad that is at once light on the palate and richly satisfying.

Since brains cannot be frozen with success—their texture becomes spongy—only specialty butchers and large supermarkets carry them. Even at these shops, brains usually must be ordered in advance. When fresh, brains are pale pink, moist, plump and evenly formed. Like all organ meats, they are highly perishable. If you cannot cook the brains at once, cover them with a damp kitchen towel to keep them moist, and refrigerate them for no longer than 24 hours.

Before they are cooked, brains should be soaked for at least one hour in acidulated water, made by adding one tablespoon [15 ml.] of vinegar to a quart [1 liter] of water. Soaking loosens the membranous cover of blood vessels that clings to each brain and makes this membrane easy to remove. If not peeled away, the membrane would contract during cooking and distort the shape of the brain, while the blood would muddy its flavor and mar its pale color.

The delicacy of brains dictates gentle poaching in liquid kept at a simmer that barely murmurs in the pot. After poaching and cooling, however, brains become firm enough to be handled easily and cut neatly into slices or dice. The irregularly shaped outside edges, and any scraps produced in the cutting process, need not be lost. Sieving reduces them to a purée that adds substance to the dressing; a subtle mustardy topping that contrasts with the brains' mild taste is used here.

A Spicy Cream Dressing

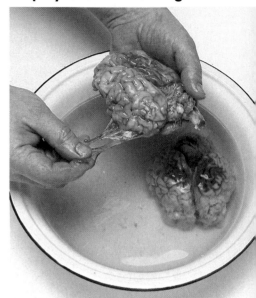

1 **Peeling the brains.** Soak the brains in cold acidulated water for at least an hour. With your finger tips, peel away the membrane *(above),* loosening it by repeatedly dipping the brains in the water. If the brains are blood-stained, soak them in fresh water, changing it until the liquid is clear.

5 **Presenting the brains.** Pour a thin stream of heavy cream into the dressing, stirring vigorously *(above).* Taste the dressing and correct the seasoning. Arrange the slices of brain on a platter. Pour the dressing over them. If you like, garnish with sprigs of mustard cress and slices of cooked carrot from the court bouillon *(right).*

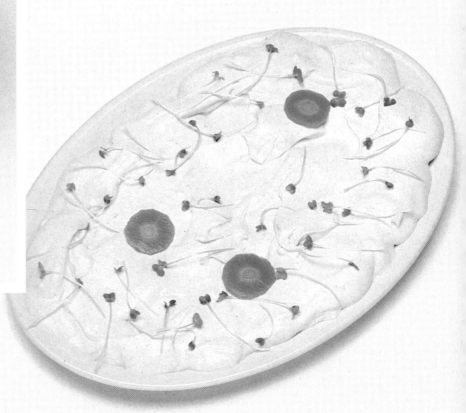

2 **Poaching the brains.** In a pan of water, simmer wine vinegar, onion, carrot, leek, celery, an unpeeled garlic clove, parsley, thyme and a bay leaf for 30 minutes. Add whole peppercorns. Gently slide each brain into the liquid *(above)*; partly cover the pan and simmer for 15 to 20 minutes.

3 **Cooling the brains.** Skim off any scum from the surface of the liquid, then lift out the brains with a slotted spoon or a mesh skimmer and place them on a plate. To keep the brains moist and to prevent them from discoloring, cover them with a damp towel dipped in the court bouillon *(above)*.

4 **Sieving the brains.** When the brains are cool, trim off the irregular edges and slice the brains crosswise. Cover the slices with the towel again. Put lemon juice, salt, pepper and Dijon mustard in a bowl. To add body to the dressing, press the scraps of brain through a sieve into the bowl *(above)*.

Vinaigrette Colored with Spinach and Herbs

1 **Making the dressing.** Stem a handful of spinach, and blanch it for two minutes in boiling salted water. Drain the spinach, squeeze it dry, then chop it coarse and purée it through a food mill or in a food processor. In a mixing bowl, stir vinegar, salt and pepper until the salt dissolves; mix in the spinach, then add fines herbes and chopped watercress. Stir in olive oil *(above)*.

2 **Presenting the dish.** Spread the dressing evenly on a large serving platter and arrange slices of poached and cooled brains on top *(above)*. Alternatively, you could cut the brains into large dice and gently toss them with the dressing. Either presentation may be garnished with more fines herbes.

Ringing Changes on Chicken Salad

Poached or roasted chicken and turkey breasts yield neat, uniform slices. Served with a vivid dressing, the delicate meat makes a striking salad. Here, slices of chicken breast are arranged on a bed of tomato-flavored vinaigrette *(recipe, page 167)*. As an alternative, you could color the vinaigrette with puréed spinach and perhaps flavor it with fines herbes.

Breasts bought separately retain their juiciness best when poached. Whole birds may be either poached or roasted, and their leg and wing meat can become a second, more robust salad with a green mayonnaise dressing *(opposite, bottom; recipe, page 166)*.

To carve a whole bird neatly, remove the wishbone before cooking: Pull back the neck skin and cut the bone from the flesh. Season the cavity and truss the wings and legs to the body. Undercook the bird to keep the breast moist. The 3-pound [1½-kg.] chicken here was roasted for one hour at 325° F. [160° C.]. The dark meat, still pink, was then cooked separately for another 10 to 15 minutes.

Perfect Breast Slices in a Pinwheel Design

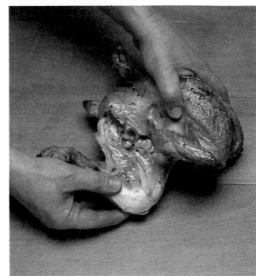 

1 **Removing the first leg.** Roast a chicken and let it rest for 15 minutes. Remove the trussing string. Steady the chicken with one hand and, using a sharp knife, cut the skin between the thigh and the body. Bend the leg down to locate the hip joint *(above)* and cut through it to sever the whole leg.

2 **Removing the wings.** Move the wing back and forth to locate its joint with the collarbone and shoulder blade. Cut through the corner of the breast to the shoulder joint, then sever the wing from the body at the joint *(above)*. Turn the bird; remove the other leg and wing.

6 **Making the dressing.** Simmer peeled, seeded and chopped tomatoes, uncovered, over low heat to make a thick purée. Season and cool the purée. Prepare a vinaigrette with lemon juice, using six parts of oil to one of lemon. Stir enough purée into the vinaigrette to give it a rich color *(above)*.

7 **Presenting the salad.** Spread the dressing on a serving platter and arrange the slices of chicken breast in a pinwheel pattern on top. Garnish with a neat rosette of fresh herbs, green leafy vegetables or, as here, watercress.

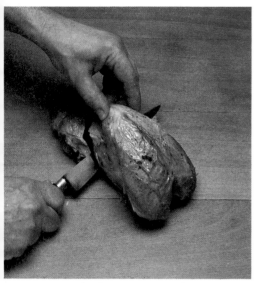
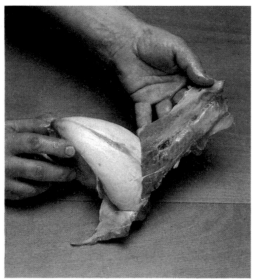
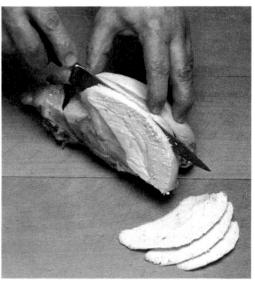

3 **Freeing the breast.** Return the legs to the oven to cook until done, about 10 to 15 minutes; reserve the legs and wings for another preparation. Meanwhile, starting from its tail end, cut the chicken just below both sides of the rib cage *(above)* to sever the breast from the backbone.

4 **Removing the skin.** Steady the bird with one hand. With your other hand, firmly grasp the edge of the skin at the narrow, pointed end of the breast and pull it away in one piece *(above)*.

5 **Carving the breast.** Steady one side of the breast with your finger tips, and carve the opposite side into thin slices *(above)*. Hold the breast bone while carving the second side of the breast. Reserve the carcass for stock.

Natural Cups for Chunks of Chicken

1 **Cutting up the chicken.** Skin and pick every scrap of meat from a roasted chicken's legs and wings, and chop the meat into chunks *(above)*. Parboil spinach in salted water. Drain the spinach, squeeze it dry and purée it with a food mill or processor.

2 **Serving.** Into mayonnaise *(page 17)*, stir the spinach and chopped watercress, scallions, celery and fines herbes. Toss this with the chicken and serve it on a bed of greens or, as here, on leaves of red Verona chicory. Garnish the salad, if you like, with parsley and bits of tomato *(above)*.

4
Fish and Shellfish
Matching the Method to the Ingredient

The catch from oceans, rivers and lakes produces a panoply of salads as varied and appealing as the fish and shellfish themselves: sweet lobster morsels laced with vinaigrette, chunks of rich mackerel drenched with wine sauce, succulent mussels tossed with lemony mayonnaise, and a multitude of other delectable combinations.

Tender enough to be eaten straight from the water, seafood is sometimes served raw in salads such as the Latin American-inspired *seviche* opposite *(pages 66-67)*. More conventionally, the fish and shellfish for salad making are cooked by the moist-heat methods that preserve their innate flavor and texture: steaming, braising, poaching or boiling.

The character of the seafood dictates which method suits it best. Steaming over a shallow layer of boiling liquid is ideal for bivalves such as clams and mussels; these shellfish open when done and their natural juices would be diluted if they were submerged *(pages 68-69)*. Braising in a minimum of liquid keeps soft, fatty fish—mackerel, tuna or herring, for example—intact during cooking. Poaching, which involves complete immersion, is appropriate for such firm-fleshed fish and thin-shelled crustaceans as salmon, haddock or shrimp. With both braising and poaching, the liquid must be kept trembling gently at about 175° F. [85° C.]; higher temperatures will dry out and break up such seafood. By contrast, crabs and lobsters should be cooked in vigorously boiling liquid so that the heat quickly penetrates their thick shells *(pages 70-71)*.

Plain or salted water will serve for boiling crabs or lobsters, but a wide range of seasoned liquids may be used to advantage in steaming, braising or poaching other seafood. A cooking liquid based on wine, vinegar or milk and such aromatics as onions and herbs will enhance the flavor of the fish or shellfish. Moreover, the liquid can be boiled down afterward, providing a rich broth to augment salad dressings and carry the flavor of the seafood to every element of the assembly.

Dressings for seafoods may be thick or thin, mild or tangy, and enriched with broth, herbs or spices, as the cook chooses. The overriding factor with dressing a seafood salad is timing. The fish or shellfish should be tossed with vinaigrette, mayonnaise or cream dressing while still at room temperature and served as soon as possible. Chilling would mute the delicate flavors of seafood and dressing alike.

A trickle of olive oil lends gloss to the avocado slices and escarole leaves surrounding a refreshingly simple *seviche*. For this unusual salad, bite-sized cubes of red snapper were first marinated in lime juice, which reacted with the protein of the fish to firm it, and then tossed with onion rings, chives and tiny circles of hot red chili.

63

Enhancing Flavor with a Court Bouillon

Braising and poaching are the best ways to cook fish destined for the salad plate: The fish emerges from the pot firm yet moist, and with its characteristic texture unaltered. While plain water can serve as the cooking medium, the flavor of any fish is improved by using a rich liquid called a court bouillon, made with white or red wine, vinegar or milk plus aromatic vegetables and herbs.

Fatty fish such as the mackerel used in the top demonstration on these pages contain enough oil to give them an assertive taste. These fish benefit from a pungent court bouillon, based on wine or wine vinegar, that includes forceful flavorings such as garlic, fennel and coriander *(recipe, page 165)*.

A milk court bouillon, on the other hand, complements the mild flavor of lean fish—whiting, halibut or cod are typical—and it helps to keep their flesh pearly white. Milk court bouillon also provides a creamy contrast to smoked fish, such as the haddock used in the demonstration at bottom right *(recipe, page 142)*. Unlike wine and vinegar mixtures, milk court bouillon needs no advance simmering.

To avoid overcooking and thus drying out the fish, a braising or poaching liquid should be kept at the barest tremble. Fresh fish should be simmered for no more than 10 minutes for each inch [2½ cm.] of thickness, measured at its thickest part; the fish is done when the flesh has become opaque and firm enough to offer just slight resistance to the tip of a skewer or knife. Smoked fish, too, demands gentle cooking until its flesh is just tender, although well-cured specimens may take as long as an hour.

After the braising or poaching is completed, the court bouillon can be used to dress the fish. A winy broth can perform this role, either as is, or chilled to produce a light jelly. And any court bouillon can be incorporated with a mayonnaise, tart cream or vinaigrette dressing. In the case of the smoked-haddock salad, the milk court bouillon does triple duty—flavoring first the fish, then the rice, then a tart cream dressing *(page 16)*.

Double Duty for a Wine-based Medium

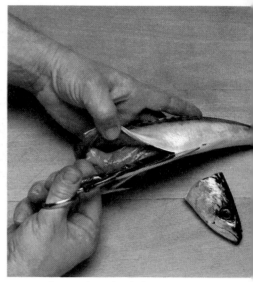

1 **Making a court bouillon.** In a saucepan, bring some dry white wine to a boil. Add salt and aromatics — here, carrots, onions, unpeeled garlic cloves, bay leaves, coriander, fennel and thyme. Reduce the heat, cover and simmer for 15 minutes; add a few peppercorns just before removing from the heat.

2 **Eviscerating the fish.** Cut off the head of each fish — in this case, mackerel — with a large, sharp knife. With kitchen scissors, slit the belly *(above)*. Pull out the viscera and the thin membrane that lines the belly. Cut off the tails, and slice the fish into pieces 1½ inches [4 cm.] wide.

A Moderating Role for Milk

1 **Poaching the fish.** Line a nonreactive pot with onion rings and top them with chopped fresh herbs. Place the fish — in this instance, smoked haddock — in the pot, and add more onion rings and herbs. Cover the fish completely with milk and poach until barely tender, about one hour. Remove the fish to a platter; strain and reserve the court bouillon.

2 **Slicing the fish.** Pick off bits of onion or milk froth clinging to the fillets. With a knife, ease away any surface membrane and trim off the thinner portion of each fillet *(above)*; reserve the trimmings. Slice the thick part of each fillet into serving portions and marinate them in a lemony vinaigrette.

3 **Braising the fish.** Place the fish in a stainless-steel, enameled or tin-lined sauté pan just large enough to hold the pieces in a single layer so that they will cook evenly. Add court bouillon to cover them about halfway, and simmer over low heat until the pieces are cooked through — about 10 minutes.

4 **Serving the salad.** Arrange the fish in a shallow dish and pour the court bouillon and aromatics over the pieces. Let the fish cool to room temperature before serving *(above)*. To intensify the flavors, you may cover the salad and put it in the refrigerator for up to three days; the court bouillon will jell lightly.

3 **Preparing rice.** In a separate pot, immerse rice in twice its volume of boiling, strained court bouillon, cover and simmer for 15 minutes. Flake the reserved fish trimmings into the cooked rice, add vinegar, olive oil and chopped parsley; toss and season to taste. Cool the rice to room temperature.

4 **Assembling the salad.** Mound the rice on a platter and overlap the fish slices on top of it. Border the salad with lemon wedges and pitted black olives, and garnish it with parsley and marinated onion rings. Serve with a dressing made of tart cream thinned with a little court bouillon and lemon juice.

The Felicitous Alliance of Citrus and Seafood

The cuisines of every continent celebrate salads uniting cooked or raw fish with fresh citrus juices—from lemons, limes, grapefruits or the bitter Seville oranges sometimes found in specialty food stores. These juices, with their aromatic oils and light, natural sugars, can substitute for sharper-tasting vinegars in marinades and dressings.

If marinated in citrus juice for several hours and served raw, fish becomes the basis of the Latin American salad known as *seviche*. It can be made with such shellfish as scallops, shrimp or conch, or with any firm-textured fish—sole or bass, for example, or the red snapper used in the demonstration at top right.

To make *seviche*, bite-sized pieces of fish or shellfish are bathed with citrus juice in a glass or ceramic bowl; a metal bowl would react with the acids in the juice to adversely affect the flavor of the seafood. The fish or shellfish is then marinated in the refrigerator for up to six hours. During this time, the acids in the juice act on the proteins in the flesh to whiten and firm it and make it opaque. Before serving, the seafood is tossed with olive oil—which counters the acidity of the marinade—and with seasonings and garnishes *(recipes, pages 139-140)*.

Although lengthy marinating of raw seafood produces changes that resemble those of cooking, it does not kill parasites that, in rare cases, could cause stomach upset or worse. A salad based on cooked fish or shellfish—and enhanced with citrus—is entirely safe to eat: All parasites are killed at a temperature of 105° F. [40° C.]. For the tangy shrimp salad demonstrated below, the shellfish is poached in a court bouillon that incorporates wine. This cooking liquor is then reduced and mixed with a lively lemon-and-lime vinaigrette that serves both as a marinade and as a dressing.

A Dramatic Transformation of Raw Fish

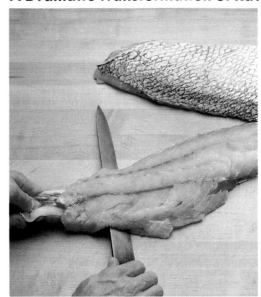

1 **Skinning the fillets.** Lay a fillet — in this case, red snapper — skin side down. Insert a sharp knife between the skin and the flesh at its narrow end. Grasp the skin firmly and, angling the knife slightly downward, cut away from yourself with short strokes.

2 **Marinating the fish.** Cut the fillets into cubes and drop them into a ceramic or glass bowl. Squeeze enough citrus juice — lime is used here — to cover the fish at least halfway, and pour it over the cubes. Toss the fish in the juice, cover the bowl and refrigerate for one hour.

A Tart Accent for Cooked Shellfish

1 **Poaching the shrimp.** Prepare a basic court bouillon *(recipe, page 165)*. Let the liquid cool slightly, then add the shrimp. Cover the pan, simmer until the shrimp turn pink — five to eight minutes — and then immediately remove the pan from the heat.

2 **Draining the shrimp.** Pour the shrimp and court bouillon into a colander set over a deep bowl. Transfer the drained shrimp to another bowl. Return the court bouillon to the pan and boil down the liquid to half its original volume.

3 **Marinating the fish.** After one hour, the flesh should begin to look opaque. To ensure that all pieces marinate evenly, toss the fish again and re-cover. Let the pieces steep in the marinade for another two to four hours, tossing them occasionally.

4 **Adding the garnishes.** When the fish is firm and completely opaque, drain off the marinade. Add seasonings and garnishes — here, olive oil, salt, pepper, cut chives, rings of red onion and hot chili — and toss the salad.

5 **Serving the seviche.** Spoon the fish mixture onto a serving plate and add any garnishes. This salad includes escarole and avocado slices, both dressed with a lime-juice-and-olive-oil vinaigrette *(recipe, page 167).*

3 **Marinating the shrimp.** Shell the warm shrimp, leaving the tail shells on the most attractive shrimp to create a garnish. Marinate the shrimp for about an hour in a mixture of lime juice, lemon juice, olive oil, salt and pepper. Add the shells to the court bouillon.

4 **Making the dressing.** Simmer the shells in the court bouillon for five to 10 minutes. Purée this mixture a little at a time in a food processor, then strain it, using a cheesecloth-lined strainer. Drain the shrimp and whisk their marinade into the strained liquid.

5 **Serving the shrimp.** Mound the shelled shrimp on a platter, then drape the large shrimp with tails over the top as a garnish. Surround the shrimp with a ring of lemon and lime slices and spoon the dressing over them.

Succulent Candidates for Steaming

Bivalves such as mussels and hard- or soft-shell clams yield succulent morsels of flesh perfectly suited to salads. The easiest way to cook them is also the best: in a tightly covered pot with just enough liquid to envelop the clams or mussels in steam. This method keeps the flesh tender, and any natural juices that escape can be retrieved by straining the cooking broth, boiling it down and incorporating it into the salad dressing.

Before cooking clams, soak them for an hour or two in several changes of cold salted water to let them expel any sand or grit. Mussels, used in this demonstration, live on rocks rather than in the sandy bottoms; hence, they need only a brief plunge into cold water to refresh them and loosen surface mud.

Scrub the clams or mussels clean, remove the beards of mussels *(Step 1)*, and test bivalves of any kind to make sure that they are alive and safe to eat. Live clams and mussels usually keep their shells shut tight. To guard against dead specimens that have been sealed by mud, slide closed shells laterally; if they move, discard them. Test slightly open shells by tapping them against a bowl *(Step 2)*; they will snap shut if the clams or mussels are alive.

As the clams or mussels steam, shake the pot to ensure even cooking, and remove the lid often to check on their progress. When a bivalve is fully cooked, its shell pops open. Mussels and soft-shell clams need about five minutes' steaming; hard-shell clams may have to cook for 10 to 15 minutes.

Once they are opened, soft-shell clams must be trimmed of their long necks, or siphons—tough scraps that can be incorporated into the dressing if peeled and then chopped or puréed. Steamed mussels or hard-shell clams, on the other hand, can be simply scooped from their shells and tossed with a vinaigrette or mayonnaise to make a delicious salad. Here, both kinds of dressing are used: vinaigrette as a marinade and mayonnaise as a final dressing. Clam and mussel salads can be further elaborated by introducing such complementary vegetables as shredded, blanched celeriac, steamed fennel slices or boiled whole new potatoes *(recipe, page 148)*.

1 Cleaning the mussels. Soak the mussels in ice water for 10 minutes or so to refresh them. Scrub the shells with a stiff-bristled brush. Then, holding each mussel firmly in one hand, grip the ropy beard running along the edge of the shell and jerk the beard back and forth until it tears off *(above)*.

2 Testing. Tap the hinged side of each opened mussel against a bowl and discard any shell that does not shut immediately. Check each closed mussel by grasping it firmly between your thumb and forefinger, then trying to slide the shell halves in opposite directions. If the halves slide, the mussel is dead.

6 Blending the dressing. With a pestle or spoon, press the mussel purée through a strainer into the mayonnaise. Whisk the two together thoroughly. Add enough of the reduced broth to thin the dressing to the consistency of heavy cream.

7 Dressing the mussels. Taking care not to tear the mussels, gently fold enough of the dressing into them so that each mussel is lightly coated. Reserve the remaining dressing.

3 **Steaming the mussels.** In a large pot prepare a court bouillon — here made with white wine, shallots and herbs. Add the mussels and cover the pot. Cook over high heat for about five minutes, shaking the pot often while holding the lid and pot with a towel.

4 **Marinating the mussels.** Remove the mussels with a skimmer; discard any closed shells. Shell the warm mussels and toss them with olive oil and lemon juice. Set aside any torn mussels to flavor the dressing; reserve the nicest shells for a garnish. Prepare a thick mayonnaise *(page 17)*, omitting the lemon juice.

5 **Making a mussel purée.** Strain the cooking broth through a sieve lined with a coffee filter (cheesecloth will not catch fine particles); then boil the broth until it is reduced by half. In a mortar, make a paste of the torn mussels and fresh herbs. Add enough of the cooled broth to make a thin purée.

8 **Assembling the platter.** Mound the mussels in the center of a serving platter and arrange a border of shells around them *(above)*. Garnish the platter with lemon wedges and parsley *(right)*. Serve with the reserved dressing.

Making the Most of a Crustacean's Sweet Flesh

The sweet flesh of lobster or crab, moistened with a vinaigrette that includes the crustacean's own juices and decorated with its own carapace, makes an opulent salad. Here, lobster meat is presented on a bed of chicory—for a tart contrast of flavors—and garnished with walnuts for a textural complement. Lobster or crab also could be dressed with mayonnaise—enriched, perhaps, with whipped cream or capers—and ringed with slices of avocado and tomato (recipe, page 144).

Essential to any such salad is freshly cooked shellfish, bought live on the day it is to be served. Allow about ½ to 1 pound [¼ to ½ kg.] of live weight for each serving. Lobsters ranging from 1 to 4 pounds [½ to 2 kg.] are the ones most commonly available; the pair shown here weigh 1¼ pounds [⅔ kg.] apiece. Depending on variety, crabs can vary in size from ½ to 3 pounds [¼ to 1½ kg.] each.

The most humane way to dispatch lobsters or crabs is to plunge them headfirst into a pot of boiling water. Because their circulatory organs are centered in the head, the extreme temperature will kill them instantly. Then, with the shellfish totally submerged, simply cover the pot and boil them until they are done.

Do not start timing the shellfish until the water returns to a boil. Then cook lobsters for 10 minutes a pound [½ kg.], adding four minutes for each additional ½ pound [¼ kg.]. For crabs, allow about eight minutes for each pound. To test a lobster or crab for doneness, remove it from the pot with tongs, grasp one of the legs and jerk it sharply. If the leg comes off, the lobster or crab is done; if not, cook it for another two or three minutes and then test it again.

When they have cooled, disjoint lobsters and remove the meat from the tail and claws (Steps 1-6). For crabs, twist off the legs and claws, crack them and peel the shells from the meat. Snap off the tail flap from the underside, and pull off the top shell in one piece. Then, discard the gravel sac (stomach), cut away the gills and split the body shell down the middle; pick out the meat from the crevices.

Both crabs and lobsters yield tomalley (liver), and female specimens also contain coral (roe)—splendid treats when reserved and added to the dressing.

1 **Removing the tail.** Drop lobsters into a pot of boiling salted water, cover and boil over high heat until they redden and a leg can be easily torn off. Set them on a cutting board to cool. Holding one lobster at a time over a bowl to catch its juices, twist off the tail section. Upend the body to drain it and collect any loose bits of tomalley.

5 **Removing the tail meat.** Pull off the tail fins and reserve them. Then, holding the tail in one hand, use scissors to cut the center of the undershell. Spread the shell and ease the tail meat out whole. Discard the shell.

6 **Extracting the claw meat.** Using a mallet, crack each claw in the center and on both pincers. Pull away the shell fragments to extract the meat in one piece. Twist off each claw from the two jointed segments. Cut open the joints (above) and remove the meat. Disjoint the second lobster similarly.

7 **Preparing the dressing.** Add a little red wine vinegar to the lobster juices and solids, and whisk until the mixture is smooth. Whisk in oil—in this case, walnut oil—to finish the dressing, using a ratio of approximately four parts of oil to one part of vinegar.

2 **Removing legs and claws.** Hold the lobster with its soft undershell facing up, grasp each leg where it meets the body and twist it off. Twist off the claws where their joints meet the body. Reserve the legs and claws.

3 **Removing the undershell.** Hold the body over the bowl containing the juices and slip your thumb under the hard upper shell. Pull away the soft undershell in one piece: The feathery gills will come with it. Discard the undershell and inedible gills.

4 **Extracting the tomalley.** With a spoon, scoop out the greenish tomalley from the upper shell and add it to the juices in the bowl. If the lobster is a female, as here, scoop out the reddish coral from near the head; add it to the juices. Remove and discard the gravel sac from between the eyes. Set the upper shell aside.

8 **Assembling the salad.** Slice the tail meat crosswise into medallions. Brush the body shells, tail fins and legs with oil to give them a sheen. Then prepare a bed of greens — here, chicory — moistening each piece with a vinaigrette flavored with some lobster dressing *(left)*. Arrange the shells and meat on the greens. Garnish the salad with walnuts marinated in oil and spoon the dressing over it *(above)*.

5
Composed Salads
Assemblies to Please Both Eye and Palate

The proper cooking of pasta
Tenderizing grains
A dressing based on coconut milk
A traditional use of herring
Pairing cheese with meat
Creating a mousse with jellied stock

The most sophisticated products of the salad maker's art are what the French refer to as *salades composées*—combinations of diverse savory elements usually presented in formal arrangements. Almost any raw or cooked food that can be enjoyed cold may become part of the final composition; eggs, cheeses and starches all qualify, along with vegetables, fruits, meats and seafood.

In some classic formulas, the composition is a simple, light amalgam of cooked and raw vegetables. *Salade Dubarry,* for example, combines sliced radishes and sprigs of watercress with boiled cauliflower florets. More often the composition unites elements of so much substance that the result practically qualifies as a meal in itself: In *Salade Francillon,* potatoes and mussels are set off by strips of herring and slices of truffle (*recipe, page 148*).

Although useful as guides, recipes cannot begin to encompass all of the possibilities of the composed salad. However, creativity needs to be tempered by common sense. Too many bits of this and pieces of that produce a cacophony. The key to success lies in choosing a dominant ingredient and then picking other foods that—used as generous complements, not as mere accents—balance and enhance the base. As a rule, when the base is mild, its complements should be more assertive, and vice versa. Similarly, crisp textures balance soft ones. And the visual traits of the ingredients—shapes, sizes and colors—should be coordinated in a way that produces a pleasing design before the salad is tossed.

Greenery is the most versatile starting point for composed salads (*pages 74-75*). Beds or borders of firm lettuces and other leaves serve as a light background for almost any leftover or fresh vegetable or fruit. Grains ranging from the exotic Middle Eastern cracked wheat called bulgur to the commonplace white rice provide a more substantial base (*pages 76-77*). So does pasta that has been cooked until it is *al dente*— approximately "firm to the bite" (*pages 78-79*).

Dressings ordinarily supply the final touch that marries ingredients: vinaigrette when tartness is in order, mayonnaise and cream dressings for a mellow effect. A spectacular alternative is to encase a composition of ingredients in jelly, a binder that not only displays foods like jewels but pervades the salad with a unifying flavor (*pages 86-87*).

A dollop of oil polishes the ingredients of this shell-pasta salad, a giant bull's-eye pattern of contrasting tastes, textures, colors and shapes. The unassertive pasta is an apt background for the stronger-tasting circles of ripe olives, cubed feta cheese, chunks of tomato and whole rocket and basil leaves.

Vivid Arrays of the Materials at Hand

Although countless formulas exist for composed salads, the most pleasing versions often are impromptu creations inspired by leftovers from the refrigerator or produce from the garden: herbs and flowers, hard-boiled eggs, cooked meat or seafood, raw or cooked vegetables. Depending on their nature, the salad ingredients can be used whole, chopped, sliced, diced or—in the case of eggs and large vegetables—even hollowed and stuffed. The salad can be served from the bowl it is mixed in *(below)* or arranged in formal display on a platter *(box, opposite page)*.

Lettuces and other leaves play an important part in marrying the elements of such assemblies, and simple dressings such as lemon and cream or vinaigrette *(recipes, pages 165 and 167)* provide another unifying theme. When vinaigrette is the choice, it can be made early and used as a marinade to brighten the flavors of most kinds of cooked vegetables, meat and fish, as well as raw onion. But leaves and green beans should be dressed at the last moment to retain crispness.

1 **Making a vinaigrette.** In a salad bowl, grind a cut-up garlic clove, salt and pepper with a wooden pestle *(above)* until they form a paste. Add vinegar, stirring until the salt dissolves. Then add olive oil, using four parts for each part of vinegar, and mix thoroughly.

2 **Starting the marinating.** Place into the salad bowl ingredients that will benefit from marinating. In this case, strips of broiled, peeled and seeded green, red and yellow peppers *(page 42)* are torn into strips and then marinated along with sliced red onions and anchovy fillets.

5 **Tossing the salad.** Place the remaining ingredients on top: in this case, boiled green beans, tomato wedges, quartered hard-boiled eggs, nasturtium leaves and blossoms, purple hyssop flowers and parsley *(left)*. Slip out the servers and toss the salad with the servers or by hand *(above)*.

3 Coating the ingredients. Using the pestle or your hands, stir the ingredients until they are thoroughly coated with the dressing, taking care not to crush the soft pieces. Taste the dressing and adjust the seasoning. Marinate the ingredients at room temperature for up to 30 minutes.

4 Adding the leaves. To keep the leaves out of the dressing until the salad is tossed, cross salad servers over the bottom of the bowl. Lay some larger leaves (here, red-tipped oakleaf lettuce) on the servers and fill the bowl with the remaining leaves: purslane, rocket and basil are shown.

Two Schemes for Display

Arranging ingredients in rows. Lay broiled peppers down the center of a platter; border them with rows of green beans, tomato slices and rocket. Decorate the rows with anchovies, onion rings, purslane, basil and chopped hard-boiled eggs. Dress with vinaigrette and sprinkle with hyssop flowers *(above)*.

Using stuffed tomatoes and eggs. Cover a platter with leaves — red-tipped oakleaf lettuce are shown. Peel and hollow tomatoes and fill with beans. Mash hard-boiled egg yolks with anchovies and mustard and fill the whites. Place the tomatoes and eggs on the platter; garnish with nasturtiums and pepper strips.

Substantial Foundations of Grain

Cooked grains provide mild flavors and chewy textures that afford a flattering background for almost any raw or cooked vegetable, as well as for leftover meat, poultry or seafood.

The best grains for salads are those that keep their shape and stay somewhat firm when they are cooked and dressed: long-grain white rice, brown rice, or the cracked wheat variously called bulgur or *burgul*. Wild rice, which has a softer texture and a more pronounced taste when it is cooked, offers yet another option.

Choose the rest of the salad ingredients carefully, so that their flavors do not clash; extra character can be derived from the addition of imaginative seasonings and dressings. In the Middle Eastern *tabbouleh* shown at right, top *(recipe, page 153)*, bulgur is mixed with tomatoes and scallions, scented with fresh herbs and dressed with lemon juice and olive oil. In the bottom demonstration, a salad of white rice, mushrooms, onions and tomatoes is dressed with a vinaigrette and perfumed with chopped fresh tarragon *(recipe, page 152)*.

As in any grain salad, the preparation of both the bulgur and the white-rice mixtures begins with softening or cooking the grain. Before it is sold, the wheat is cooked and sun-dried; all the cook needs to do is soak it in cold water. Rice should be boiled or steamed until just tender. The cooking time will depend on the variety of rice you use. The white rice shown here needs to be boiled for 15 to 20 minutes; wild rice takes about 45 minutes and brown rice about 50 minutes.

Once the grains are ready, they must be rid of excess liquid. Properly drained, the grain will absorb some of the dressing, resulting in a cohesive mixture that can—if you choose—be presented as a molded dish *(Steps 3 and 4, bottom)*.

An Aromatic Assembly from Cracked Wheat

1 **Soaking the bulgur.** In a bowl, soak bulgur in cold water for at least half an hour. Then bite a few grains: When they are soft but still slightly chewy, the bulgur is ready. Scoop up the grains, squeeze out the water *(above)* and put the bulgur in a mixing bowl. Drain the last few grains through a strainer.

2 **Assembling the salad.** Add finely chopped parsley, mint, scallions and chives to the bulgur in the bowl. Then put in peeled, seeded and chopped tomatoes. Season with salt and pepper and add fresh lemon juice. Toss the ingredients thoroughly with your hands.

A Centerpiece of Molded Rice

1 **Preparing the rice.** Bring a large quantity of salted water to a boil, add the rice, cover, and simmer until tender—15 minutes. Meanwhile, make vinaigrette *(recipe, page 167)* in a large bowl. Drain the rice in a strainer and empty it onto a kitchen towel. Fold the towel over the rice and pat it dry.

2 **Assembling the salad.** Transfer the rice to the bowl containing the vinaigrette. Add mushrooms that have been blanched in lightly salted water, finely chopped onions, fresh tarragon and peeled, seeded and chopped tomatoes. Toss the ingredients together with your hands.

3 **Adding olive oil.** Pour some olive oil over the salad *(above)* and mix it in by hand. Continue to add oil and toss the salad until the ingredients stick together. Taste the salad and, if necessary, add some more salt and lemon juice.

4 **Serving the cracked-wheat salad.** Arrange lettuce on a serving platter and mound the bulgur mixture on top. Garnish with a few sprigs of mint and serve with a bowl of extra lettuce leaves. To eat the salad in the traditional Middle Eastern way, use a lettuce leaf to roll up a bite-sized morsel of the wheat mixture.

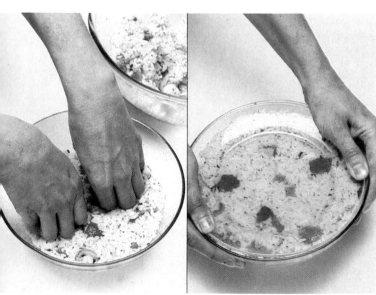

3 **Packing the mold.** Serve the salad straight from the mixing bowl or, as demonstrated here, mold it first. Transfer the salad to a smaller bowl. Then, with your knuckles, push the salad down tight, taking care not to crush the ingredients *(above, left)*. When the bowl is filled to the top, use a plate *(right)* to press the salad down, thus completing the molding and creating a smooth base.

4 **Unmolding the rice salad.** Let the salad rest for about 10 minutes. Remove the plate and invert a serving platter on top of the bowl. Hold the platter and the bowl firmly together and turn them over. Carefully lift the bowl away to unmold the rice salad *(above)*. Garnish the salad with leaves of crisp lettuce or corn salad — tossed, if you like, in a vinaigrette.

Noodles: An Unobtrusive Base for Bold Flavors

Properly cooked noodles make a perfect basis for a composed salad: Their mild taste and subdued color invite the addition of bright, boldly flavored ingredients and tart dressings. The choice of noodles is wide. For instance, Italian pasta— made from wheat flour—is commercially available as ribbons, tubes, bows, spirals and the shell shapes shown at top right *(recipes, page 155)*. For a different effect, salads may include the thin, translucent noodles made of rice flour and available in Oriental markets *(bottom; recipe, page 154)*. Preparation of either type of noodle is simple, but care must be taken to protect their texture.

Pasta noodles must be boiled. To prevent them from turning into a gummy mass, large quantities of salted water— at least 4 quarts [4 liters] per pound [½ kg.] of pasta—must be used, and cooking should be brief. Plunge the noodles into rapidly boiling water and begin to test their texture after one minute for fresh pasta, after four minutes for dried pasta; bite into ribbons or tubes, or test small noodles as shown in Step 1 at right. When the noodles are tender but still firm, drain them and immediately add oil to keep them from sticking as they cool.

Oriental rice noodles should be deep fried in 3 inches [8 cm.] of peanut or vegetable oil heated to 375° F. [190° C.] *(Step 3, bottom)*. They will puff up and twist into crisp nests.

The cook has an unlimited scope for improvisation with either type of noodle. Pasta marries well with acidic and salty foods: peppers and anchovies, for example, or the tomatoes and feta cheese chosen for the salad at right. Usually a pasta salad is dressed with a vinaigrette or, if its components are sufficiently sharp-tasting, with oil alone, as here.

The crispness of rice noodles can occasion a complex play of textures. In the salad shown below, shredded raw cabbage and poached duck are added along with a crunchy, fried duck-skin garnish. The dressing combines garlic, ginger, scallions, chilies, oil and two Chinese sauces: sweetish *hoisin* and salty soy.

A Mediterranean Meld

1 **Checking for doneness.** Drop the pasta—this is shell pasta—into boiling salted water. After about four minutes, use a slotted spoon to transfer a few of the shells onto a plate and pinch through the shells with your thumbnail. The shells should be slightly hard and resistant, not soft.

An Oriental Collage

1 **Preparing the duck.** Poach a duck, covered, for one hour, or until the juices run clear when the thick part of a leg is pierced. Remove the duck; strain the stock. Cut off the legs and wings, skin the breast, slice it thin *(above)* and moisten it with stock. Shred the skin. Save the remaining meat for other use.

2 **Preparing vegetables.** Shred red cabbage *(page 24)* and toss it with vinegar. Shred scallions by slicing them diagonally. Then chop fresh ginger, garlic and chilies. In a wok, lightly brown sesame seeds; cool them on paper towels. Add vegetable oil, brown the duck skin and drain it.

3 **Frying the noodles.** Add oil to a depth of 3 inches [8 cm.] and heat it until a test noodle puffs almost instantly. Drop in a handful of noodles. After they puff and rise to the surface, turn and cook them for a few seconds more. Drain, and repeat with the rest of the noodles.

2 **Readying the pasta.** Immediately drain the cooked pasta in a colander set in a sink; shake the colander vigorously several times to drain the shells thoroughly. Then transfer the pasta to a serving bowl.

3 **Seasoning the pasta.** To prevent the shells from sticking together as they cool, lightly toss them with oil — the oil used in this demonstration was flavored with basil leaves *(page 13)* — or with vinaigrette. Season with salt and pepper.

4 **Assembling the salad.** In separate bowls dress peeled, seeded and chopped tomatoes, cubed feta cheese and ripe olives with basil-flavored oil. Surround the pasta with rocket and basil leaves. Add tomatoes and olives in concentric circles, then insert feta-cheese cubes as accents.

4 **Making the sauce.** Pour the oil from the wok and add a thin film of sesame-seed oil. Fry the ginger and garlic for about 30 seconds over medium heat. Add *hoisin* sauce, a little duck stock and soy sauce, and heat through. Add the chilies and scallions and heat for 30 seconds. Mix in the sesame seeds.

5 **Dressing the noodles.** Place the wok on a trivet or pad close to the serving platter. Hold one clump of the fried noodles over the wok and gently spoon sauce over it. Set the coated noodles in the center of the platter.

6 **Completing the salad.** Dip the duck slices in the sauce and arrange them on the noodles. Top with the shredded duck skin. Edge the platter with the red cabbage and dribble the remaining sauce over it. Garnish the cabbage with coriander sprigs.

When Dressings Take Center Stage

Dressing, when it is rich and complex in flavor, may step out of its category as a salad complement to act as a centerpiece for a wide-ranging assembly of salad elements. In the South of France, for example, an array of foods from artichokes to salt cod may be served with the strongly flavored garlic mayonnaise known as aioli *(recipe, page 152)*. In Italy, a similar mélange may be presented with *bagna cauda*, a warm, anchovy-based sauce. Another such salad is the Javanese *gado gado* shown here, which centers on a fiery dressing enriched by coconut milk and ground peanuts *(recipe, page 129)*.

In *gado gado*, as in other compositions of its type, the vegetables vary in taste and texture to provide a spectrum of vehicles for the sauce. Here, for instance, delicate green beans, bean sprouts, flat-stemmed Chinese chives and spinach are steamed—cooked over boiling water just long enough to tenderize them. These are set off by crisp raw cabbage and, for another sort of contrast, bland fried potatoes and bean curd, a versatile ingredient often marketed as *tofu*. (Available where Oriental foods are sold, fresh bean-curd cakes will look creamy white. Their excess moisture should be removed before cooking by wrapping the cakes in paper towels, then weighting them with a heavy object such as a frying pan.)

The dressing used for these vegetables demands fairly extensive preparation. The first ingredient required is a coconut so fresh that its liquid gurgles audibly when the coconut is shaken. This bitter milky liquid, however, is used only for keeping the meat of the opened coconut moist. The so-called coconut milk that forms the base of the dressing is an extract made by grinding the white meat with water, then straining out the essences *(Steps 1-3)*.

Further nuttiness is provided by peanuts ground in a nut mill or, as here, in a food processor. Spice and sweetness come from fresh ginger root and brown sugar; fire comes from fresh hot chilies, available at Oriental, Caribbean and other specialty food markets.

1 Opening a coconut. With an ice pick or a screwdriver, puncture the three eyes at one end of the coconut. Drain its liquid through them into a bowl. With the dull side of a cleaver, hammer around the coconut *(above)* until a crack encircles it. Strike sharply on the crack; the coconut will split in half.

2 Removing the meat. Break the halves into smaller pieces with the cleaver. Pry the white meat from the shell with a small paring knife *(above)*. Pare off the papery brown skin and put the meat in the reserved coconut liquid to prevent its drying out.

6 Deep frying. Cut boiled and peeled potatoes into slices ¼ inch [6 mm.] thick. Heat 4 inches [10 cm.] of vegetable oil to a temperature of 375° F. [190° C.]. Deep fry the slices, turning them, until they are golden; drain them on paper towels. Deep fry the bean-curd cakes in the same hot oil until they are golden, then drain them. Cut the cakes into ¼-inch [6-mm.] slices.

7 Steaming. Bring 1 inch [2½ cm.] of water to a boil in a wok. Over it place layered Chinese steamer tray containing the longest-cooking vegetable — green beans, in this case. Put a tray of shorter-cooking bean sprouts and chives over the beans. Fragile leaves such as spinach should be on top. Cover, and steam the vegetables for five to eight minutes, until the spinach is just softened.

3 **Making coconut milk.** Grind small portions of coconut in a food processor, gradually adding an equal amount of hot water. When the meat is pulped, pour the mixture into a cheesecloth-lined strainer set over a bowl. Squeeze the cloth into a ball to force out the remaining coconut milk.

4 **Preparing the dressing.** Sauté sliced onions and chopped garlic in olive oil until the onions are soft. Add water and bring to a boil. Stir in brown sugar, grated ginger root and chopped chilies; simmer for several minutes. Add ground peanuts and salt, and stir over high heat until the mixture looks dry *(above)*.

5 **Adding coconut milk.** Reduce the heat to low and pour in the coconut milk. Stirring often, simmer uncovered for about 15 minutes, or until the dressing is thick enough to hold its shape in a spoon. Set the pan aside off the heat.

6 **Arranging.** Remove the outer leaves of a red cabbage. Shred the rest and toss it with lemon juice to set its color. Cut the ribs from the outer leaves *(above)* and arrange them on a platter to form a basket, bracing it with egg and cucumber slices. Fill the basket with cabbage shreds, bean sprouts and chives. Border it with potato slices, green beans, *tofu* and spinach. Dress each portion after serving.

Strategies for Using Cheese

Given the great range of tastes and textures among cheeses, it is hardly surprising that their usefulness as salad components varies considerably.

Very strong-tasting cheeses such as Roquefort and Parmesan, for instance, should be used only as flavorings or garnishes *(page 23)* — and sparingly even then, lest the cheese overwhelm the other ingredients. Delicate ripened cheeses such as Brie and Camembert are too soft to be used in salads. But between these two extremes can be found a plethora of cheeses that, imaginatively dressed and garnished, make substantial and distinctive salads *(recipes, pages 150-151)*.

In the top demonstration, for example, chunks of mozzarella, a mild cheese firm enough for slicing, provide a foil for spicy salamis. Gruyère and sausage, Cheddar and ham, or provolone and prosciutto are other agreeable combinations. These salads require tart greens that balance the richness of the cheese: rocket, lettuces such as escarole, or the watercress used here. Vegetables such as tomatoes, peppers or olives all are effective additions.

Cottage, farmer's and ricotta cheeses are complemented by a similar range of leaves and vegetables, but they require preliminary preparations to give them form and character. In the bottom demonstration, for instance, cottage cheese is enriched with whipped cream, enlivened with various flavorings, then chilled in a perforated, cheesecloth-lined mold that allows excess liquid to drain away, thus firming the cheese. A flowerpot is used here, but any perforated mold—even a strainer or colander—would do. Once firm, the cheese can be served with a bright array of crisp, colorful vegetables.

In cheese salads, as in all composed salads, the dressing confers unity on the disparate ingredients. For the mozzarella and salami salad, the cheese is marinated with olive oil and basil leaves, the meat with vinegar and shallots. When the two marinades are combined, the result is a vinaigrette redolent of both meat and cheese. Similarly, the molded cottage cheese and the milder vegetables served with it are flavored with vinegar, a sharp accent that links the different tastes. In each case, salt is used sparingly: Most cheese is quite salty enough.

A Firm Cheese Partnered with Meats

1 Preparing the cheese. Pour a thin layer of olive oil into a shallow container. Slice the mozzarella ¼ to ½ inch [6 mm. to 1 cm.] thick and layer the slices in the oil with pieces of fresh basil. Drizzle more oil over the top layer. Cover the container tightly and set it aside at room temperature for three or four hours.

2 Preparing the meats. Slit the salami casings lengthwise. Then peel and slice the salamis —*copa toscana, sopressata* and pepperoni are used here. In a shallow container, layer the slices with vinegar and chopped shallots. Cover the container, and marinate the meats for three or four hours.

A Cheese Mold Ringed with Vegetables

1 Enriching cottage cheese. Beat heavy cream into softly drooping peaks. Gradually whisk in creamed cottage cheese — use 1 pound [½ kg.] of cheese for each cup [¼ liter] of cream. Blend in vinegar; add chopped scallions, parsley and broiled red peppers *(page 42)*.

2 Draining. Soak a clay flowerpot in water to rid it of any clay flavor. Line it with a double layer of cheesecloth, set in a shallow dish and spoon in the cheese mixture *(left)*. Fold the cloth over the mixture *(right)* and let it drain for two hours, pouring off liquid as necessary.

3 **Assembling the salad.** Line a serving bowl with watercress. Stack the marinated meat slices and cut them into bite-sized pieces *(above)*; cube the cheese and add both meat and cheese to the bowl in alternating layers.

4 **Making the dressing.** Pour the shallot-and-vinegar marinade used on the meats into a bowl and season it with salt and pepper. Whisk in the oil used to marinate the cheese, and add more vinegar and oil *(above)* to produce enough viniagrette to dress the salad.

5 **Dressing the salad.** Spoon the dressing over the salad. Arrange several sprigs of purple basil over the meats and cheese as a garnish.

3 **Preparing the vegetables.** Parboil small carrots for five minutes, then drain and toss them while hot with oil and mint. Slice radishes and toss them with oil. Cut off strips of peel from cucumbers and core them. Slice the cucumbers with a knife or mandolin *(above)* and toss them in vinaigrette. Julienne zucchini, salt it, let it sit for 10 minutes, then squeeze it dry. Add broiled pepper strips to the zucchini and toss with vinaigrette. Slice mushrooms and toss with lemon juice, oil and tarragon.

4 **Serving the salad.** Unwrap the cloth from the top of the flowerpot. Place a spatula over the cheese mixture, invert the pot onto a platter and slide out the spatula. Arrange the vegetables around the pot and then lift the pot, holding the cheesecloth against the platter as you do. Peel off the cloth gently and moisten the mold, if desired, with tart cream *(page 16)*.

A Full-Meal Salad Founded on Herring

Few fish are as meltingly tender as the type of salt-cured herring that the Dutch call *matjes,* or immature, herring. Because the fish are cured whole to retain their juices and are salted lightly, their flavor is mild compared to dry-salted or brine-packed fillets. Taste and texture alike make *matjes* herring an excellent base for a main-course salad.

In the robust creation demonstrated here, the fish are set off by slices of boiled, peeled potatoes, cubes of baked, peeled beets and slices of red onions. Other foods that balance the flavor of herring include raw apples, celery or fennel, wilted cabbage, boiled turnips or carrots and—for the most substantial salads—poached or braised veal *(recipe, page 137).*

Before *matjes* herring can be used, they must first be boned and trimmed *(Steps 1-3).* Although they are already eviscerated, the fish may contain a sac of linked lobes holding the male milt or female roe. Both of these delicacies should be reserved and can be sieved into the dressing for the salad.

To mute their salinity, *matjes* herring should be soaked in cold water for an hour or so. Dry-salted fillets also must be soaked—sometimes for as long as 24 hours with several changes of water to leach out their excess salt. Brine-packed fillets need only be rinsed.

Any kind of salt herring profits from being steeped in a cooked vinegar-and-spice marinade for six to 12 hours. The marinade then can serve as the base for the dressing: Simply whisk some of it with oil and add chopped fresh dill or other herbs—parsley, chives, fennel or lovage would all complement the herring's flavor. For richer effect, the salad could be dressed with sour cream that has been thinned with a spoonful of the marinade or—if beets are part of the salad—with a little beet juice.

1 **Opening the herring.** Extend the existing slit along the belly and remove the roe or milt sac. Cut off the head, but leave the tail on for easy handling. Keeping the knife flat, cut along one side of the backbone to sever the ribs.

2 **Boning the fish.** With the tail facing away, grasp the end of the backbone. Scrape away the flesh from the opposite side of the backbone *(above)* and pull out the bone and ribs. Cut under the remaining ribs to free them.

6 **Assembling the salad.** Using dill and substituting strained marinade for vinegar, make a vinaigrette *(recipe, page 167).* Toss cooked potato slices and beet cubes separately with this dressing. Place the potatoes in a bowl and strew marinated onion rings over them. Remove the herring tails, separate the two fillets and cut the fillets in chunks. Add the herring and beets to the bowl.

3 **Trimming the fish.** Cut away rough edges from the outside of the herring. Place the fish in a bowl of cold water and soak them for at least one hour, changing the water several times until the liquid tastes barely salty.

4 **Draining the fish.** Boil cider vinegar with peppercorns, allspice, juniper, bay leaf and parsley for 10 minutes. Cool to lukewarm. Line a casserole with onion rings and herbs — in this demonstration, lovage is used. Drain the fish.

5 **Marinating the herring.** Place the fish skin side up in the casserole and pour the lukewarm vinegar marinade over them. Top with more onion rings and herb leaves, cover the casserole and refrigerate for six to 12 hours.

7 **Serving the salad.** Moisten sprigs of watercress with the remaining marinade-flavored vinaigrette, and scatter the sprigs over the contents of the bowl. Just before serving, dribble a little additional oil onto the salad to add a gloss to its ingredients.

A Shimmering Interplay of Aspic and Mousse

A jelly—the combination of liquid and gelatin described on page 32—holds together the elements of a composed salad while unifying the flavors with its own taste. Clear jelly displays salad elements in whatever arrangement the cook ordains. When it is mixed with whipped cream and mayonnaise, jelly also can create an opaque mousse.

The two-tiered salad demonstrated on these pages exemplifies both approaches. A poached, boned fish (salmon is shown here) is suspended in aspic jelly based on the fish's poaching liquid *(recipe, page 159)*. The same aspic is used instead of plain gelatin to set a vegetable mousse—watercress, in this case, though spinach or cucumber could be substituted *(recipe, page 156)*. Molded together, the mixtures produce an interplay of color and texture unattainable by any other means.

Success depends on the aspic, which must be clear and pure in flavor. To achieve this, the poaching liquid must be clarified: simmered with egg shells and whites to collect impurities that may then be lifted away *(Step 4)*.

1 Poaching the salmon. Prepare a poaching liquid—in this case, basic court bouillon *(recipe, page 165)*—and let it cool until tepid. Wrap a large cross section of salmon in cheesecloth to keep it from breaking during cooking, and knot the cloth. Lower the salmon into the liquid and poach 10 minutes for each inch [2½ cm.] of its thickness.

2 Removing the skin. Lifting the cheesecloth bundle with a fork, and supporting it from below, transfer the fish to a platter. Unwrap the cloth. Strain the poaching liquid into a clean pot. Cut the fin from the fish. Then make a shallow incision down the length of the fish along the back. With your fingers, peel the skin from the top of the fish.

5 Assembling. Set a mold in ice and spoon in a ½-inch [1-cm.] layer of aspic. Arrange blanched tarragon in the aspic and refrigerate to set it. Arrange half of the salmon over the layer. Cover with aspic *(above)*, refrigerate, then add the remaining salmon and cover it with aspic. Refrigerate.

6 Preparing watercress. Blanch watercress, drain it, refresh it under cold running water to arrest its cooking, and drain it again. Gather the watercress into a ball in a towel and squeeze out the excess moisture. Chop the watercress into fine pieces.

7 Making the mousse. Mix the chopped watercress with mayonnaise *(above)*. Stir in a ladleful of the remaining liquid aspic, then gently fold in whipped cream. Refrigerate until the mousse is slightly thickened but not set—approximately 30 minutes.

3 **Boning the salmon.** Insert a spatula into the fish just above the ribs *(left)*. Slide the spatula over the ribs to separate the flesh from the backbone. Place your palm over the top half of the fish, then turn the spatula so that the flesh is reversed onto your hand; transfer the piece to a platter *(right)*. Peel the backbone and the ribs attached to it away from the bottom half of the fish. Pick out the remaining bones. Turn the fish over, peel off the cheesecloth and skin, transfer the fish to the platter and cut it into serving pieces. Cover, and refrigerate for an hour.

4 **Clarifying.** Warm the poaching liquid, add softened gelatin and whisk until the gelatin dissolves. Then add beaten egg whites and their broken shells and heat the liquid just to a boil. Remove from the heat; after 10 minutes, lift out the coagulated egg whites *(above)*. Strain the aspic through cheesecloth into a bowl to cool.

5 **Serving.** Spoon watercress mousse over the salmon aspic to fill the mold to the top *(above)*. Refrigerate for at least three hours, until the salad has set. Unmold by inverting the mold onto a platter as demonstrated on page 32. Garnish with halved Bibb lettuce hearts dressed with vinaigrette.

Tomatoes Carved into Colorful Fans

The versatile tomato commonly is cut into slices, chunks or wedges to color and perfume composed salads. More artfully, tomatoes are sliced into fans *(right)* or hollowed into shells *(box, below)* to display the cook's choice of fillings.

A shell may be made from a peeled tomato *(page 26)* if the flesh is firm and the hollow loosely packed with a filling such as blanched asparagus tips or the green beans shown on page 75. Otherwise, the skin should be kept intact so the shell can support a weightier filling: rice, for example *(pages 76-77)*, or mayonnaise-bound mussels *(pages 68-69)*.

With a fan, the fillings always are kept light and used sparingly; because the fillings exert little pressure, the tomato skin can be removed safely. Here, an unctuous anchovy-and-olive *tapenade* and a basil-based pesto *(recipes, page 163)* are interspersed with slices of hard-boiled egg. Other appropriate fillings include garlic mayonnaise *(recipe, page 166)*, marinated cucumber, and chopped shrimp bound with tart cream dressing.

1 Slicing the tomatoes. Position each peeled tomato stem end down. Using a sharp knife, cut vertically about three quarters of the way through the tomato at ½- to ¾-inch [1- to 2-cm.] intervals so that the segments will be strong enough to support fillings.

2 Removing seeds. Holding the tomato over a bowl, open the first segment and ease the seeds out with your finger. Remove the seeds from the other segments in the same way. To draw out excess moisture, sprinkle salt between the segments and drain the tomatoes on towels for 30 minutes.

A Shell for Stuffing

Hollowing a tomato. Slice off the round top of the tomato. With a grapefruit knife, cut down almost to the base about ¼ inch [6 mm.] inside the skin. Cut around the tomato to remove the core, pulp and seeds. Salt the hollow; invert and drain the tomato.

3 Adding the fillings. Hard-boil eggs and cut them crosswise into ¼-inch [6-mm.] slices. Prepare *tapenade* and pesto. Fill the spaces between the tomato segments alternately with egg slices and spoonfuls of one of the sauces.

4 Serving the tomatoes. Arrange the filled tomato fans in a radiating pattern on a serving platter. Garnish them with watercress lightly moistened with vinaigrette *(recipe, page 167)*.

Anthology of Recipes

Drawing upon the cooking traditions and literature of more than 30 countries, the editors and consultants for this volume have selected 207 published salad recipes for the Anthology that follows. The selections range from the simple to the elaborate—from homely coleslaw to an exotic Siamese concoction of chicken, pork and shrimp, tossed with rose petals.

Many of the recipes were written by world-renowned exponents of the culinary art, but the Anthology, spanning nearly five centuries, also includes selections from now rare and out-of-print books and from works that have never been published in English. Whatever the sources, the emphasis is always on fresh, natural ingredients that blend harmoniously.

Since many early recipe writers did not specify amounts of ingredients, the missing information has been judiciously added. Where appropriate, clarifying introductory notes have also been supplied; they are printed in italics. Modern terms have been substituted for archaic language, but to preserve the character of the original recipes and to create a true anthology, the authors' texts have been changed as little as possible. Some instructions have necessarily been expanded, but in any circumstance where the cooking directions still seem somewhat abrupt, the reader need only refer to the appropriate demonstrations in the front of the book to find the technique explained.

In most cases, the recipes are organized by their main ingredients, with salads combining diverse ingredients placed at the end of each category (molded salads, however, constitute a separate category). Tomatoes, botanically classed as fruit, are treated as vegetables for organizational purposes; avocados are grouped with fruit. Recipes for standard preparations—court bouillon or mayonnaise, for example—appear at the end of the Anthology. Unfamiliar cooking terms are explained in the combined General Index and Glossary.

Apart from the primary components, all recipe ingredients are listed in order of use, with the customary U.S. measurements and the new metric measurements provided in separate columns. The metric quantities given here reflect the American practice of measuring such solid ingredients as flour or sugar by volume rather than by weight, as European cooks do.

To simplify measuring, many figures have been rounded off to the gradations now standard on metric spoons and cups. (One cup, for example, equals 237 milliliters; wherever practicable in these recipes, however, a cup appears as a more readily measurable 250 milliliters.) Similarly, weight, temperature and linear metric equivalents are rounded off slightly. Thus the American and metric figures are not equivalent, but using one set or the other will produce equally good results.

Raw Vegetable Salads

Bean Sprout Salad

This is an adaptation of a Thai dish.

	To serve 6	
1 lb.	fresh bean sprouts	½ kg.
2 tbsp.	soy sauce	30 ml.
2 tbsp.	rice vinegar	30 ml.
2 tbsp.	sesame-seed oil	30 ml.
1	cucumber, peeled, seeded and chopped	1
1	bunch scallions, chopped	1
2	small icicle radishes, chopped	2
2 tsp.	freshly ground black pepper	10 ml.
1 tbsp.	chopped fresh parsley (optional)	15 ml.
½ lb.	shrimp, cooked in lightly salted water for 3 to 4 minutes, drained and peeled (optional)	¼ kg.

Pick over the bean sprouts, wash them quickly, and drain them in a colander. Pour boiling water over them in the colander, then run cold water over them to cool them. Combine the bean sprouts, cucumber, scallions and radishes in a large bowl. Chill. Before serving, toss the salad with the soy sauce, vinegar and sesame oil, beaten together and seasoned with black pepper. If desired, garnish the salad with parsley and cooked shrimp.

MERRY WHITE
COOKING FOR CROWDS

Pickled Bean Sprouts

	To serve 4	
1 lb.	fresh bean sprouts, washed and drained	½ kg.
1	medium-sized carrot, shredded	1
1	large scallion, cut crosswise into 2-inch [5-cm.] pieces and cut lengthwise into julienne	1
1	whole bamboo shoot, washed, sliced thin and cut into julienne	1
1 tbsp.	salt	15 ml.

Mix all of the ingredients together and pour in enough water to cover them. Let the mixture stand at room temperature for at least three hours, but preferably all day; it will keep for about two days in the refrigerator. Drain before serving.

JILL NHU HUONG MILLER
VIETNAMESE COOKERY

Beet Salad with Yogurt

Rote-Rüben-Salat mit Joghurt

	To serve 4	
4 or 5	small young raw beets (about 10 oz. [350 g.]), peeled and thinly sliced	4 or 5
2	apples, peeled, cored and sliced	2
1 cup	plain yogurt or sour cream	¼ liter
	salt	
½ tsp.	sugar	2 ml.
3 to 4 tbsp.	strained fresh lemon juice	45 to 60 ml.
3 tbsp.	mayonnaise (recipe, page 166)	45 ml.
1	small onion, chopped, or 2 tsp. [10 ml.] grated fresh horseradish	1

Mix the beets and apples together. Season the yogurt or sour cream with the salt, sugar and lemon juice; add the mayonnaise and stir this mixture into the beets and apples. Sprinkle on the chopped onion or grated horseradish, and serve.

JOZA BŘÍZOVÁ AND MARYNA KLIMENTOVÁ
TSCHECHISCHE KÜCHE

Buttermilk Coleslaw

The technique of shredding cabbage is shown on page 24.

	To serve 6	
1½ quarts	shredded cabbage	1½ liters
¼ cup	thinly sliced onion	50 ml.
1 cup	thinly sliced or julienned carrot	¼ liter
¾ cup	mayonnaise (recipe, page 166)	175 ml.
¾ cup	buttermilk	175 ml.
1 tsp.	salt	5 ml.
2 tbsp.	finely cut fresh dill leaves	30 ml.

Mix the cabbage, onion and carrots in a large bowl. Combine the mayonnaise, buttermilk and salt, stirring until smooth. Add this dressing to the vegetables and stir in the dill.

THE GREAT COOKS' GUIDE TO SALADS

Coleslaw

The technique of shredding cabbage appears on page 24.

	To serve 4	
½	head small cabbage (about 8 oz. [¼ kg.]), cored and finely shredded	½
2	large carrots, finely shredded	2
1	medium-sized onion, finely chopped	1
1	green pepper, halved, seeded, deribbed and thinly sliced (optional)	1
½ cup	mayonnaise *(recipe, page 166)*	125 ml.
1½ to 2 tbsp.	fresh lemon juice	22 to 30 ml.
	salt and freshly ground black pepper	

Put all of the vegetables in a large mixing bowl. Add the mayonnaise and stir to combine. Stir in the lemon juice and plenty of salt and pepper, and continue stirring until all of the vegetables are evenly coated with the mayonnaise.

Transfer the coleslaw to a serving dish. Cover, and chill in the refrigerator until required.

JENI WRIGHT
THE ALL COLOUR COOKERY BOOK

Shredded Raw Carrot

Carottes Râpées Crues

	To serve 4	
6	medium-sized carrots (about 1 lb. [½ kg.])	6
	salt and pepper	
2 tbsp.	strained fresh lemon juice	30 ml.
½ cup	heavy cream	125 ml.
	chopped fresh parsley	

Peel or scrape the carrots, wash carefully, dry, and shred only the red part of the carrots (that is to say, remove the cores). Season with salt and pepper. Stirring constantly, pour the lemon juice gradually into the cream. Then pour this dressing over the carrots. Mix well and sprinkle with the chopped parsley.

MADAME SAINT-ANGE
LA CUISINE DE MADAME SAINT-ANGE

Carrot and Onion Salad

	To serve 4	
3	carrots, scraped	3
2	onions, peeled	2
2	fresh hot green chilies, stemmed and seeded	2
1	small piece fresh ginger root, scraped	1
	salt	
about 3 tbsp.	vinegar or fresh lime juice	about 45 ml.

Put the carrots, onions, chilies and ginger through a food grinder or chop them very fine. Add salt and vinegar or lime juice to taste and mix well.

ISIDORE COELHO
THE CHEF

Raw Cauliflower Salad

Chou-fleur Cru en Salade

	To serve 6	
1	firm cauliflower, trimmed and separated into florets	1
1 tbsp.	prepared French mustard	15 ml.
	salt and freshly ground pepper	
3 or 4 tbsp.	olive oil	45 or 60 ml.
1 tbsp.	fresh lemon juice	15 ml.
1	bunch watercress, stems removed	1
3	tomatoes, quartered	3

Wash the cauliflower florets quickly and dry them well. Put them into a salad bowl. To make the vinaigrette, put the mustard in a bowl with a good pinch of salt and two or three grindings from the pepper mill. Add 1 tablespoon [15 ml.] of the oil and blend well. Then, little by little, add the remaining oil, stirring continuously. Finally, add the lemon juice. Pour this dressing over the cauliflower florets and let them marinate for one hour.

Put the watercress and tomatoes in the salad bowl and mix well immediately before serving.

ODETTE KAHN
LA PETITE ET LA GRANDE CUISINE

Capered Celeriac in Mustard Sauce

If you do not have a food processor, you can shred the celeriac by hand. You will need about 1½ pounds [¾ kg.] of celeriac as purchased to obtain 1 pound [½ kg.] peeled.

To serve 4 to 6

1 lb.	peeled celeriac	½ kg.
6 tbsp.	fresh lemon juice	90 ml.
1 tsp.	salt	5 ml.
	freshly ground black pepper	
1 cup	heavy cream	¼ liter
2 tbsp.	Dijon mustard	30 ml.
2 tbsp.	capers, rinsed and dried	30 ml.
3 to 4 tbsp.	finely chopped fresh parsley	45 to 60 ml.

Shred the celeriac by hand or cut it into pieces and pass these through a food processor, using the shredder plate. Immediately toss it well with the lemon juice, salt and ½ teaspoon [2 ml.] of pepper. Beat the cream and mustard together, pour the mixture over the shredded celeriac and mix it well. Cover and chill thoroughly.

At serving time, toss the celeriac with the capers and sprinkle with the parsley. Offer additional pepper.

SHIRLEY SARVIS
WOMAN'S DAY HOME COOKING AROUND THE WORLD

Celery and Apple Salad

Salade Angèle

To serve 4

1	bunch celery, trimmed and cut into fine julienne	1
2	small apples, peeled, cored and cut into fine julienne	2
1	cold cooked potato, peeled and cut into fine julienne	1
1	small cold cooked beet, peeled and cut into fine julienne	1
Walnut oil dressing		
about ¼ cup	walnut oil	about 50 ml.
¼ cup	strained fresh lemon juice	50 ml.
1	hard-boiled egg yolk, finely chopped	1
½ tsp.	chopped fresh chervil	2 ml.
	salt and pepper	

Tastefully arrange the celery, apples, potato and the beet in a salad bowl. Serve with a dressing made with the walnut oil, lemon juice, egg yolk and chervil and seasoned with salt and pepper. Before serving, mix in the dressing well.

ALFRED SUZANNE AND C. HERMAN SENN
A BOOK OF SALADS

Cucumber Salad with Nut Sauce

Khiyār Tèrètùru

To blanch the walnuts or almonds called for in this recipe, place them in a bowl and pour boiling water over them. Then drain the nuts and rub off their skins.

The leaves of purslane make a nice salad with the nut sauce. Broccoli, cauliflower or spinach, previously scalded, also makes a good salad with the same sauce.

To serve 4

1 or 2	cucumbers, peeled and thinly sliced	1 or 2
	salt and white pepper	
2 tbsp.	olive oil	30 ml.
Nut sauce		
⅔ cup	walnuts or almonds (about 3½ oz. [100 g.]), blanched	150 ml.
½ tsp.	salt	2 ml.
3 or 4	garlic cloves	3 or 4
1	slice firm homemade-style white bread with the crusts removed, soaked in warm water then squeezed almost dry	1
⅔ cup	wine vinegar or ⅓ cup [75 ml.] strained fresh lemon juice	150 ml.

Pound the nuts in a stone mortar. Add the salt and the garlic to the nuts and pound again. Mix in the bread and pound until a smooth paste is formed. Gradually pour in the vinegar or the lemon juice, stirring continuously with a wooden spoon, and then slowly add enough water to bring the paste to the consistency of cream.

Put the sliced cucumber in a dish, season with a little salt and white pepper, and pour the sauce over it. Pour the olive oil over the salad and serve.

TURABI EFFENDI
TURKISH COOKERY BOOK

Wilted Cucumber Salad

Salade de Concombres

	To serve 3 or 4	
2	young tender cucumbers, peeled and sliced into very thin rounds	2
	salt	
2 or 3	large scallions, each stuck with 1 whole clove	2 or 3
6 tbsp.	olive oil	90 ml.
2 tbsp.	wine vinegar	30 ml.
	pepper	

Place the cucumber slices in a bowl and sprinkle them with salt. Add the scallions stuck with cloves and set aside at room temperature to macerate for at least 12 hours, turning the cucumber slices from time to time to pickle them thoroughly. Remove and discard the scallions. Drain the cucumber slices and place them in a salad bowl. Mix with the oil, vinegar and very little pepper, and serve.

NICOLAS DE BONNEFONS
LES DÉLICES DE LA CAMPAGNE

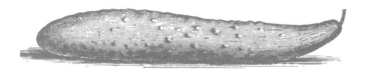

Cucumber and Yogurt Salad

Talattouri

	To serve 6 to 8	
3	medium-sized cucumbers, peeled, quartered lengthwise, seeded and thinly sliced	3
1 to 4	garlic cloves, pounded to a purée	1 to 4
	salt	
2 tbsp.	dried mint	30 ml.
1 cup	plain yogurt	¼ liter
	olive oil (optional)	

Mix the cucumbers and the garlic together. Layer the cucumber slices in a bowl, sprinkling each layer lightly with salt, and let them stand for 30 minutes. Pour off the liquid that has formed, pressing the cucumbers firmly. Crumble the mint over the cucumbers. Beat the yogurt until smooth and pour it over the cucumbers; mix and add a little olive oil if you like. Serve the salad very cold.

AMARANTH SITAS
KOPIASTE

Almond-Cucumber Salad

	To serve 6	
¼ cup	chopped almonds	50 ml.
2	cucumbers, peeled and very thinly sliced	2
	salt	
1 cup	sour cream	¼ liter
2 tbsp.	finely cut fresh chives	30 ml.
1 tsp.	fresh lemon juice	5 ml.

Place the cucumber slices in layers in a colander, sprinkling each layer with salt. Mix the sour cream, chopped almonds, chives, lemon juice and ½ teaspoon [2 ml.] of salt to make a dressing. Drain the cucumber slices and sponge them dry. Put them in a salad bowl, pour on the dressing, and serve.

HELEN EVANS BROWN
HELEN BROWN'S WEST COAST COOK BOOK

Cucumber and Fennel with Yogurt

Cacik

This simple salad is a Bulgarian and Russian specialty.

	To serve 4	
1	cucumber, peeled and thinly sliced	1
1 or 2	fennel bulbs, thinly sliced	1 or 2
2 cups	plain yogurt	½ liter
	salt	
2 tbsp.	olive oil	30 ml.

Layer the cucumber slices in a bowl, sprinkling each layer with salt, and let them drain for at least 30 minutes. Rinse and drain the cucumber slices, then dry them gently.

Pour a layer of yogurt into the bottom of a salad bowl. Cover with a layer of cucumber slices and then a layer of the fennel slices; sprinkle with a few drops of the olive oil. Continue to make alternating layers of yogurt, cucumber and fennel in the same way until all of the ingredients are used.

Chill the salad before serving.

PIERRE ANDROUET
LA CUISINE AU FROMAGE

Cucumber Salad with Goat's Cheese

Salade de Concombre au Fromage de Chèvre

The crottin cheese called for in this recipe is a small, round, soft goat's-milk cheese. You can substitute Montrachet or any other soft goat's-milk cheese.

	To serve 2	
2	medium-sized cucumbers (about 1 lb. [½ kg.]), peeled, halved, seeded and coarsely grated	2
	salt	
2 oz.	young spinach leaves, cut into strips	75 g.
4 oz.	lettuce leaves, cut into strips	125 g.
1	*crottin* cheese (about 2 oz. [75 g.]), rind removed, cut into strips	1
10	ripe olives, preferably oil-packed Greek olives	10
Yogurt and garlic dressing		
½ cup	plain yogurt, preferably made from goat's milk	125 ml.
2	garlic cloves, finely chopped	2
	salt (optional)	
	freshly ground pepper	
1 tbsp.	olive oil	15 ml.

Sprinkle the grated cucumbers lightly with salt and put them in a strainer set over a bowl to drain for three hours in the refrigerator.

Prepare the dressing in the salad bowl by beating the yogurt with the garlic, a little salt if desired, pepper to taste, and the olive oil.

Mix the spinach and lettuce together. Stir in the cucumbers. Put everything in a salad bowl. Garnish with the cheese and the olives. Serve immediately.

SYLVIE THIÉBAULT
SALADES ET ASSIETTES FROIDES

Fresh Fennel Slices in Salad

	To serve 6	
3	large fennel bulbs, thinly sliced	3
1	garlic clove, quartered	1
⅛ tsp.	sugar	½ ml.
2 tbsp.	red wine vinegar	30 ml.
6 tbsp.	olive oil	90 ml.
½ tsp.	salt	2 ml.
	freshly ground pepper	
	lettuce leaves (optional)	

In a large bowl, marinate the garlic with the sugar and vinegar for at least one hour. Press the garlic pieces against the side of the bowl to extract what juice and flavor you can; discard the pieces. Add the oil to the bowl and whisk briskly until this dressing becomes cloudy. Add the salt and pepper (use a liberal amount of pepper in this case). Toss the dressing and fennel slices together just before serving. The fennel may be arranged on lettuce leaves or not, as you prefer.

JOE FAMULARO AND LOUISE IMPERIALE
THE FESTIVE FAMULARO KITCHEN

Lettuce with Almonds or Walnuts

Laitue Fermière

To blanch almonds or walnuts, place them in a bowl and pour boiling water over them. Drain the nuts and rub off their skins. To make the almond milk, pound ½ cup [125 ml.] of blanched nuts in a mortar and slowly add 1 cup [¼ liter] of water, or pulverize the nuts with the water in a processor. Strain the mixture in a sieve lined with two layers of damp cheesecloth. Twist the cloth to squeeze out the almond milk.

	To serve 4	
1	head romaine lettuce, leaves separated, halved lengthwise and the ribs trimmed or removed	1
1 cup	blanched almond or walnut halves	¼ liter
¾ cup	cream or almond milk	175 ml.
2	eggs, hard-boiled and sliced	2
2 tbsp.	fines herbes, mixed with 1 finely crushed garlic clove and 2 to 3 tsp. [10 to 15 ml.] vinegar	30 ml.

Place two almond or walnut halves on each lettuce-leaf half and roll up the leaf. Arrange the leaves on a salad dish and cover them with a little cream or almond milk. Garnish with hard-boiled egg slices and sprinkle with the fines herbes.

LA CUISINE LYONNAISE

Caesar Salad

If the salad is to be eaten in the traditional fashion —with the fingers —leave the lettuce leaves whole.

	To serve 8	
2	heads romaine lettuce	2
2 cups	diced firm white bread, preferably homemade	½ liter
¾ cup	olive oil	175 ml.
3	garlic cloves, crushed	3
1 tsp.	salt	5 ml.
12 to 15	oil-packed flat anchovy fillets, rinsed, patted dry and finely cut	12 to 15
2 tbsp.	fresh lemon juice	30 ml.
1	egg, raw, or coddled for 1 minute	1
1 tsp.	freshly ground pepper	5 ml.
½ to ¾ cup	freshly grated Parmesan cheese	125 to 175 ml.

Wash the romaine thoroughly and dry it well. Wrap it in a tea towel or paper towels, and refrigerate until you are ready to serve the salad.

Sauté the diced bread in ¼ cup [50 ml.] of the olive oil with the garlic cloves. Shake the pan well and cook over medium heat until the croutons are delicately browned and crisp. Add additional oil if necessary. Remove the garlic and drain the croutons on absorbent paper.

In a chilled salad bowl, break the greens into bite-sized pieces. Add the remaining ½ cup [125 ml.] of olive oil and toss well so that each leaf is coated. Add the croutons, salt, anchovies, pepper and lemon juice. Break the egg into the bowl. Toss again and add the grated Parmesan cheese.

JAMES BEARD
JAMES BEARD'S AMERICAN COOKERY

Mixed Herb Salad

La Salade de Plusieurs Herbes

This recipe is adapted from a 16th Century French translation of a book originally published in Latin in 1474. At the time the author was writing, the term "herb" was applied to almost any type of small, green leafy vegetable. The intention of the author, apparently, was to include as many complementary herbs as possible, or available, in early summer. Other greens and herbs such as dandelion, rocket, hyssop and salad burnet may be included or substituted if desired.

	To serve 6	
1	head lettuce	1
1	small head escarole	1
1 handful	young, tender borage leaves	1 handful
1 handful	chopped fresh mint leaves	1 handful
1 handful	fresh lemon-balm leaves	1 handful
1 handful	tender fennel shoots and flowers	1 handful
1 handful	fresh chervil leaves	1 handful
2 tbsp.	chopped fresh parsley	30 ml.
1 tbsp.	oregano or marjoram flowers and leaves	15 ml.
	salt	
⅓ cup	olive oil	75 ml.
2 tbsp.	wine vinegar	30 ml.

Wash the lettuce and herbs well, dry them and place them in a large dish. Sprinkle with salt, add the oil and finally the vinegar. Let the salad stand a while before serving. Eat the salad heartily, crunching and chewing well.

BAPTISTE PLATINE DE CRÉMONNE
LE LIVRE DE L'HONNESTE VOLUPTÉ

Lettuce with Cream

	To serve 6 to 8	
3	heads lettuce, trimmed and cut into large pieces	3
2	eggs, hard-boiled, the yolks mashed and the whites finely chopped	2
1	egg yolk	1
	salt	
1 tsp.	prepared mustard	5 ml.
⅓ tsp.	white pepper	1½ ml.
1 to 2 tbsp.	vinegar	15 to 30 ml.
¾ cup	heavy cream	175 ml.

Pound the mashed egg yolks with the raw egg yolk, and season with a pinch of salt, the mustard and the white pepper. Add the vinegar and the cream gradually, stirring well. Mix the lettuce well with the dressing. Sprinkle with the chopped egg whites and serve.

INGA NORBERG
GOOD FOOD FROM SWEDEN

Mrs. Eaton's Mixed Green Salad

The author suggests that fresh pennyroyal, sage or balm leaves may be added in small quantities if desired. Elder vinegar is made by steeping dried elder flowers in vinegar for several weeks, then straining and bottling the vinegar. Dried elder flowers are obtainable from stores that specialize in herbs. If not available, raspberry vinegar or dry white wine may be substituted.

To serve 4 to 6

1	head lettuce	1
4 oz.	young sorrel leaves	125 g.
4 oz.	young spinach	125 g.
8	tender mint-sprig tips	8
2 or 3	scallions, chopped	2 or 3
Egg yolk and cheese dressing		
2	hard-boiled egg yolks	2
1 tbsp.	freshly grated Parmesan cheese	15 ml.
1 tsp.	prepared mustard	5 ml.
1 tbsp.	tarragon vinegar	15 ml.
1½ tbsp.	homemade ketchup or tomato purée	22 ml.
¼ cup	oil	50 ml.
1 tbsp.	elder vinegar	15 ml.

Wash and trim the lettuce leaves, sorrel, spinach and mint. Drain well and arrange them in a salad bowl, together with the chopped scallions.

Mix the egg yolks, cheese, mustard, tarragon vinegar and ketchup or tomato purée. When these are stirred well together, add the oil and elder vinegar and beat to a smooth consistency. Pour the dressing over the salad and serve.

MRS. MARY EATON
THE COOK AND HOUSEKEEPER'S COMPLETE AND
UNIVERSAL DICTIONARY, 1822

Lettuce with Sour Cream, Russian-Style

Salade de Laitue à la Crème Aigre

The variety of cucumber called for in the original version of this recipe is the agourci, or brown-nettled, cucumber. Native to Russia, it has a patterned olive-green skin and is oval in shape. Any variety of cucumber may be substituted.

To serve 4

1	head tender lettuce, separated into leaves	1
1	thinly sliced cucumber	1
Sour-cream and herb dressing		
½ cup	sour cream	125 ml.
4	hard-boiled egg yolks	4
	salt and pepper	
about 1 tbsp.	vinegar	about 15 ml.
2 tsp.	chopped fresh chervil	10 ml.
2 tsp.	chopped fresh fennel leaves	10 ml.
2 tsp.	chopped fresh tarragon	10 ml.

To prepare the dressing, mash the egg yolks in a bowl and add the sour cream; mix well and then press the mixture through a sieve into a bowl. Season with salt, pepper, vinegar and the chopped chervil, fennel and tarragon. Stir well.

Place the lettuce in a salad bowl, pour the dressing over the leaves, and toss the lettuce with the dressing. Garnish with thin slices of cucumber, and serve.

JOSEPH FAVRE
DICTIONNAIRE UNIVERSEL DE CUISINE PRATIQUE

Nasturtium Flower Salad

Làtin Chìcheghi Sàlatassi

To serve 4

48	young nasturtium flowers	48
1 tbsp.	chopped fresh chervil	15 ml.
½ tsp.	salt	2 ml.
2 to 3 tbsp.	olive oil	30 to 45 ml.
2 to 3 tbsp.	fresh lemon juice	30 to 45 ml.

Put the nasturtium flowers in a salad bowl with the chervil; sprinkle in the salt, olive oil and lemon juice; toss the salad with a spoon and fork until well mixed, and serve.

TURABI EFFENDI
TURKISH COOKERY BOOK

Mushroom Salad

Insalata di Funghi

	To serve 4	
1 lb.	fresh mushrooms, sliced	½ kg.
½ cup	olive oil	125 ml.
	salt and pepper	
2 tbsp.	chopped fresh parsley	30 ml.
3	salt anchovies, filleted, soaked in water for 30 minutes, drained, patted dry and chopped	3
3 to 4 tbsp.	fresh lemon juice	45 to 60 ml.

Mix the mushrooms with the other ingredients in a salad bowl, and let them marinate for 30 minutes before serving.

JANET ROSS AND MICHAEL WATERFIELD
LEAVES FROM OUR TUSCAN KITCHEN

Onion and Anchovy Salad

Insalata di Cipolla e Alici

	To serve 6	
1 lb.	small onions, cut in thin slivers	½ kg.
6	salt anchovies, filleted, soaked in water for 30 minutes, drained and patted dry	6
¼ cup	olive oil	50 ml.
½ tsp.	salt	2 ml.
¼ tsp.	freshly ground pepper	1 ml.
2 tbsp.	wine vinegar	30 ml.

Soak the onion slivers in ice-cold water, changing it a couple of times, for at least three hours. Drain the slivers and wrap them in two or three layers of paper toweling to remove as much water as possible before placing them in a salad bowl.

Cut the anchovy fillets into 1-inch [2½-cm.] lengths and add them to the onion slivers. Dress with the olive oil, toss, add the salt and pepper, mix well and add the vinegar. Toss the salad again and serve.

MARGARET AND G. FRANCO ROMAGNOLI
THE ROMAGNOLIS' MEATLESS COOKBOOK

Smashed Radishes

	To serve 6	
20	radishes, trimmed	20
	salt	
1 tbsp.	soy sauce	15 ml.
2 tbsp.	white or cider vinegar	30 ml.
1 tsp.	white or light brown sugar	5 ml.
1 tsp.	peanut oil or ½ tsp. [2 ml.] sesame-seed oil	5 ml.

Lay each radish on its side and crush it lightly by pounding decisively once or twice with the side of a heavy knife or cleaver, or with the bottom of a heavy glass. (The radish should split open, but not break apart.) Sprinkle the radishes lightly with salt. Let them stand for 10 minutes, then drain and transfer them to a bowl.

In a cup, combine the soy sauce, vinegar and sugar with ½ teaspoon [2 ml.] of salt, blending well. Pour this dressing over the vegetables, tossing well to coat them. Refrigerate, covered, only to chill (about 20 minutes). Sprinkle the salad with the peanut or sesame-seed oil, toss again and serve.

GLORIA BLEY MILLER
THE THOUSAND RECIPE CHINESE COOKBOOK

Tomato Salad

Salade de Tomates

Lovers of tomato salad eat the tomatoes thinly sliced without peeling or seeding. This, of course, holds only for young, firm-fleshed tomatoes.

	To serve 4	
4	medium-sized tomatoes (about 1 lb. [½ kg.]), cored, halved vertically, then each half cut into thin slices	4
⅓ cup	vinaigrette *(recipe, page 167)*, made with 1 tsp. [5 ml.] prepared mustard	75 ml.
	fines herbes	

Arrange the tomato slices in a dish and pour the vinaigrette over them. Toss the slices until they are thoroughly coated with the dressing. Sprinkle on fines herbes, and serve.

H. HEYRAUD
LA CUISINE À NICE

Stuffed Tomatoes Aioli

The author suggests using such fish as salmon, cod, whiting or sole—and increasing the volume of the stuffing, if necessary, by adding two chopped hard-boiled eggs.

To serve 4 to 6

4 to 6	medium-sized ripe tomatoes	4 to 6
	salt and freshly ground black pepper	
1 cup	flaked leftover poached fish	¼ liter
½ cup	freshly shelled peas, cooked in boiling salted water for 4 to 6 minutes	125 ml.
1 tbsp.	finely chopped fresh parsley	15 ml.
1 tbsp.	finely cut fresh chives	15 ml.
about 2 tbsp.	fresh lemon juice	about 30 ml.
	Boston lettuce leaves	

Aioli

1	garlic clove, mashed	1
1	large egg	1
1 tsp.	wine vinegar	5 ml.
½ to ¾ cup	olive oil	125 to 175 ml.
	salt and freshly ground black pepper	

Cut the tops off the tomatoes and set the tops aside. Carefully scoop out the pulp of the tomato cases without breaking the skins; reserve the pulp for sauces and stocks. Sprinkle the tomatoes with salt and pepper, turn them upside down on a plate and let them drain for 30 minutes to one hour.

For the aioli, combine the garlic, egg, vinegar and a little salt and pepper in the container of a blender. Blend the mixture at top speed for 30 seconds. Still blending, dribble in the oil until the mixture starts to thicken, then add the remaining oil in a light stream. Blend this mayonnaise until it is thick and creamy and does not absorb any more oil. Taste and correct the seasoning, then set the aioli aside.

In a bowl, combine the fish, peas, parsley, chives and lemon juice. Fold ¼ cup [50 ml.] of the aioli into the mixture, reserving the remaining aioli for another use. Chill the fish mixture for 30 minutes. Taste and correct the seasoning, then fill the tomatoes with the fish mixture and cap them with the tomato tops. Chill until serving time. Just before serving, line a serving platter with lettuce leaves and arrange the tomatoes on top.

PERLA MEYERS
THE PEASANT KITCHEN

Grated Zucchini with Fresh Basil

Courgettes Rapées au Basilic Frais

This salad should be prepared at the last possible moment. If fresh basil is not available, substitute fresh tarragon.

To serve 4

4 or 5	young zucchini, 4 to 6 inches [10 to 15 cm.] long, ends removed, passed through the medium blade of a rotary shredder, or coarsely grated	4 or 5
10 to 12	fresh basil leaves, finely chopped	10 to 12
⅓ cup	vinaigrette *(recipe, page 167)*, made with 1 tsp. [5 ml.] Dijon mustard	75 ml.

Add two thirds of the basil to the vinaigrette and pour this dressing over the zucchini. Transfer the zucchini mixture to a salad dish, sprinkle with the rest of the basil, and serve.

MARTINE JOLLY
RÉUSSIR VOTRE CUISINE

Japanese Cucumber and Tomato Salad

Kyuri Akanasu Gomasu Sarada

The fried bean curd called for in this recipe is soybean curd that has been sliced and fried in deep fat until golden. The fried curd is available fresh or canned from Oriental grocers.

This salad has a delicious, slightly nutty flavor, thanks to the ground sesame seeds and the bits of fried bean curd that are in the dressing covering the cucumber and tomato.

To serve 4

1	cucumber, peeled, halved lengthwise, seeded and sliced	1
1	large tomato, sliced	1
½ tsp.	salt	2 ml.
2 tbsp.	rice or cider vinegar	30 ml.
1 tsp.	coarsely ground roasted sesame seeds	5 ml.
1 tsp.	soy sauce	5 ml.
1 tbsp.	fried bean curd, dipped in hot water for a few seconds to remove oil, squeezed dry and finely shredded	15 ml.

Sprinkle the cucumber and tomato with salt, and set aside for about 30 minutes. To make the dressing, mix together the vinegar, sesame seeds and soy sauce. Drain all of the juices from the cucumber and tomato slices, and dry them gently in a towel. Stir the bean curd into the dressing, pour it over the cucumber and tomato slices, and toss the mixture like an ordinary salad.

SIGRID SCHULTZ (EDITOR)
OVERSEAS PRESS CLUB COOKBOOK

Vietnamese Cucumber Salad

The nuoc mam called for in this recipe is a fermented fish sauce, obtainable where Vietnamese foods are sold. The quantities called for in this recipe will yield enough nuoc mam dressing for two or three meals. The prepared dressing can be stored in the refrigerator for two to three months in a tightly closed bottle or jar.

To serve 4

2	large cucumbers, peeled, halved, seeded, sliced paper-thin and soaked in salted water to cover for 30 minutes or more	2
¼ cup	sesame seeds	50 ml.
½ lb.	shrimp, boiled for 3 to 4 minutes with a crushed scallion, then peeled and sliced lengthwise	¼ kg.
½ lb.	lean pork, poached, cooled and sliced into thin strips	¼ kg.
about 20	fresh mint leaves, coarsely chopped	about 20

Nuoc mam dressing

¼ cup	*nuoc mam*	50 ml.
½ tsp.	finely diced fresh hot chili	2 ml.
1	garlic clove	1
1 tsp.	sugar	5 ml.
½	lime, peeled and seeded	½
1 tbsp.	vinegar	15 ml.
1 tbsp.	water	15 ml.

To make the dressing, crush the chili, garlic and sugar together in a mortar. Add the lime pulp and continue to pound the mixture until well mashed. Mix in the vinegar and water, then stir in the *nuoc mam.*

In a small pan over low heat, roast the sesame seeds until they become a light golden color, shaking the pan to keep the seeds from burning. Then crush the seeds slightly to bring out their flavor.

Drain the cucumber slices in a cloth-lined strainer and twist the muslin to squeeze out the water thoroughly. Mix the cucumbers, shrimp and pork together in a bowl. Add about 1 tablespoon [15 ml.] of the *nuoc mam* dressing and taste the salad. Add more dressing as you like.

Just before serving, add the sesame seeds to the salad along with the chopped mint, and mix them well. Serve in small, individual bowls.

JILL NHU HUONG MILLER
VIETNAMESE COOKERY

Bean Curd and Peanut Salad, Shanghai-Style

To serve 4 to 6

4	cakes fresh bean curd, cut into ½-inch [1-cm.] cubes	4
½ cup	roasted peanuts, coarsely chopped	125 ml.
½ cup	diced celery	125 ml.
½ cup	diced green pepper	125 ml.
1 tsp.	sugar	5 ml.
2 tbsp.	light-colored soy sauce	30 ml.
1 tsp.	Oriental sesame-seed oil	5 ml.
	salt and white pepper	

Place the bean curd, peanuts, celery and green pepper in a salad bowl. Dissolve the sugar in the soy sauce in a small bowl, and stir in the sesame-seed oil. Then pour this dressing over the bean-curd mixture and mix all carefully. Season to taste. Serve at room temperature.

MARGARET GIN AND ALFRED E. CASTLE
REGIONAL COOKING OF CHINA

Provençal Salad

La Macédoine ou Salade Provençale

This salad should be prepared one hour before serving.

To serve 4

6	small tomatoes, halved, seeded, salted, drained for 1 hour, and patted dry	6
6	small new potatoes, boiled, peeled and thinly sliced	6
2 or 3	small onions, sliced	2 or 3
½	garlic clove, finely chopped (optional)	½
1	sprig fennel, finely chopped (optional)	1
¼ cup	ripe oil-packed Mediterranean olives	50 ml.

Caper sauce

2 tbsp.	capers, rinsed and drained	30 ml.
3 or 4	salt anchovies, filleted, soaked in water for 30 minutes, drained and patted dry	3 or 4
3 to 4 tbsp.	fresh lemon juice	45 to 60 ml.
½ cup	olive oil	125 ml.

To make the caper sauce, or *tapenade,* pound the capers with the anchovy fillets, incorporate the lemon juice and, finally, the oil. Taste for pepper and salt. Combine the tomatoes, potatoes, onions, garlic and fennel with the sauce, mix thoroughly and garnish with the olives.

AUSTIN DE CROZE
LES PLATS RÉGIONAUX DE FRANCE

Niçoise Salad

La Salada Nissarda

To prepare the artichokes called for in this recipe, see the editor's note for Artichoke Salad with Orange and Celery, page 108. The prepared artichokes may be dipped in lemon juice to prevent them from blackening.

The author recommends using Niçoise olives, which are very small, half-ripened black, violet or greenish olives preserved in herbed brine.

This fresh, tomato-based salad consists solely of raw vegetables (apart from a few hard-boiled eggs) and is prepared by salting the tomatoes three times and sprinkling them with a little oil—no vinegar! The people of Nice occasionally add anchovies or tuna to the salad.

	To serve 6	
10	medium-sized tomatoes (about 2½ lb. [1¼ kg.]), quartered, lightly salted and left to drain for 30 minutes	10
	salt	
1	garlic clove, halved	1
1	small cucumber, peeled, halved, seeded and thinly sliced	1
1 cup	shelled young broad beans (about ½ lb. [¼ kg.]) or 12 very young artichokes about 2 inches [5 cm.] high, turned and thinly sliced into rounds (optional)	¼ liter
2	green peppers, stem ends removed, seeded and cut into thin rings	2
6	scallions, sliced	6
3	eggs, hard-boiled and quartered or sliced	3
6	salt anchovies, filleted, soaked in water for 30 minutes, drained, patted dry and each cut into 3 or 4 pieces	6
about ⅔ cup	ripe olives (preferably half-ripened Niçoise) (3½ oz. [100 g.])	about 150 ml.
Basil dressing		
6	fresh basil leaves, torn into pieces	6
6 tbsp.	olive oil	90 ml.
	salt and pepper	

Drain the tomatoes and lightly resalt them. Rub the base and sides of a salad bowl with the garlic. Put all of the salad ingredients into the bowl, arranging them decoratively to set off their brilliant contrasting hues.

To make the dressing, blend the basil, olive oil and seasoning together. Pour the dressing over the salad. Chill thoroughly in the refrigerator before serving.

JACQUES MÉDECIN
LA CUISINE DU COMTÉ DE NICE

Swiss Salad

	To serve 6 to 8	
5 or 6	medium-sized ripe tomatoes (about 1½ lb. [¾ kg.]), peeled, seeded and cut into wedges	5 or 6
2	cucumbers, unpeeled but thinly sliced	2
6	eggs, hard-boiled and sliced	6
2	small green peppers, halved, seeded, deribbed and very thinly sliced	2
½ lb.	Gruyère or Emmenthal cheese, cut into julienne	¼ kg.
½ cup	pitted black olives, sliced	125 ml.
2	small onions, thinly sliced and separated into rings	2
1	garlic clove, split	1
Anchovy dressing		
10	oil-packed flat anchovy fillets, rinsed, patted dry and crushed	10
¾ cup	oil	175 ml.
¼ cup	red wine vinegar	50 ml.
1½ tbsp.	fresh lemon juice	22 ml.
1 tbsp.	sharp brown mustard	15 ml.
½ tbsp.	minced oregano	7 ml.
	salt and freshly ground white pepper	

Prepare the anchovy dressing and set it aside in a cool place for at least four hours.

To make the salad, prepare the ingredients, rub the bowl or tureen with the cut side of the garlic clove and discard it, then combine all of the ingredients in the bowl. Stir very carefully so that the eggs do not break. Present the salad, pour over the dressing, and mix before serving.

LILLIAN LANGSETH-CHRISTENSEN
HOW TO PRESENT AND SERVE FOOD ATTRACTIVELY

Belgian Endive, Mushroom and Cucumber Salad

To serve 8 to 10

6	heads Belgian endive, trimmed, cored and cut into julienne	6
1 lb.	fresh button mushrooms, cleaned in 1 quart [1 liter] water mixed with 1 tbsp. [15 ml.] lemon juice, stems trimmed, thinly sliced	½ kg.
2	cucumbers, peeled and thinly sliced	2
2 tbsp.	finely chopped fresh parsley	30 ml.
2 tbsp.	finely chopped shallots	30 ml.
½ cup	vinaigrette (recipe, page 167)	125 ml.

Place the Belgian endive julienne, mushroom slices and cucumber slices in a chilled bowl and sprinkle with the parsley. Add the chopped shallots to the vinaigrette and, just before serving, pour this dressing over the vegetables and toss.

JULIE DANNENBAUM
MENUS FOR ALL OCCASIONS

Mixed Salad with Mushrooms

Salade Mélangée aux Oronges

The original version of this recipe calls for oronges, or amanita caesarea, known as Caesar's mushrooms, which grow wild in the woods of Southern Europe. These, however, are similar in appearance to other, poisonous, members of the Amanita family. Firm, unopened cultivated mushrooms are a satisfactory substitute even though their flavor is different.

To serve 4

3	tomatoes, seeded, sliced and well drained	3
½ lb.	firm fresh mushrooms, cleaned and sliced	¼ kg.
½ lb.	roasted or poached chicken meat, skin removed, meat cut into strips (about 1 cup [¼ liter])	¼ kg.
3½ oz.	Port Salut or Fontina cheese, diced (about ¾ cup [175 ml.])	100 g.
2	eggs, hard-boiled and sliced into rounds	2
3 to 4 tbsp.	fresh lemon juice	45 to 60 ml.
	salt and freshly ground pepper	
⅓ cup	olive oil	75 ml.

Line the bottom of a salad bowl with the tomato slices, then add the mushrooms, chicken, cheese and eggs. In a small bowl, mix the lemon juice with salt and pepper, then add the oil, stirring well. Pour this dressing over the salad, mix it gently and serve.

F. AND T. RARIS
LES CHAMPIGNONS, CONNAISSANCE ET GASTRONOMIE

Mixed Salad with Ham and Mushrooms

Salade à la Beaucaire

To prevent them from discoloring, the celeriac and apples for this recipe should be incorporated into the dressing as soon as they are julienned.

To serve 6 to 8

1	celeriac, cut into julienne	1
1	bunch celery, cut into julienne	1
3 or 4	heads Belgian endive, cut into julienne	3 or 4
1	beet, wrapped in foil, baked in a 325° F. [160° C.] oven for 3 to 4 hours, peeled, one half cut into julienne, the other half thinly sliced	1
½ cup	vinaigrette (recipe, page 167), made with 1 tbsp. [15 ml.] prepared mustard	125 ml.
½ lb.	lean cooked ham, cut into julienne	¼ kg.
⅔ cup	fresh mushrooms, sautéed briefly in butter until tender, and cut into julienne	150 ml.
2 or 3	tart cooking apples, peeled, cored and cut into julienne	2 or 3
3 to 4 tbsp.	mayonnaise (recipe, page 166)	45 to 60 ml.
2	potatoes, boiled, peeled and thinly sliced	2
1 tbsp.	finely chopped mixed fresh parsley, chervil and tarragon	15 ml.

Put the julienned celeriac, celery, Belgian endive and beet into a bowl. Mix well with the vinaigrette and leave to marinate for an hour. Mix in the ham, mushrooms and apples, bind the salad with mayonnaise and transfer it to a large shallow salad bowl or serving dish. Encircle the mixture with alternating slices of beet and potatoes. Sprinkle with the chopped parsley, chervil and tarragon, and serve.

PHILÉAS GILBERT
LA CUISINE DE TOUS LES MOIS

Vegetables with Coconut Dressing

Urap

The technique of opening a coconut is shown on page 80. The trassi called for in this recipe is a cake of dark-colored, fermented shrimp paste. It is obtainable from stores specializing in Southeast Asian foods.

Almost any combination of vegetables can be prepared in this way. You may use either cooked or raw vegetables, but do not mix cooked and raw.

To serve 4 to 6

1	bunch watercress	1
2	small carrots, chopped	2
¼	small white cabbage, cored and shredded	¼
5 or 6	radishes, sliced	5 or 6
1	small cucumber, sliced	1
2 or 3	scallions, chopped	2 or 3
1 tbsp.	chopped fresh mint	15 ml.

Spiced coconut dressing

½	small coconut	½
1 tsp.	*trassi*	5 ml.
1 tsp.	oil	5 ml.
1	garlic clove	1
	salt	
	sugar	
½ tsp.	cayenne pepper	2 ml.
2 to 3 tsp.	strained fresh lime juice	10 to 15 ml.

To prepare the dressing, first break open the coconut and remove the flesh. Peel the brown skin from half of the flesh, and grate the pure white coconut. (Reserve the remaining half—wrapped tightly and refrigerated—for another use.)

Fry the *trassi* in the oil over high heat for one minute on each side. Remove the *trassi* from the pan, and pound it into a coarse paste with the garlic, a little salt, a pinch of sugar and the cayenne pepper. Mix the grated coconut into this paste, then add the lime juice.

In a deep bowl, mix the watercress, carrot, cabbage, radishes, cucumber, scallions and mint. Add the spiced coconut dressing, or *bumbu,* and toss well. Serve the salad in an oblong or oval dish.

SRI OWEN
THE HOME BOOK OF INDONESIAN COOKERY

Greek Salad

Salata

	To serve 4	
6 cups	bite-sized pieces of greens (lettuce, chicory, escarole, romaine, endive, etc.)	1½ liters
1	garlic clove, halved	1
2	tomatoes, cut into wedges	2
1	cucumber, sliced	1
1	green pepper, halved, seeded, deribbed and sliced	1
2	scallions, chopped	2
2	small onions, sliced	2
4 or 5	radishes, sliced	4 or 5
¼ cup	chopped fresh parsley	50 ml.
4	oil-packed flat anchovy fillets, rinsed and patted dry	4
⅓ cup	ripe olives, pitted	75 ml.
½ cup	feta cheese (about 2 oz. [75 g.])	125 ml.
3 tbsp.	fresh lemon juice or wine vinegar	45 ml.
½ cup	olive oil	125 ml.
	salt and pepper	
	oregano	
	mint	

Rub a large wooden salad bowl with the garlic. Then put into the bowl all of the vegetables, the anchovies, olives and cheese; chill. In a small bowl, combine the lemon juice or vinegar, oil, salt and pepper to taste, oregano and mint. Mix well and, immediately before serving, pour the dressing on the salad and toss gently.

THE WOMEN OF ST. PAUL'S GREEK ORTHODOX CHURCH
HEMPSTEAD, LONG ISLAND, NEW YORK
THE ART OF GREEK COOKERY

Fruit Salads

Waldorf Salad

This recipe, first published in 1896, records the original formula for the now-famous —if widely varied —salad as conceived by Oscar of the Waldorf.

	To serve 4	
2	apples, peeled, cored and cut into small pieces, about ½ inch [1 cm.] square	2
1 cup	celery, cut into ½-inch [1-cm.] pieces	250 ml.
about ¼ cup	mayonnaise *(recipe, page 166)*	about 50 ml.

Combine the apples and celery. Be careful not to let any seeds of the apples be mixed in. The salad must be dressed with a good mayonnaise.

OSCAR TSCHIRKY
OSCAR OF THE WALDORF'S COOK BOOK

Apple-Grape "Salade Alice"

	To serve 6	
6	large ripe apples with stems	6
about 1⅓ cups	red grapes, halved and seeded	about 325 ml.
1	lemon, cut in half	1
about 1⅓ cups	walnuts or blanched almonds, roughly chopped	about 325 ml.
½ to ¾ cup	heavy cream	125 to 175 ml.
	salt	
3	lettuce hearts, halved	3

Slice the tops off the apples, taking care to leave the stems intact. Rub the exposed flesh with the cut lemon. Set the apple tops aside. Cut away the remaining flesh from the insides of the apples, leaving only enough flesh so that thin, freestanding shells remain. Rub the inner walls of these shells with the lemon. Reserve the lemon. Discard the cores and seeds of the apples and dice the remaining flesh.

Pour water into one of the apples and then into a measuring cup. Note the level of the water and then discard it.

Measure out twice this amount of diced apple and combine it with equal amounts of grapes and nuts.

Just before serving, squeeze as much juice as you can out of the reserved lemon and combine the juice with ½ cup [125 ml.] of heavy cream. Add salt to taste, then gradually stir the lemon-and-cream blend into the fruit-salad mixture. Add more cream, if needed, to coat the salad completely.

Fill the apple shells with the salad. Put the tops back on the apples and arrange them on a serving platter, alternating the apples with the lettuce hearts.

THE GREAT COOKS' GUIDE TO SALADS

Four Pyramids Salad

This is a typical Mexican dish that takes its name, no doubt, from the great Pyramids of the Sun and the Moon, and others, which rise out of the hills surrounding Mexico City. This is a very good summer salad —and a good way of using up an overripe avocado. In Yucatán, four pyramids are served — one of mashed avocado, one of chopped onion, one of small chunks of tomato, and the fourth of a mixture of dry grated bread crumbs and goat's-milk cheese. Everyone helps himself to as much, or as little, of each as he wishes.

	To serve 4	
1	ripe avocado, halved, pitted and peeled	1
2	small onions, finely chopped	2
2	large tomatoes, peeled, seeded and chopped	2
⅛ tsp.	paprika	½ ml.
	salt and freshly ground black pepper	
1 tbsp.	fresh lemon juice	15 ml.
	lettuce leaves	

Mash the avocado with the onions and the tomatoes. Add the paprika, and salt and pepper to taste. When all is well mixed, add the lemon juice, and stir rapidly once more. Serve the mixture in four neat pyramids on lettuce leaves (the Mexicans serve it on tortillas).

LESLEY BLANCH
AROUND THE WORLD IN EIGHTY DISHES

Avocado Stuffed with Roquefort Cream

Avocats Farcis à la Crème de Roquefort

To serve 4

4	ripe avocados, halved, pits removed, flesh scooped out and diced, shells reserved	4
	Boston or Bibb lettuce heart, cut into a chiffonade	

Roquefort cream

¼ cup	Roquefort cheese (about 2 oz. [75 g.])	50 ml.
4 tbsp.	butter, softened	60 ml.
½ cup	pot or farmer cheese, drained in a strainer for 1 or 2 hours	125 ml.
	salt and pepper	
	pungent paprika	

In a bowl, blend together the Roquefort, butter and pot or farmer cheese to form a smooth paste. Season with salt and pepper and a dash of paprika.

Gently mix the diced avocados with the Roquefort cream. Fill the empty avocado shells with the mixture and refrigerate them until needed. Serve on a bed of lettuce.

PIERRE ANDROUET
LA CUISINE AU FROMAGE

Green Banana Salad

La Salade de Leyritz

This recipe comes from Martinique, in the Caribbean.

To serve 6 to 8

4	green bananas	4
	salt	
1	large tomato, peeled, seeded and coarsely chopped	1
1	medium-sized cucumber, peeled and coarsely chopped	1
1 cup	sliced celery	¼ liter
2	medium-sized carrots, scraped and shredded	2
1	medium-sized avocado, halved, peeled, pitted and sliced	1
	lettuce leaves	
½ cup	vinaigrette *(recipe, page 167)*, made with 2 tsp. [10 ml.] Dijon mustard	125 ml.

Peel the green bananas by cutting through the skin lengthwise in two or three places, then peeling the skin off in sec-

tions. Put the bananas into a saucepan with enough cold water to cover them, and add a little salt. Bring the water to a boil. Reduce the heat, cover and cook for about 10 minutes or until the bananas are tender. Drain, cool, and cut the bananas crosswise into slices ½ inch [1 cm.] thick.

Mix the bananas, tomato, cucumber, celery, carrots and avocado lightly with the vinaigrette. Line a salad bowl with the lettuce leaves and fill with the banana mixture.

ELISABETH LAMBERT ORTIZ
THE COMPLETE BOOK OF CARIBBEAN COOKING

Fresh Fig and Mint Salad

Salade de Figues Fraîches à la Menthe

To serve 5 or 6

2 to 2½ lb.	ripe figs	1 kg.
3	thin slices prosciutto, fat removed, cut into fine julienne about 1 inch [2½ cm.] long	3
12 to 15	leaves fresh mint	12 to 15
3 to 4 tbsp.	strained fresh lemon juice	45 to 60 ml.
	salt	
¾ cup	heavy cream, preferably not ultrapasteurized	175 ml.

Peel the figs and cut each one halfway down from the stem end, making two incisions in the form of a cross. Press gently from the sides to open the incisions slightly (as one does with a baked potato). Arrange the figs closely on a serving dish and chill for about one hour in the coldest part of the refrigerator (but not in the freezer).

Crush about half of the mint leaves in the lemon juice and let them macerate for 20 to 30 minutes, then discard them. Dissolve a pinch of salt in the lemon juice and slowly stir the cream into the juice: Adding the cream a small quantity at a time—with continued stirring—encourages the thickening. Taste for salt.

Sprinkle the figs with half of the prosciutto, spoon over the cream sauce, distribute the remaining prosciutto on top, and decorate the dish with the remaining mint leaves.

RICHARD OLNEY
SIMPLE FRENCH FOOD

Berry Best Salad in Orange Cups

To serve 12

1 cup	fresh blueberries	¼ liter
1 cup	fresh raspberries	¼ liter
2 cups	fresh strawberries, hulled	½ liter
6	large oranges	6
1½ cups	plain yogurt	375 ml.
¼ cup	honey	50 ml.
1 tbsp.	grated orange peel	15 ml.
3 tbsp.	fresh orange juice	45 ml.
½ tsp.	grated nutmeg	2 ml.
12	fresh mint sprigs	12

Thoroughly blend the yogurt, honey, orange peel and juice, and nutmeg. Refrigerate this dressing for several hours.

Cut each of the oranges in half and remove the pulp. Trim the bottom of each orange half so it will stand upright. Combine the berries with as much orange pulp as desired and spoon the mixture into the orange shells. Spoon the dressing over the berries when ready to serve. Garnish each salad with a sprig of fresh mint.

MARGARET WOOLFOLK
COOKING WITH BERRIES

Grapefruit, Romaine and Red Onion Salad

The grapefruit sections called for in this recipe are prepared by the technique used for the orange sections on page 28.

To serve 4

2	grapefruits	2
1	head romaine lettuce, leaves torn into pieces	1
1	red onion, thinly sliced	1
⅓ cup	vegetable oil	75 ml.
2 tbsp.	vinegar	30 ml.
2 tbsp.	heavy cream	30 ml.
½ tsp.	sugar	2 ml.
¼ tsp.	salt	1 ml.

Place the lettuce in a salad bowl. Add the onion slices. Peel the grapefruits, separate them into sections and remove the membranes, reserving 2 tablespoons [30 ml.] of the grapefruit juice. Place the sections in the bowl with the lettuce.

In a small bowl, mix the oil, vinegar, grapefruit juice, heavy cream, sugar, salt and pepper with a wire whisk. Pour the dressing over the salad.

MICHELE EVANS
THE SALAD BOOK

Mango-Papaya Salad

To serve 6

3	firm ripe mangoes, peeled, pitted and cut into bite-sized pieces	3
3	firm ripe papayas, peeled, seeded and cut into bite-sized pieces	3
¼ cup	freshly shredded coconut	50 ml.
¼ cup	slivered almonds	50 ml.
⅓ cup	mayonnaise *(recipe, page 166)*	75 ml.
1½ tbsp.	fresh lemon juice	22 ml.

Mix the fruits well. Sprinkle them with the coconut and slivered almonds. Chill. In a small bowl, blend the mayonnaise and lemon juice. Top the salad with the mayonnaise dressing before serving.

CALIFORNIA BICENTENNIAL CELEBRATION COMMITTEE
OFFICIAL CALIFORNIA BICENTENNIAL COOKBOOK

Summer Fruit Special

To serve 8

1	cantaloupe	1
1	honeydew melon	1
1	papaya	1
2 or 3	pears, peeled, halved, cored and cut into wedges	2 or 3
1 cup	strawberries, hulled	¼ liter
Avocado dressing		
1	fully ripe avocado, halved, pitted, peeled and diced or mashed	1
2 tbsp.	fresh lemon juice	30 ml.
½ tsp.	salt	2 ml.
½ cup	fresh orange juice	125 ml.
2 tbsp.	honey	30 ml.
½ cup	mayonnaise *(recipe, page 166)*	125 ml.
	dash of Tabasco sauce (optional)	

To make the dressing, beat or whirl in a blender the avocado with the lemon juice. Add the remaining ingredients and beat or whirl until smooth. Alternate thin lengthwise slices of peeled cantaloupe, honeydew melon and papaya on chilled salad plates. Add wedges of freshly peeled pears and the strawberries. Serve with the avocado dressing.

HAZEL BERTO
COOKING WITH HONEY

Melon Curry Salad

Curry powder may be made of as many as 20 different spices, the most common of which are ginger, turmeric, fenugreek, cloves, cumin, cinnamon, and red and black pepper. The best curries to use for spicy effect are those made in, or in the style of, Madras, India.

	To serve 3 or 4	
3 cups	small cubes of cantaloupe or watermelon	¾ liter
1 tsp.	curry powder	5 ml.
1 tbsp.	fresh lemon juice	15 ml.
1 tbsp.	cider vinegar	15 ml.
⅓ cup	heavy cream	75 ml.
	lettuce leaves	

Mix the curry powder, lemon juice and cider vinegar in a small bowl. Let the dressing stand for five minutes. Whip the cream until thick but not really stiff. Stir the curry mixture gently into the whipped cream, then carefully mix in the melon cubes. Chill for 10 minutes. Serve spooned into individual lettuce leaves.

ELIZABETH ALSTON
THE BEST OF NATURAL EATING AROUND THE WORLD

Orange, Onion and Olive Salad

Munkaczina

A salad brought from the East by Anatole France.

	To serve 4	
4	oranges, peeled, sliced crosswise, seeds and white membrane in the middle of the rounds removed	4
1	small onion, finely chopped	1
⅔ cup	ripe olives, pitted	150 ml.
	cayenne pepper	
	salt	
3 tbsp.	olive oil	45 ml.

Arrange a bed of orange slices in a dish and cover with the chopped onion. On top of the onion place a bed of olives, and sprinkle them with cayenne pepper, salt and olive oil.

MRS. C. F. LEYEL AND MISS OLGA HARTLEY
THE GENTLE ART OF COOKERY

Walnut and Watercress Salad

Walnut oil has a strange and marvelous flavor. It is delicious on salads. You can buy it in health-food stores, but the taste is not so pronounced as that of the French walnut oil. If you can get the French kind, all the better.

	To serve 4	
1 cup	walnut halves	¼ liter
1	bunch watercress, tough stems cut off	1
1	apple, peeled, cored and diced	1
¼ cup	diced Gruyère cheese (about 2 oz. [75 g.])	50 ml.
2 tsp.	chopped Spanish onion	10 ml.
8	ripe olives	8
3	eggs, hard-boiled and halved (optional)	3
	Walnut oil vinaigrette	
½ cup	walnut oil	125 ml.
1 tbsp.	red wine vinegar	15 ml.
½ tsp.	Dijon mustard	2 ml.
	coarse salt and freshly ground black pepper	

In a salad bowl combine the walnut halves, cress, apple, cheese, onion, olives and the eggs, if using. Make a dressing of the walnut oil with the vinegar, mustard, salt and pepper. Pour onto the salad, mix well, and serve.

MOIRA HODGSON
COOKING WITH FRUITS AND NUTS

Orange, Lettuce and Walnut Salad

Shlada Bellecheen

	To serve 6	
3	navel or Temple oranges	3
1	head romaine lettuce, separated into leaves	1
¾ cup	chopped walnuts	175 ml.
2 tbsp.	lemon juice	30 ml.
2 tbsp.	sugar	30 ml.
	salt	
	ground cinnamon	
1 tbsp.	orange-flower water	15 ml.

Peel the oranges and remove all the outside membranes, using a small serrated knife and employing a seesaw motion. Section the oranges by cutting away all the membranes from the orange flesh. As you work, lift out each section and place it in a small mixing bowl. Squeeze the juice from the remainder of the orange over the sections to keep them moist. Cover the bowl and keep chilled.

Make a dressing by mixing the lemon juice, sugar, salt, ½ teaspoon [2 ml.] of cinnamon, the orange-flower water and 2 tablespoons [30 ml.] of the orange juice. Blend well, then taste—the dressing should be sweet.

Just before serving, shred the lettuce and arrange it in a glass serving dish. Pour the dressing over and toss. Make a design around the edges with overlapping sections of orange, then sprinkle the salad with the chopped walnuts and dust with cinnamon. Serve immediately.

PAULA WOLFERT
COUSCOUS AND OTHER GOOD FOOD FROM MOROCCO

Nut Salad

The author of this 1897 recipe suggested that the salad is exceedingly nice to serve with roasted duck, or with game.

To serve 4

1 cup	walnuts, the kernels kept in perfect halves, if possible	¼ liter
2 cups	chicken stock *(recipe, page 164)*	½ liter
1	bay leaf	1
2 tbsp.	chopped onion	30 ml.
1 tbsp.	chopped carrot	15 ml.
1	sprig parsley	1
1	truffle, finely chopped	1
12	mushrooms, finely chopped	12
	lettuce or chicory leaves	
1	orange, halved, seeded, and the pulp scooped out and reserved	1
	vinaigrette *(recipe, page 167)*, made with fresh orange or lemon juice	

Cover the walnuts with boiling water, boil for five minutes and then remove the skin carefully from all the little crevices. Put the walnuts into a saucepan; cover with the stock; add the bay leaf, the chopped onion, the chopped carrot and the sprig of parsley. Simmer gently for 20 minutes and then drain; stand away until cold.

When ready to serve, line a salad bowl with lettuce or chicory leaves. Put the pieces of orange pulp over the lettuce leaves, then add a sprinkling of the chopped truffle and mushrooms, then the walnut kernels, and then the remaining mushrooms and truffles. Send to the table with the vinaigrette; mix and serve.

MRS. S. T. RORER
NEW SALADS

Pear Salad with Ham

To serve 4

4	small firm pears, peeled and cored	4
3 oz.	lean cooked ham, finely diced	100 g.
4	scallions, white parts only, chopped, or 1 small onion, chopped	4
½ cup	cottage, farmer or pot cheese	125 ml.
2 tbsp.	sour cream	30 ml.
3 to 4 tbsp.	fresh lemon juice	45 to 60 ml.
	lettuce or cress (optional)	
	parsley sprigs	

Mix the ham and scallions with the cheese and sour cream. Slice the pears into 2-by-½-inch [5-by-1-cm.] pieces, dropping them into the lemon juice and turning them to prevent discoloration. Pile the cheese mixture onto four small plates or one large one (on lettuce or cress if you like). Garnish with the pieces of pear. Top with sprigs of parsley.

GAIL DUFF
FRESH ALL THE YEAR

Pear and Potato Salad

To grate the onion called for in this recipe, use the smallest holes of a box grater.

To serve 6

2	large, firm, slightly underripe pears, peeled, cored and thinly sliced	2
5	medium-sized potatoes, boiled, peeled and sliced while still warm	5
¼ cup	white wine vinegar	50 ml.
¼ tsp.	pepper	1 ml.
½ tsp.	salt	2 ml.
½ tsp.	sugar	2 ml.
1 tsp.	grated onion	5 ml.
½ cup	oil	125 ml.

Mix the vinegar, pepper, salt, sugar, onion and oil together. Combine this dressing with the potato and pear slices, being careful not to break the potatoes. This salad may be served warm, at room temperature, or chilled.

CHARLOTTE ADAMS
THE FOUR SEASONS COOKBOOK

Pear, Melon and Cucumber Salad

A cool and refreshing salad for a hot day, and best served as a course by itself. It holds up well for at least a day, so don't worry about leftovers.

	To serve 4	
2	medium-sized Bartlett or Anjou pears	2
⅓	honeydew melon	⅓
2	small cucumbers	2
⅓ cup	oil	75 ml.
2 tbsp.	vinegar	30 ml.
¼ tsp.	salt	1 ml.
1	scallion, sliced, or 1 teaspoon [5 ml.] finely cut fresh chives	1
	fresh black pepper	

Chill the fruit and, before you cut it up, make the dressing. Mix the oil, vinegar, salt, scallion or chives, and a good grinding of pepper in a serving bowl. Use a stainless-steel knife to cut up the fruit. Peel the rind off the melon; cut the flesh into smallish, bite-sized chunks. Mix the melon gently with the dressing. Peel the cucumbers, cut them into bite-sized chunks and mix them with the dressing. Peel the pears or not, cut them in quarters, remove the cores and slice the pears thin. Mix the pear slices with the dressing. The salad can be served right away or chilled for one hour.

ELIZABETH ALSTON
THE BEST OF NATURAL EATING AROUND THE WORLD

Cooked Vegetable Salads

Asparagus in Vinaigrette

Although the title suggests a contemporary volume, the cookbook from which this recipe comes was published in 1773.

	To serve 4	
4 lb.	asparagus, thick ends peeled	2 kg.
½ cup	vinaigrette *(recipe, page 167)*	125 ml.

Tie the asparagus in a bundle and let them be boiled in water with salt for seven to eight minutes: Observe that they be not too much done. Drain the asparagus, place on a dish and remove the string. Pour over the vinaigrette and serve.

VINCENT DE LA CHAPELLE
THE MODERN COOK

Artichoke Salad with Orange and Celery

To prepare the artichoke bottoms called for in this recipe, first break off the stem of each artichoke and snap off the large leaves. Slice off the top half of the remaining inner leaves, pare the bottom to remove the bases of the outer leaves, trim the top of the artichoke down to the tightly packed central leaves, and scrape out the hairy choke with a teaspoon.

	To serve 4	
4	artichoke bottoms, chokes removed, parboiled for 10 minutes and quartered	4
3	oranges, peeled, bitter pith and white membrane removed, cut into sections	3
2	celery hearts, leaves removed and reserved, ribs blanched for 5 minutes and cut into 1-inch [2½-cm.] lengths	2
2 tbsp.	olive oil	30 ml.
1 tbsp.	fresh lemon juice	15 ml.
½ tsp.	salt	2 ml.
¼ tsp.	paprika	1 ml.

Mix together the orange sections, celery pieces, olive oil, lemon juice, salt and paprika. Heap together lightly on a serving dish and surround the mixture with the artichoke hearts; wreathe with the celery leaves and serve.

JANET MCKENZIE HILL
SALADS, SANDWICHES, AND CHAFING-DISH DAINTIES

Artichoke Salad with Asparagus

	To serve 4	
6	cold cooked artichoke bottoms, sliced	6
1⅓ cups	cold cooked asparagus tips (about ½ lb. [¼ kg.])	325 ml.
2 tbsp.	chopped salted almonds, pounded	30 ml.
3 to 4 tbsp.	fresh lemon juice	45 to 60 ml.
	salt and pepper	
½ cup	heavy cream	125 ml.

Combine the pounded almonds, lemon juice, salt and pepper, and then gradually stir in the cream. Mix the artichokes and asparagus tips lightly together and serve with the salad dressing poured over them.

MRS. C. F. LEYEL AND MISS OLGA HARTLEY
THE GENTLE ART OF COOKERY

Green Bean Salad

Haricots Verts à l'Huile

The burnet called for in this 1739 recipe is an herb whose leaves have a delicate, cucumber-like flavor when young and tender, but become bitter with age. Burnet does not dry well. If fresh young burnet is unavailable, borage, lovage, fennel or even celery leaves may be substituted.

To serve 4 to 6

1½ lb.	small tender green beans, trimmed	¾ kg.
	salt	
1 tbsp.	butter	15 ml.
1	garlic clove, halved	1
2 tbsp.	finely chopped fresh chervil	30 ml.
2 tbsp.	finely chopped, fresh young burnet leaves	30 ml.
2 tbsp.	finely chopped fresh tarragon	30 ml.
2 tbsp.	finely cut fresh chives	30 ml.
2 tbsp.	finely chopped fresh watercress	30 ml.
	olive oil	
	tarragon vinegar	
	freshly ground black pepper	

Cook the beans in boiling salted water with the butter until just tender, then drain them. Rub a salad bowl with the garlic clove and arrange the beans pleasingly in the bowl. Mix the herbs together and arrange them in a ring around the beans. Season the salad at the table with the olive oil, tarragon vinegar and a little black pepper.

FRANÇOIS MARIN
LES DONS DE COMUS

Green Bean Salad with Anchovies

Haricots Verts en Salade

The original version of this recipe calls for onions that have been baked whole in the ashes of a fireplace. Alternatively, the onions may be wrapped individually in foil and baked in a preheated 350° F. [180° C.] oven for about 40 minutes.

To serve 4 to 6

1½ lb.	green beans, parboiled for 3 to 5 minutes, refreshed in cold water and drained	¾ kg.
4 or 5	salt anchovies, filleted, soaked in water for 30 minutes, drained and patted dry	4 or 5
3 or 4	onions, baked, peeled and sliced	3 or 4
2	beets, cooked, peeled and sliced	2
	fines herbes	
	salt and freshly ground pepper	
	olive oil	
	wine vinegar	

Place the beans in a salad bowl and garnish with the anchovies, onions, beets and salad herbs. The salad is seasoned at table with salt, pepper, oil and vinegar.

A. BEAUVILLIERS
L'ART DU CUISINIER

Beet-Green Salad

Beets can be a perfect vegetable if only they are not boiled. When this is done, the vegetable sodium that the beets contain is just thrown away. Beets are delicious if cooked in wax paper in a casserole dish, with the stems left on and only lightly scrubbed, and eaten while hot with melted butter. Beets are also delightful when cooked in cinders, like a baked potato, and served hot in a folded napkin, seeing that the skin is not bruised. As a salad, beets are best shredded very fine in the raw state—a decorative and valuable salad ingredient if kept away from the vinegar bottle.

To serve 4

1 lb.	beet greens, steamed 7 to 10 minutes, squeezed dry and finely chopped	½ kg.
1	raw beet, peeled and grated	1
2 tbsp.	fresh lemon juice	30 ml.
1 tbsp.	honey	15 ml.
⅓ cup	oil	75 ml.
1	egg, hard-boiled and thinly sliced	1

Let the beet greens cool, and serve them as a salad garnished with the raw, grated beet and dressed with the lemon juice, honey and oil, well shaken together. Decorate the salad with the egg slices.

MARGERY BRAND
FIFTY WAYS OF COOKING VEGETABLES IN INDIA

Broccoli with Oil and Lemon

Broccoli all'Olio e Limone

Broccoli, cauliflower, green beans, chard, spinach—practically all vegetables can be cooked *al dente* and served as in the following recipe; it is perhaps the favorite Italian way of eating greens.

To serve 4		
2½ lb.	broccoli, florets cut apart, stems peeled and cut into 3-inch [8-cm.] pieces, and larger stems also split lengthwise	1¼ kg.
½ to ⅔ cup	olive oil	125 to 150 ml.
3 to 4 tbsp.	strained fresh lemon juice	45 to 60 ml.
	salt and freshly ground pepper	

Cook the broccoli, in just enough boiling salted water to cover it, for four to five minutes, or until tender but still crisp. Drain, and put the broccoli into a serving dish.

Combine the oil, lemon juice and a little salt and pepper, and pour over the broccoli. Serve hot or cold.

NIKA HAZELTON
THE REGIONAL ITALIAN KITCHEN

Red Cabbage Salad with Lemon Juice

Choux-Rouges en Salade

To serve 6		
1	medium-sized red cabbage	1
2 quarts	boiling salted water	2 liters
	salt and pepper	
1 tsp.	chopped fresh thyme	5 ml.
1	bay leaf	1
1 cup	strained fresh lemon juice	¼ liter

Remove the leaves from the red cabbage, cut out the ribs and shred the rest into fine julienne. Immerse the cabbage in the boiling salted water and leave it there for one minute. Drain it thoroughly, pressing it down with the back of a skimming ladle. The cabbage will begin to turn purple.

Put the cabbage into a salad bowl and season it with a very little salt, pepper to taste, the thyme and the bay leaf. Then pour the lemon juice over the cabbage. As soon as the acid comes into contact with the cabbage, the cabbage will

take on a reddish color. Cover the bowl with wax paper and let the salad stand at room temperature overnight, or for at least six hours. Discard the bay leaf before serving the salad.

H. HEYRAUD
LA CUISINE À NICE

———————◆———————

White- and Red-Cabbage Salad

Weiss- und Rotkohl Salat

To serve 6		
1	very small head white cabbage	1
1	very small head red cabbage	1
	salt	
1 cup	vinegar	¼ liter
3 oz.	slab bacon (about ⅓ inch [1 cm.] wide), cut into ⅓-inch cubes	100 g.
½ tsp.	coriander seeds	2 ml.
6	juniper berries	6
¼ tsp.	rubbed sage	1 ml.
1 to 1⅓ cups	oil (neither safflower nor olive)	250 to 325 ml.
	freshly ground pepper	
	chopped fresh parsley	

Cut each cabbage into four wedges. Cut the core off so as to discard the rough part that is too fibrous. Cut each wedge crosswise into ⅙-inch [4-mm.] strips. Keep the white and red cabbages separated.

Bring a 4-quart [4-liter] pot of water to a boil. Add a good tablespoon [15 ml.] of salt and the white cabbage. Bring back to a rolling boil. Boil for one full minute. Remove the cabbage from the hot water bath, and rinse it under cold running water. Drain and pat the cabbage dry in a tea towel. Remove it to a bowl.

Bring the hot water bath back to a boil. Add ½ cup [125 ml.] of the vinegar and the red cabbage. Bring to a full boil for one minute. Drain, rinse, and pat dry as you did the white cabbage. Keep the cabbages separated.

Render the diced bacon slowly in a frying pan until golden. Remove the bacon to a bowl; discard the rendered bacon fat. To the frying pan, add the remaining ½ cup vinegar, the coriander seeds, juniper berries, sage and a teaspoon [5 ml.] of salt. Cook together until the vinegar is reduced to about ⅓ cup [75 ml.]. Strain the mixture into a bowl. Gradually add the oil and mix with a whisk to obtain a good emulsion. Correct the salt, add pepper and mix in more coriander and sage if you desire.

Toss each cabbage separately with half of the dressing and present them in a glass bowl, alternating the colors. Sprinkle with the reserved bacon and chopped parsley.

MADELEINE M. KAMMAN
WHEN FRENCH WOMEN COOK

Red Cabbage Salad

Salade de Choux Rouge

The technique of shredding the cabbage is shown on page 24.

To serve 4 to 6

1	small red cabbage (about 1 lb. [½ kg.]), cored, leaves separated and ribs removed	1
about 2 tbsp.	salt	about 30 ml.
½ cup	vinaigrette (recipe, page 167)	125 ml.

Cut the cabbage leaves into julienne. Layer the cabbage in a bowl, sprinkling each layer with salt, and set the cabbage aside at room temperature for four hours.

Roll the julienne in a towel to wipe off all of the moisture, then put the cabbage into a salad bowl. Season with vinaigrette, and serve.

LÉON ISNARD
LA CUISINE FRANÇAISE ET AFRICAINE

Sweet-and-Sour Cabbage, Peking-Style

Ts'u Lu Pai Ts'ai

I call this cabbage dish a hot salad because the cabbage should be crisp and the sauce is like a hot dressing. It is also excellent when cooked a day ahead of time and served as a cold dish. To make sweet-and-sour cabbage, Szechwan-style, add four whole dried hot chilies to the oil to brown them, then add the cabbage.

To serve 4 to 8

1	small head cabbage (about 1 lb. [½ kg.])	1
½ tsp.	salt	2 ml.
2 tbsp.	sugar	30 ml.
½ tsp.	cornstarch	2 ml.
2 tbsp.	soy sauce	30 ml.
2 tbsp.	distilled white vinegar	30 ml.
2 tbsp.	peanut oil	30 ml.

Remove the tough outer layers of leaves from the cabbage and discard. Cut the cabbage into quarters, cutting out and discarding the hard core from each quarter. Then cut the cabbage quarters into 1½-by-1-inch [4-by-2½-cm.] chunks and separate the leaves to make about 6 cups [1½ liters].

Combine the salt, sugar, cornstarch, soy sauce and vinegar in a cup. Set aside near the cooking area.

Sprinkle the cabbage with a little water to prevent burning during cooking. Heat a wok, add the peanut oil and stir fry the cabbage over high heat for two minutes. Stir the sauce in the cup, making sure the sugar has dissolved. Add the sauce to the wok. Stir and mix well over high heat for another minute. Serve hot or cold.

FLORENCE LIN
FLORENCE LIN'S CHINESE REGIONAL COOKBOOK

Sauerkraut Salad

Sauerkrautsalat

If the sauerkraut is very salty, dip it into cold water, then squeeze it gently to remove the water. This salad also may be made with a mayonnaise dressing.

To serve 4

1 lb.	mild sauerkraut, drained and roughly chopped	½ kg.
1 or 2	apples, peeled, cored and grated	1 or 2
1	small onion, finely chopped	1
2 or 3	sour gherkins, roughly chopped, or 1 tomato, peeled, seeded and roughly chopped	2 or 3
3 tbsp.	oil	45 ml.
1 tbsp.	fresh lemon juice	15 ml.
2 tbsp.	wine vinegar	30 ml.
1 tsp.	sugar	5 ml.
	freshly ground black pepper	

Loosen the shreds of the sauerkraut by tossing it with your finger tips, then add the apple, onion and gherkin or tomato, and mix well. In a small bowl blend the oil, lemon juice, vinegar, sugar and pepper. Season the salad well with this dressing, and serve.

HERMINE KIEHNLE AND MARIA HÄDECKE
DAS NEUE KIEHNLE KOCHBUCH

Spiced Carrot Salad

To serve 4

1 lb.	carrots, peeled	½ kg.
1	garlic clove	1
⅛ tsp.	ground cinnamon	½ ml.
¼ tsp.	ground cumin	1 ml.
½ tsp.	sweet paprika	2 ml.
	cayenne pepper	
3 tbsp.	fresh lemon juice	45 ml.
⅛ tsp.	sugar	½ ml.
	salt	
	olive oil	
	chopped fresh parsley	

Boil the carrots whole in water with the garlic until they are barely tender. Drain. Discard the garlic, and then dice or slice the carrots.

Combine the cinnamon, cumin, paprika and a pinch of cayenne with the lemon juice, sugar and salt, and pour over the carrots. Chill. Sprinkle the carrots with oil and parsley just before serving.

PAULA WOLFERT
COUSCOUS AND OTHER GOOD FOOD FROM MOROCCO

Cauliflower with Mustard-Seed Butter

Cauliflower Raita

To serve 4 to 6

1	medium-sized cauliflower	1
2 tbsp.	fresh lemon juice	30 ml.
4 tsp.	coarse salt	20 ml.
2 cups	plain yogurt	½ liter
3 tbsp.	mustard seeds	45 ml.
6 tbsp.	clarified butter	90 ml.

Cut the cauliflower into medium-sized florets. With a small, sharp knife, trim the heavy skin from their stems.

Put the cauliflower into a large enameled or stainless-steel pan with cold water to barely cover, and add the lemon juice. Bring to a boil, sprinkle with 3 teaspoons [15 ml.] of the coarse salt and simmer for four to five minutes. Drain immediately and thoroughly.

Beat the yogurt with the remaining teaspoon [5 ml.] of salt until creamy smooth. Toss the cooled, dry cauliflower in the yogurt and refrigerate.

In a small, enameled cast-iron pot with a cover, fry the mustard seeds over high heat in the clarified butter. When you begin to hear popping and spattering sounds, count to 50 and remove the pot from the heat. Do not lift the lid for another five minutes.

Drizzle the butter-and-mustard-seed mixture over the cauliflower and yogurt, and swirl together lightly with a wooden spoon. Do not overmix—this *raita* should have a streaky appearance.

THE GREAT COOKS' GUIDE TO SALADS

Marinated Celery

Selino Marinato

Marinated celery must be made in advance, and will keep for up to one week. This marinade may also be used for artichokes, beans, fennel, leeks or mushrooms.

To serve 4

1	bunch celery, tough ribs scrubbed and scraped, all ribs cut diagonally into 1½-inch [4-cm.] pieces and wide pieces halved lengthwise	1
½ cup	olive oil	125 ml.
4 to 5 tbsp.	strained fresh lemon juice	60 to 75 ml.
2 tbsp.	chopped fresh fennel leaves	30 ml.
1 or 2	sprigs fresh thyme, chopped	1 or 2
2	sprigs fresh parsley, chopped	2
1	small bay leaf	1
	salt and freshly ground pepper	
about ½ cup	water	about 125 ml.

In an enameled, glass or stainless-steel pan large enough to accommodate all of the celery, combine the oil, lemon juice, herbs, seasonings and water. Bring this marinade to a boil over high heat, then drop in the celery and add more water, if necessary, to half-cover the celery. Cover the pan, and simmer over low heat for 15 minutes, or until the celery is tender but still crisp. Remove the pan from the heat and let the celery cool in the marinade.

Store, marinade and all, in a covered glass jar in the refrigerator. If the marinade is very watery, boil it down in a small saucepan over high heat and pour it over the celery.

Serve the marinated celery garnished with lemon slices and fresh fennel leaves.

VILMA LIACOURAS CHANTILES
THE FOOD OF GREECE

Christmas Celeriac Salad

Weihnachtssalat aus Sellerie

To serve 4

1 lb.	celeriac, peeled and sliced	½ kg.
1 cup	boiling salted water	¼ liter
2 tsp.	vinegar	10 ml.
2	cubes sugar	2
1	onion, finely chopped	1
	pepper	
3 tbsp.	olive oil	45 ml.
1 tbsp.	fresh lemon juice	15 ml.
2 tbsp.	chopped walnuts	30 ml.

Drop the celeriac into a pan of boiling salted water as soon as it has been peeled and sliced; add the vinegar and sugar, and cook until the celeriac is soft—about 20 minutes. Reserving the broth, drain the celeriac; place it in a bowl and sprinkle it with the chopped onion and a little pepper. Stir the oil and lemon juice into the celeriac broth and pour the broth over the celeriac. Garnish with the chopped walnuts. The salad has a better flavor if left to stand for 24 hours.

JOZA BŘIZOVÁ AND MARYNA KLIMENTOVÁ
TSCHECHISCHE KÜCHE

Celeriac Salad

To serve 4

1	celeriac, peeled and cut into thin slices, blanched for 3 minutes in boiling water, drained and cut into coarse julienne	1
	salt and pepper	
½ tsp.	dry English mustard	2 ml.
2 tbsp.	vinegar	30 ml.
½ cup	oil	125 ml.

Sprinkle the blanched celeriac julienne with salt and let them stand for 30 minutes. Then wash the celeriac thoroughly and dry them in a towel. An hour before serving, mix the mustard, salt and pepper with the vinegar, add the oil, and mix thoroughly together with the celeriac.

ALFRED SUZANNE AND C. HERMAN SENN
A BOOK OF SALADS

Chicory Salad

Salade de Chicorée Cuite

When this recipe was written in the 18th Century, salads were sometimes dressed ahead of time with a vinaigrette, but most often vinegar, olive oil, salt and pepper were served at the table and each guest seasoned his or her salad to taste. The decorative presentation was important, and the most usual garnishes were salt anchovies that had been filleted, soaked, rinsed and dried; tuna preserved in oil; quartered, sliced or chopped hard-boiled eggs; beets baked in ashes, peeled and thinly sliced; capers; purslane and other wild greens; fines herbes; and often flowers such as nasturtiums, pot marigold petals, rose petals, violets and hyssop blossoms.

Celery hearts that have been trimmed, split in half lengthwise, and either left raw or parboiled for 10 minutes may be substituted for the chicory.

To serve 4 to 6

2 or 3	heads chicory with the outer leaves discarded, left whole but washed thoroughly	2 or 3
1	beet, wrapped in foil, baked in a 325° F. [160° C.] oven for 3 to 4 hours, peeled and thinly sliced	1
1 tbsp.	capers, rinsed and drained	15 ml.
3½ oz.	cooked tuna, broken into pieces (about ⅔ cup [150 ml.])	100 g.
	salt and pepper	
	wine vinegar	
	olive oil	

Blanch the chicory in boiling salted water for two to three minutes; rinse in cold water and dry thoroughly by pressing the heads in a cloth; then cut out the cores and slice the chicory heads crosswise. Arrange the chicory slices in a salad dish and garnish them with the beet, capers, tuna and anything else you find suitable. Serve accompanied by salt, pepper and cruets of vinegar and oil.

GILLIERS
LE CANNAMELISTE FRANÇAIS

Chicory Cooked in Court Bouillon
Gourilos

To serve 8 to 10

20	hearts of chicory or other lettuce, trimmed	20
	Lemon court bouillon	
¼ cup	strained fresh lemon juice	50 ml.
1¼ cups	water	300 ml.
¼ cup	olive oil	50 ml.
	salt	
8 to 10	peppercorns	8 to 10
8 to 10	coriander seeds	8 to 10
½ tsp.	fennel seeds	2 ml.
1	celery rib	1
1	sprig fresh thyme	1
1	bay leaf	1

Put the chicory into an enameled, glass or stainless-steel saucepan with the water, lemon juice, salt, olive oil and all of the seasonings. Bring to a boil, cover and simmer gently for 15 minutes, or until tender. Cool the chicory in its cooking liquid, drain, and serve chilled.

PROSPER SALLES AND PROSPER MONTAGNÉ
LA GRANDE CUISINE

Dandelion and Salt-Pork Salad
Salade de Pissenlits aux Lardons

To serve 6

½ lb.	dandelion greens, stems removed	¼ kg.
3½ oz.	lean salt pork with the rind removed, blanched in boiling water for 3 minutes, drained and cut into julienne	100 g.
1 tbsp.	oil	15 ml.
1	small heel of dry bread	1
1	garlic clove, cut in half	1
	freshly ground pepper	
3 tbsp.	wine vinegar	45 ml.
2	eggs, hard-boiled and quartered	2

In a skillet over medium heat, lightly brown the salt pork in the oil. Pour boiling water into a salad bowl to heat it; dis-

card the water and wipe the bowl dry. Add the dandelions, the bread rubbed with the garlic, and pepper to taste.

From now on, work rapidly: Throw the hot salt pork and its cooking fat into the salad bowl. In the same frying pan, bring the vinegar to a boil over high heat. Pour the vinegar over the salad and toss immediately. Garnish with the hard-boiled eggs and serve at once.

SYLVIE THIÉBAULT
SALADES ET ASSIETTES FROIDES

Dandelion and Smoked Herring Salad
Salade de Pissenlits

Pick the dandelion greens after a spring frost, when they have just begun to grow and have hearts of tender young yellowish-green leaves.

To serve 4

½ lb.	dandelion greens	¼ kg.
2 oz.	lean salt pork with the rind removed, blanched in boiling water for 5 minutes, drained and diced	75 g.
1 tbsp.	butter	15 ml.
3 or 4	eggs, hard-boiled and finely chopped	3 or 4
½ cup	vinaigrette (recipe, page 167), made with either olive or walnut oil, and 1 tsp. [5 ml.] prepared mustard	125 ml.
1	pickled herring, skinned, filleted and diced	1
	small crusts of bread, rubbed with garlic	

Fry the salt pork in the butter over low heat. Meanwhile, mix the chopped eggs with the vinaigrette in a salad bowl, and adjust the seasoning to taste. When the salt pork is golden, add the dandelions to the vinaigrette and toss them. Immediately add the hot pork pieces—with their fat—and the herring dice to the dandelions. Toss again and serve the salad at once, with the garlic crusts on a separate plate.

TOULOUSE-LAUTREC AND MAURICE JOYANT
L'ART DE LA CUISINE

Stuffed Eggplant

Imam Bayildi

The technique of sautéing the pine nuts called for in this recipe is shown on page 48.

To serve 6

3	small eggplants	3
2 tbsp.	chopped fresh parsley	30 ml.
¼ cup	pine nuts, sautéed	50 ml.
	Vegetable stuffing	
2	onions, thinly sliced	2
1	green pepper, halved, seeded, deribbed and cut into thin julienne	1
4	medium-sized tomatoes, cored, peeled, seeded, cut into chunks and drained	4
6 tbsp.	olive oil	90 ml.
1	garlic clove, finely chopped	1
1 ½ tsp.	salt	7 ml.
⅛ tsp.	freshly ground black pepper	½ ml.
½ tsp.	sugar	2 ml.
¼ tsp.	oregano	1 ml.
2 tbsp.	fresh lemon juice	30 ml.

Place the eggplants in a large pan and cover them with boiling water. Cook them, uncovered, over high heat for five minutes. Turn them often, using a wooden spoon so you do not puncture the skins. Transfer the eggplants to a pan of cold water to cool quickly.

Split the cooled eggplants in half lengthwise. Cut around the inside of each half, about ½ inch [1 cm.] from the edge. Next, cut the pulp into squares, leaving ½ inch of uncut pulp on the bottom of each shell. Scoop out the diced pulp.

Place the eggplant shells skin side up on a tray lined with paper towels, and chill until ready to use. The shells will become limp, but they will look fine when stuffed.

Put 3 tablespoons [45 ml.] of the olive oil in a large skillet and sauté the onions and peppers until they are just wilted—about five minutes. Add the garlic and the diced eggplant; cover and cook, stirring the vegetables occasionally, until the eggplant is tender—about seven minutes. Add the salt, pepper, sugar and oregano, stir, then cook for about two minutes. Remove the pan from the stove, then gently stir in the tomatoes.

Transfer the mixture to a large bowl. Mix in the remaining 3 tablespoons of olive oil and the lemon juice. Chill well—for at least four hours. Just before serving, pat the inside of the shells with paper towels and divide the vegetable mixture among the shells, heaping it up as much as necessary. Sprinkle each half with parsley and pine nuts.

ELEANOR GRAVES
GREAT DINNERS FROM LIFE

Spiced Eggplant

To serve 6

2 or 3	large eggplants, sliced into rounds 1 inch [2½ cm.] thick, sprinkled with salt and left to drain for 1 to 1½ hours, then dried	2 or 3
about ½ cup	oil	about 125 ml.
2	green peppers, halved, seeded, deribbed and diced	2
2	sweet red peppers, halved, seeded, deribbed and diced	2
2	sour pickles, diced	2
2¼ cups	wine or cider vinegar	550 ml.
	water	
	freshly ground black pepper	
8 to 10	fresh grapevine leaves	8 to 10

Fry the eggplant slices in the oil until soft, remove and drain them. Fry the diced peppers and pickles in the same oil until soft. Remove and drain them. Prepare a dressing by diluting the vinegar with a little water according to taste. Add some black pepper and the vine leaves, bring to a boil, and simmer for five to seven minutes.

Line the bottom of a deep dish with the vine leaves. Place a layer of eggplant on the leaves, and on top of each eggplant slice spoon the diced pepper-and-pickle mixture. Alternate layers in this way until all of the eggplant and all of the pepper mixture have been used. The dish looks most attractive when there are at least four layers of eggplant and peppers. Pour the vinegar dressing over the eggplant. Refrigerate for one to two days, to allow the eggplant and peppers to absorb the vinegar.

JESSICA KUPER (EDITOR)
THE ANTHROPOLOGISTS' COOKBOOK

Eggplant Cooked Like Mushrooms

Melanzane a Fungetielli

To serve 6

3	medium-sized eggplants (about 1 lb. [½ kg.] each), thinly peeled and cut into 1-inch [2½-cm.] cubes	3
	salt	
⅓ cup	olive oil	75 ml.
4	large ripe tomatoes, peeled, seeded and chopped	4
6 to 8	large ripe olives, pitted and chopped	6 to 8
1 tbsp.	capers, rinsed and drained	15 ml.
2 or 3	sprigs basil or parsley, finely chopped	2 or 3
1 tsp.	finely chopped oregano or marjoram	5 ml.
1	garlic clove, finely chopped	1

Place the eggplant cubes in a colander, sprinkle them lightly with salt and leave them for one hour to drain off the bitter liquid. Wipe the cubes dry.

Heat the oil in a deep pan, add the eggplant cubes and sauté over medium heat for 15 minutes. Add the tomatoes, olives and capers. Reduce the heat and continue cooking for about 15 minutes, or until the eggplant cubes are soft. Add the herbs and garlic, taste for salt and stir gently. Serve cold.

ADA BONI
ITALIAN REGIONAL COOKING

Eggplant in Yogurt

Aubergines Macérées dans du Lait Caillé

To serve 4 to 6

2	medium-sized eggplants, peeled and cut into slices ½ inch [1 cm.] thick	2
3 cups	plain yogurt, drained in a cloth-lined strainer overnight	¾ liter
	salt	
1¼ cups	olive oil	300 ml.
3	garlic cloves	3
2 tsp.	finely crumbled dried mint leaves	10 ml.

Sprinkle the eggplant slices with salt and let them stand for 15 minutes. Dry them in a towel and fry the slices, a small batch at a time, in the oil over medium heat for about 10 minutes or until golden and soft. Drain, and arrange them on a plate to cool. Pound together the garlic and a pinch of salt and mix with the yogurt. Pour the yogurt mixture over the cooled eggplant slices. Sprinkle with the mint and serve.

GEORGES N. RAYES
L'ART CULINAIRE LIBANAIS

Eggplant Salad

Melitzanosalata

To serve 6

3 or 4	long eggplants (about 3 lb. [1½ kg.] in all)	3 or 4
1	small onion, grated	1
2	garlic cloves, crushed	2
1	large tomato, peeled, seeded and chopped into small pieces	1
¾ cup	olive oil	175 ml.
1 tbsp.	vinegar	15 ml.
	salt and pepper	
	ripe olives	
1	large green pepper, stem end removed, seeded and sliced into rings	1

Prick the eggplants, place them in a baking pan, and bake in a 350° F. [180° C.] oven for about one hour, or until soft. Allow the skin to shrivel and turn black so as to give a smoky flavor to the salad. Peel the eggplants while they are still hot and chop the flesh into small pieces. Continue chopping while adding slowly the onion, garlic, tomato, oil, vinegar, salt and pepper. Put in a salad bowl, and garnish with olives and rings of green pepper.

CHRISSA PARADISSIS
THE BEST BOOK OF GREEK COOKERY

Eggplant Salad, Rabat-Style

The eggplant is traditionally grilled over a charcoal brazier; for convenience in this recipe, it is baked in the oven.

To serve 4

1	medium-sized eggplant (about 1 lb. [½ kg.])	1
1	garlic clove, slivered	1
2 tbsp.	chopped fresh parsley	30 ml.
2	sprigs fresh coriander leaves, chopped (optional)	2
½ tsp.	paprika	2 ml.
½ tsp.	ground cumin	2 ml.
2 tbsp.	olive oil	30 ml.
1 to 2 tbsp.	fresh lemon juice	15 to 30 ml.
	salt	

Stud the whole eggplant with garlic slivers, using a paring knife to form holes for the slivers. Bake the eggplant in a

400° F. [200° C.] oven until very soft (it will seem as if it has collapsed; the skin will be black and blistery). Remove from the oven to cool.

When cool enough to handle, peel the eggplant. Squeeze the pulp to release the bitter juices or scoop out the pulp with a wooden spoon and let it drain in a sieve. Discard the bitter liquid. Mash or push the eggplant pulp and garlic slivers through a food mill. (Avoid the temptation to use a blender—it destroys the character of the dish.)

Add the chopped herbs and spices and mix well. Fry in the oil over medium heat, turning the eggplant often with a perforated spatula until all of the liquid has evaporated and the eggplant has been reduced to a thick black jam. (This turning and frying will take about 15 to 20 minutes.) Sprinkle with lemon juice, taste for salt, and readjust the seasoning to taste. Serve warm or slightly cooled. (You may want to decorate this salad with cherry tomatoes.)

PAULA WOLFERT
COUSCOUS AND OTHER GOOD FOOD FROM MOROCCO

Eggplant Salad with Mushrooms

To serve 6 or more

1	medium-sized eggplant, peeled and cubed	1
1½ cups	sliced mushrooms	375 ml.
2	large tomatoes, chopped	2
1	large red onion, chopped	1
	salt	
2 tbsp.	oil	30 ml.
2	garlic cloves, finely chopped	2
½ cup	sliced, pitted ripe olives	125 ml.
	pepper	
2 tbsp.	capers, rinsed and drained (optional)	30 ml.
	vinaigrette (recipe, page 167) made with fresh lemon juice	

Put the eggplant in a colander and sprinkle it with salt. Let it sit for an hour or so to extract a little of the liquid, then sauté the eggplant in the oil and garlic until slightly tender. (Eggplant cooks rapidly.) Add the mushrooms and sauté one or two minutes more. Remove the pan from the heat and let the vegetables cool. Add the tomatoes, onion, olives, salt and pepper to taste, and capers, if desired. Refrigerate until chilled. Toss with the vinaigrette dressing.

SHARON CADWALLADER
SHARON CADWALLADER'S COMPLETE COOKBOOK

Spring Garlic Salad

Salata ot Paren Presen Chesun

Garlic, which is grown from large garlic cloves planted in the autumn, still has unformed bulbs in spring. The immature plants are widely used in Bulgaria, where they are sold in bunches. Scallions may be substituted for spring garlic.

If desired, this salad can be presented with a border of seasoned beet rounds.

To serve 5

2 to 2½ lb.	spring garlic plants, cleaned, trimmed of roots and green tops, cut into 1½-inch [3½-cm.] pieces	1 kg.
	wine vinegar	
	salt	
about ¼ cup	olive oil	about 50 ml.

Place the pieces of garlic in a bowl and pour boiling water over them. Leave the garlic in the bowl until the water cools, then drain the garlic in a colander and put it back into the bowl. Cover the garlic completely with vinegar: not too much—the pieces should not be floating. Let the garlic marinate for a day or two in a cool place or a refrigerator. Then strain the garlic and season it to taste with salt.

Arrange the garlic attractively on a wide, flat plate. Sprinkle the pieces liberally with the oil, and serve.

L. PETROV, N. DJELEPOV, E. IORDANOV, AND S. UZUNOVA
BULGARSKA NAZIONALNA KUCHNIYA

Jerusalem Artichokes

Articokks

To serve 4

2 to 2½ lb.	round Jerusalem artichokes, peeled and dropped into cold water mixed with a little lemon juice to keep them white	1 kg.
	salt	
3	garlic cloves, crushed	3
2 tbsp.	chopped fresh parsley	30 ml.
2 tbsp.	olive oil	30 ml.

Drain the artichokes, then boil them in salted water for about eight to 10 minutes, or until tender. Drain and place the artichokes on a serving dish. Sprinkle them with the garlic, parsley and oil. They may be served hot or cold.

ANNE AND HELEN CARUANA GALIZIA
RECIPES FROM MALTA

Leeks with Sweet Red Pepper

Poireaux aux Piments

A very pleasant flavor will be obtained if you blanch the skin of the lemon used in this recipe, refresh it in cold water, cut it into fine strips, and sprinkle the strips over the dish—a small spoonful should be enough.

To serve 4

1 lb.	leeks, white parts left whole and blanched in boiling salted water for 5 minutes, pale green parts diced and left raw, dark green tops discarded	½ kg.
¼ cup	olive oil	50 ml.
1	large sweet red pepper, halved, seeded, deribbed and diced	1
½ cup	dry white wine	125 ml.
1½ to 2 tbsp.	strained fresh lemon juice	22 to 30 ml.
8 to 10	coriander seeds	8 to 10
	salt and pepper	
1	bay leaf	1
1	sprig fresh parsley	1

In a pan, heat the oil over medium heat and cook the pale green parts of the leeks. When soft—after about 15 minutes—add the red pepper, wine, lemon juice, coriander, a little salt and pepper, the bay leaf and the parsley. Boil for five minutes. Add the white parts of the leeks, simmer tightly covered for a further 15 to 20 minutes and let the mixture cool. Serve very cold.

J. BERJANE
FRENCH DISHES FOR ENGLISH TABLES

Roasted Onion Salad

Salade d'Oignons

This recipe is from a 16th Century French translation of a book first published in Latin in 1474. The author recommends the salad for the digestion. The "must" called for as an ingredient is freshly pressed, unfermented grape juice; the vin cuit is must that has been cooked, reduced and skimmed, and preserved by the addition of a little brandy.

An alternative method of cooking the onions is to place them on a bed of salt and bake them in a preheated 350° F.

[*180° C.*] *oven for 40 to 60 minutes, or until the onions are soft when you squeeze them.*

To serve 6

6	large onions, unpeeled	6
	salt	
¼ cup	olive oil	50 ml.
¼ cup	must or *vin cuit*	50 ml.
	pepper or ground cinnamon (optional)	
	vinegar (optional)	

Roast the onions beneath hot ashes with embers piled on top for about one hour, or until the onions are tender all the way through. Allow the onions to cool, then peel them and chop or slice them neatly. Place them in a dish and sprinkle them with a little salt and the oil and must or *vin cuit*. Pepper or cinnamon or a little vinegar may be added if desired.

BAPTISTE PLATINE DE CRÉMONNE
LE LIVRE DE L'HONNESTE VOLUPTÉ

Okra with Tomatoes

Bamies Me Saltsa, Latheres

To serve 4

1 lb.	small, fresh okra, trimmed	½ kg.
	salt	
½ cup	vinegar	125 ml.
¾ cup	olive oil	175 ml.
2	medium-sized onions, coarsely chopped	2
4	medium-sized tomatoes (about 1 lb. [½ kg.]), peeled, seeded and chopped, or canned tomatoes, drained and chopped	4
	pepper	
1 tsp.	sugar	5 ml.

Place the okra on a dish, sprinkle with salt and the vinegar and set them aside for 30 minutes (this is to prevent the okra from splitting while cooking). Wash the okra again and then dry them thoroughly.

Heat the olive oil in a large frying pan and add the chopped onions. Cook gently until the onions are tender. Add the okra and cook, tossing lightly, until they are slightly browned. Add the tomatoes, and season with salt and pepper. Cover the frying pan and let the vegetables simmer gently for about 45 minutes, or until the okra are tender. Serve the vegetables cold.

CHRISSA PARADISSIS
THE BEST BOOK OF GREEK COOKERY

Sweet Peppers Stuffed with Shrimp

The technique of peeling a pepper appears on page 42.

Instead of shrimp, tuna can be used as the basis for the stuffing, spiced in the same way as the shrimp chutney.

	To serve 4 to 6	
3 or 4	large red or yellow sweet peppers, broiled, peeled and seeded, each cut into 3 or 4 wide strips	3 or 4
	olive oil	
	fresh lemon juice	
	watercress or shredded lettuce	
	Mauritian shrimp chutney	
¼ lb.	peeled, cooked shrimp	125 g.
4	scallions, chopped	4
1	green or red sweet pepper or ½ small fresh green or red hot chili, very finely chopped	1
about ¼ cup	olive oil	about 50 ml.
about ¼ tsp.	ground ginger or 1 tsp. [5 ml.] grated fresh ginger root	about 1 ml.
	cayenne pepper (optional)	
1	lime or ½ lemon	1
	salt	

To make the shrimp chutney, pound the peeled shrimp in a mortar with the chopped scallions. Add the chopped raw pepper or chili. Stir in enough olive oil, little by little, to make the mixture into a thick paste. Add a pinch of ground ginger, or a teaspoon [5 ml.] of grated ginger root, and, if sweet pepper has been used, a scrap of cayenne pepper. Squeeze in the juice of a fresh lime if available, or of half a lemon, and add salt if necessary. Put a small spoonful of this mixture on each strip of broiled pepper, and roll the strip into the shape of a sausage.

Arrange on a bed of watercress or shredded lettuce on a long dish. Pour a little olive oil and lemon juice over the rolled peppers.

ELIZABETH DAVID
SUMMER COOKING

Broiled Pepper Salad

Salatat Al-Foulayfila Al-Machwiyya

The original version of this recipe calls for broiling the peppers and garlic over charcoal; a broiler provides similar re-

sults—with less peril for most cooks. The technique of peeling broiled peppers is demonstrated on page 42.

Add a pinch of paprika for extra pungency, if wished. The garlic and cumin may be omitted; and some prefer simply to dress the peppers with oil.

	To serve 4	
3	medium-sized sweet red peppers (about 1 lb. [½ kg.])	3
2	garlic cloves	2
3	lemons, 1 squeezed, 2 peeled and sliced	3
	salt	
	ground cumin	
	paprika (optional)	

Broil the peppers about 2 inches [5 cm.] from the heat for four or five minutes, turning them so they blacken evenly. Peel them and remove the stems and seeds. Cut the peppers into strips and place these in a salad bowl with their juices.

Broil the garlic cloves in a pan for three to four minutes, turning them once or twice. Peel them, then pound the cloves in a mortar. Mix the lemon juice with the garlic and pour the mixture over the peppers. Add the lemon slices. Sprinkle with salt, a pinch of cumin and paprika, if using. Stir carefully and serve cold.

RENÉ R. KHAWAM
LA CUISINE ARABE

Potato Salad with Wine and Herbs

Salade de Pommes de Terre

	To serve 4	
2 lb.	potatoes, preferably a waxy, yellow-fleshed boiling variety, unpeeled	1 kg.
6 tbsp.	dry white wine	90 ml.
	salt and pepper	
2 tbsp.	vinegar	30 ml.
½ cup	oil	125 ml.
1 tbsp.	finely chopped fresh parsley	15 ml.
1 tbsp.	finely chopped fresh chervil	15 ml.
1	shallot or small onion, finely chopped (optional)	1

Boil the potatoes in salted water until barely tender—about 15 minutes. Dry them in a preheated 275° F. [140° C.] oven for about 10 minutes. Peel the potatoes while they are still hot, slice them immediately, and mix them—still hot—with the wine. Season with salt, pepper, vinegar, oil, parsley and chervil. A finely chopped shallot or onion may be added.

PAUL BOCUSE
PAUL BOCUSE'S FRENCH COOKING

Potato Salad

To serve 4 to 6

6 or 7	medium-sized waxy boiling potatoes (about 2 lb. [1 kg.]), unpeeled	6 or 7
	salt and pepper	
about 2 tbsp.	finely cut fresh chives or about 4 tbsp. [60 ml.] finely cut green scallion tops	about 30 ml.
1 cup	mayonnaise (recipe, page 166)	¼ liter
about ⅓ cup	milk	about 75 ml.
1 handful	mixed fresh parsley and mint, chopped	1 handful

Boil the potatoes in their skins, taking care that they are not overdone. As soon as they can be handled, peel and slice them, and season them with salt and pepper, and the chives or scallions. While the potatoes are still warm, pour over them the mayonnaise thinned with a little milk, and mix them carefully so that each slice receives its coating of mayonnaise without being broken. On the top of the salad, strew the parsley and the mint mixed together.

ELIZABETH DAVID
SUMMER COOKING

Swedish Potato Salad

To serve 4

2	medium-sized cold cooked potatoes (about 12 oz. [350 g.]), sliced	2
2	medium-sized cooked beets, cut into 1-inch [2½-cm.] julienne	2
2 tbsp.	capers, rinsed and drained	30 ml.
1	head lettuce, cut into chiffonade	1
2	egg yolks	2
½ tsp.	salt	2 ml.
½ tsp.	prepared mustard	2 ml.
1 tsp.	sugar	5 ml.
3 tbsp.	oil	45 ml.
1 to 2 tbsp.	vinegar	15 to 30 ml.
1 tbsp.	caper liquid	15 ml.
¼ cup	heavy cream	50 ml.

Mix the potatoes, beets, capers and lettuce in a salad bowl. In another bowl, stir the egg yolks with the salt, mustard and

sugar. Add the oil, vinegar and caper liquid gradually, stirring. Then stir in the cream. Pour this dressing over the salad, mixing well.

INGA NORBERG
GOOD FOOD FROM SWEDEN

Potato Salad from Périgord

La Salade de Pommes de Terre

A handful of diced cooked sausage or smoked ham can also be added to this potato salad.

To serve 6

2 to 2½ lb.	potatoes, unpeeled	1 kg.
1	garlic clove, cut	1
1	onion, sliced	1
2 tbsp.	chopped sour gherkin	30 ml.
1 tbsp.	capers, rinsed and drained	15 ml.
1 tbsp.	finely chopped fresh parsley	15 ml.
2 tsp.	finely cut fresh chives	10 ml.
1 tsp.	chopped fresh tarragon leaves	5 ml.
	salt and pepper	
Gribiche sauce		
2	eggs, hard-boiled, yolks mashed, whites chopped	2
3 tbsp.	vinegar	45 ml.
	salt and pepper	
¼ cup	walnut oil	50 ml.
½ cup	peanut oil	125 ml.

Steam the potatoes or, preferably, roast them in hot ashes. Peel the potatoes, cut them into thick slices and keep them warm under a cloth. It is essential to season the potatoes while still warm so that they become well impregnated with the sauce. Rub the inside of a warm salad bowl with the garlic clove. Put the potatoes into the bowl with the onion, gherkin, capers, parsley, chives and tarragon, and season with salt and pepper.

To make the sauce, work the egg yolks to a purée in a mortar. Add the vinegar and salt and pepper to taste, and mix thoroughly. Finally incorporate the walnut and peanut oils. Pour the sauce over the salad and mix well. Serve warm, adding the chopped egg whites at the last minute.

ZETTE GUINAUDEAU-FRANC
LES SECRETS DES FERMES EN PÉRIGORD NOIR

Old Yankee Potato Salad with Cooked Dressing

This recipe dates from the middle of the 19th Century.

	To serve 4 to 6	
4 cups	sliced, cold cooked and peeled potatoes	1 liter
	salt and white pepper	
2	onions, finely chopped	2
½ cup	vinegar	125 ml.
1 tbsp.	butter	15 ml.
2	egg yolks, well beaten	2
	heavy cream	
	cayenne pepper	

Salt and pepper the sliced potatoes and mix in the onions. Put the vinegar into a saucepan with the butter and let it heat slowly. Pour the beaten egg yolks into a 1-cup [¼-liter] measure and fill it with the cream; beat the egg yolks and cream together; pour them into the butter-vinegar mixture and continue cooking it. Season with salt, white pepper and a pinch of cayenne. Stir constantly until the dressing almost reaches the boiling point, then pour it over the potatoes and mix; serve cold. If, at the time of cooking, the dressing is too thin, add egg yolk; if too thick, add cream.

HELEN LYON ADAMSON
GRANDMOTHER IN THE KITCHEN

Potato Salad with Bacon

Kartoffelsalat mit Speck

	To serve 6	
6 or 7	medium-sized waxy boiling potatoes (about 2 lb. [1 kg.]), boiled, peeled and thinly sliced while still hot	6 or 7
2	thick slices bacon, diced	2
2 tbsp.	oil	30 ml.
1	small onion, finely chopped	1
¼ cup	vinegar	50 ml.
1 cup	basic stock *(recipe, page 164)*	¼ liter
	salt and pepper	

Fry the bacon in the oil until it browns. Add the onion and cook over low heat until the onion turns a light golden color. Remove the pan from the heat, cool the mixture slightly, then add the vinegar, stock, and a little salt and pepper, and mix well. Pour the bacon-and-onion dressing over the still-warm potato slices, mix gently and serve.

HERMINE KIEHNLE AND MARIA HÄDECKE
DAS NEUE KIEHNLE KOCHBUCH

Salad of Young Spinach Leaves

Salade d'Épinards Nouveaux

	To serve 4	
½ lb.	young spinach, stems removed and leaves torn up	¼ kg.
2	eggs, hard-boiled, the yolks pounded and the whites coarsely chopped	2
1 tsp.	Dijon mustard	5 ml.
¼ cup	strained fresh lemon juice	50 ml.
	salt and freshly ground pepper	
⅔ cup	olive oil	150 ml.
¼ lb.	thinly sliced bacon, diced	125 g.
2 tbsp.	red wine vinegar	30 ml.

Wash the spinach leaves in several changes of water, drain them, and dry them in a towel.

In a round-bottomed salad bowl, blend the hard-boiled egg yolks with the mustard, lemon juice and a little salt and pepper. Beating rapidly with a wire whisk, slowly incorporate the oil into the yolk mixture.

In a small skillet, brown the bacon; remove the bacon and drain it on paper towels. Pour all but about 1 tablespoon [15 ml.] of the fat from the skillet, and set the skillet aside.

Mix the spinach leaves with the dressing in a salad bowl, tossing thoroughly, then sprinkle the egg whites and hot bacon pieces over all.

Return the skillet to medium heat and deglaze it with the vinegar. Just before serving, pour the boiling vinegar juices over the salad and toss again.

JEAN AND PIERRE TROISGROS
THE NOUVELLE CUISINE OF JEAN & PIERRE TROISGROS

Salad of Swiss Chard Ribs

Chard is a variety of beet having large succulent stalks to the leaves. These stalks, or ribs, should be cut before they are old and tough, tied in a bundle like asparagus, and then trimmed to an equal length. The green leaves may be used for other preparations.

	To serve 4	
4 lb.	Swiss chard ribs, tied in a bundle	2 kg.
	salt	
about ¾ cup	vinaigrette *(recipe, page 167)*	about 175 ml.

In enough salted water to cover them completely, boil the chard ribs until they are tender, about 10 to 12 minutes. Drain, then untie the ribs. Dress the ribs with vinaigrette while they are still warm, but serve them cold.

MAXIMILIAN DE LOUP
THE AMERICAN SALAD BOOK

Zucchini with Saffron

Courgettes au Safran

The court bouillon called for in this 1931 recipe should be brought to a boil and simmered uncovered for about 15 minutes before the zucchini are added. The technique of peeling peppers is demonstrated on page 42.

	To serve 8	
8	zucchini, each quartered lengthwise	8
¾ cup	cooked rice	175 ml.
4	sweet red peppers, broiled, peeled, seeded and diced	4
about 2 tbsp.	chopped fresh parsley	about 30 ml.

Saffron court bouillon		
½ tsp.	ground saffron	2 ml.
½ cup	oil	125 ml.
1¼ cups	water	300 ml.
3 to 4 tbsp.	fresh lemon juice	45 to 60 ml.
1	celery rib	1
1	stalk fennel or thyme	1
1	bay leaf	1
1 tsp.	coriander seeds	5 ml.
	salt and pepper	

Prepare the court bouillon by combining all of the ingredients. Cook the zucchini in the court bouillon for about 10 minutes, or until tender but still firm. When cooked, let the zucchini cool in the liquor.

When the zucchini are cool, drain and place them on a long serving dish. Spoon the rice onto both ends of the dish and make a border with the diced red peppers. Sprinkle the zucchini and rice with some of the court bouillon and a little chopped parsley, and serve.

J. BERJANE
FRENCH DISHES FOR ENGLISH TABLES

Sweet-and-Sour Zucchini

Zucchine alla Scapece

This is the best-loved of all the Neapolitan ways of preparing small, tender zucchini. The word *scapece* comes from a degeneration over the centuries of the name Apicius, the ancient Roman gastronome. Today, in the Naples area, *scapece* is used to describe food (mostly vegetables or fish) that is prepared in the same style as this zucchini: a method that

reflects Apicius' own recipes. There must be a perfect balance between the sharpness of the vinegar and the sweetness of the sugar: Neither must predominate.

	To serve 4	
8	small young zucchini, thinly sliced	8
½ cup	olive oil	125 ml.
2 or 3	garlic cloves, very thinly sliced	2 or 3
	fresh mint leaves, torn up	
	salt and freshly ground black pepper	
2 tbsp.	superfine sugar	30 ml.
2 tbsp.	mild malt vinegar	30 ml.

Heat the oil until it is very hot and fry the zucchini slices, a few at a time, until golden on both sides. Be careful not to burn them. Drain and dry well on absorbent paper.

Put a layer of zucchini slices on a flat dish and strew them with the garlic, mint, salt and pepper. Sprinkle with a little of the sugar and a little of the vinegar. Build up layers in this way until all of the zucchini slices are used.

FRANCO LAGATTOLLA
THE RECIPES THAT MADE A MILLION

Marinated Turnips with Dill Dressing

	To serve 6	
2	large turnips (about 1 lb. [½ kg.]), peeled and cut into rectangles 1 by ½ inch [2½ by 1 cm.], each rectangle trimmed to an oval shape	2
5 tsp.	salt	25 ml.
4 tbsp.	sugar	60 ml.
1½ cups	white wine vinegar	375 ml.
3 tbsp.	fresh lemon juice	45 ml.
½ cup	dry white wine	125 ml.
2 tsp.	white pepper	10 ml.
1 tbsp.	finely cut fresh dill leaves	15 ml.

Place the turnips in a pan and cover them with water. Add 1 teaspoon [5 ml.] of the salt and 1 tablespoon [15 ml.] of the sugar to the water. Cook the turnips for 15 minutes and drain them. Mix the remaining salt and the remaining sugar with the vinegar, lemon juice, wine and pepper. Add the mixture to the turnips, stir, and set the turnips aside to marinate for 24 hours. Before serving, drain the turnips and sprinkle them with the finely cut dill.

CHARLOTTE ADAMS
THE FOUR SEASONS COOKBOOK

Middle Eastern Chick-pea Salad

To serve 4 to 6

1 to 1½ cups	dried chick-peas	250 to 375 ml.
½ tsp.	baking soda	2 ml.
1 tbsp.	red wine vinegar	15 ml.
3 to 6 tbsp.	fresh lemon juice	45 to 90 ml.
6 tbsp.	olive oil	90 ml.
¼ tsp.	dry mustard	1 ml.
1 tsp.	Dijon mustard	5 ml.
1	garlic clove, mashed to a paste	1
1	large ripe tomato, cubed	1
1	cucumber, peeled, halved, seeded and diced	1
1	green pepper, halved, seeded, deribbed and diced	1
6	radishes, diced	6
3 tbsp.	finely chopped scallion	45 ml.
2 tbsp.	finely chopped fresh parsley	30 ml.
	salt and freshly ground black pepper	

Put the chick-peas into plenty of water to cover them. Add the baking soda and let them stand overnight.

The next day, drain the chick-peas and place them in a heavy casserole. Cover the chick-peas with boiling water and place the casserole, tightly covered, in a 325° F. [160° C.] oven. Cook for two to three hours, or until the chick-peas are tender. Do not salt until the chick-peas are almost done. Remove the casserole from the oven and let the chick-peas cool in their cooking liquid before draining them.

In a large glass serving bowl, combine the vinegar, 3 tablespoons [45 ml.] of lemon juice, the olive oil, mustards and garlic. Whisk the mixture until this dressing is well blended, then add the drained chick-peas, the tomato, cucumber, green pepper, radishes, scallion and parsley. Toss the salad, season it with salt and pepper, and chill it for two to four hours.

Thirty minutes before serving, bring the salad back to room temperature. Correct the seasoning, adding more lemon juice if necessary; the salad should be quite tangy.

PERLA MEYERS
THE PEASANT KITCHEN

American Three-Bean Salad

The cooking times for dried chick-peas and beans vary from one to two hours, depending on the age and dryness of the legumes. Check the peas and beans for tenderness frequently to avoid overcooking them.

You can vary this salad as you like; I often put in some black beans as well, or as a substitute if I am out of white beans. The salad can be made the day before you need it. If you do this, do not put in the parsley and chives until the day you eat it. An important point is to put the beans hot into the vinaigrette dressing so that they absorb the flavor.

To serve 4 to 6

½ cup	dried chick-peas, soaked in water overnight and drained	125 ml.
½ cup	dried white beans, soaked in water overnight, drained and parboiled for 10 minutes	125 ml.
½ cup	dried red kidney beans, soaked in water overnight, drained and parboiled for 10 minutes	125 ml.
½ cup	chopped scallions or onion	125 ml.
2	garlic cloves, finely chopped	2
1 handful	chopped fresh parsley and chives	1 handful
⅓ cup	olive oil	75 ml.
1 tbsp.	wine vinegar or fresh lemon juice	15 ml.
	salt and pepper	
	sugar	

Immerse the chick-peas in water to cover by 2 inches [5 cm.], bring to a boil, reduce the heat and simmer for two hours, adding the white beans after one hour. Keep an eye on the pot so that the white beans are not overcooked to the bursting point. Cook the kidney beans for one and a half hours in a separate pot, as they dye the water and anything that is cooked with them.

Mix the remaining ingredients in a bowl, adjusting the seasonings to your taste. Put in the drained hot beans, turning them over well in the dressing. Let the salad cool, then cover and put it in the refrigerator to chill. Scatter some extra parsley and chives over the top before serving.

JANE GRIGSON
JANE GRIGSON'S VEGETABLE BOOK

North African Lentil Salad

To serve 4

1 cup	dried lentils	¼ liter
1 quart	water	1 liter
2 tsp.	salt	10 ml.
¼ cup	finely chopped red onion	50 ml.
¼ cup	diced green pepper	50 ml.
⅓ cup	diced celery	75 ml.
⅓ cup	seeded, diced cucumber	75 ml.
¼ cup	finely chopped, peeled, seeded tomato	50 ml.
½ cup	sliced pitted ripe olives	125 ml.
3 tbsp.	finely chopped fresh parsley	45 ml.
¼ cup	olive oil	50 ml.
¼ cup	strained fresh lemon juice	50 ml.
1	medium-sized garlic clove, crushed	1
½ tsp.	ground cumin	2 ml.
½ tsp.	crushed dried oregano	2 ml.
	salt and freshly ground black pepper	
1 cup	unflavored yogurt	¼ liter
	romaine or leaf-lettuce leaves	
2	eggs, hard-boiled and quartered	2
	radish roses made by cutting down partway along four sides of each radish and then slicing off each top	

In a heavy saucepan, bring the water and 2 teaspoons [10 ml.] of the salt to a boil over high heat. Add the lentils, boil for a minute, reduce the heat to low, partially cover, and simmer for 30 minutes, or until the lentils are just tender. Do not overcook. Drain thoroughly and place the lentils in a mixing bowl. Add the onion, green pepper, celery, cucumber, tomato, olives and 2 tablespoons [30 ml.] of the parsley.

In another bowl, beat together the oil, lemon juice, garlic, cumin, oregano, and salt and pepper with a fork or whisk until well blended. Pour this dressing over the lentil mixture and toss gently but thoroughly. Taste and adjust the seasoning. Cover and chill.

Shortly before serving, fold in the yogurt until well blended. Taste again for seasoning. Transfer to a serving dish lined with the lettuce leaves. Sprinkle with the remaining 1 tablespoon [15 ml.] of parsley, garnish with the eggs and radish roses, and serve.

SONIA UVEZIAN
THE BOOK OF YOGURT

Breton Salad

La Salade Bretonne

Corn salad is also known as lamb's-lettuce.
This salad can also be served as an accompaniment to grilled mutton chops or roast leg of lamb.

To serve 6

1½ cups	freshly cooked white beans	375 ml.
4	small beets (about 10 oz. [350 kg.]), wrapped in foil, baked at 350° F. [180° C.] for 1 hour, peeled and sliced	4
10 oz.	corn salad	350 g.
	vinaigrette (about ¾ cup [175 ml.]) (recipe, page 167)	
1 tbsp.	chopped fresh parsley	15 ml.

Mix together the hot beans and beets, and the corn salad. Season with vinaigrette as for an ordinary salad. Add a little finely chopped parsley.

AUSTIN DE CROZE
LES PLATS RÉGIONAUX DE FRANCE

Dandelion and Potato Salad

Salade Comme en Ardèche

To serve 4

½ lb.	dandelion leaves	¼ kg.
2	potatoes, boiled, peeled and sliced while hot	2
3 oz.	lean salt pork with the rind removed, blanched in boiling water for 5 minutes, drained, diced and fried until crisp	100 g.
2	eggs, hard-boiled and sliced	2
⅓ cup	ripe olives, preferably oil-packed	75 ml.
2	tomatoes, sliced	2
Tomato-purée vinaigrette		
¼ cup	puréed tomato	50 ml.
1 tbsp.	wine vinegar	15 ml.
	salt and pepper	
½ cup	olive oil	125 ml.

In a salad bowl mix together the puréed tomato, vinegar, salt and pepper, then add the olive oil. Add the hot potatoes to the tomato vinaigrette and let them macerate until the slices cool. Add the other ingredients and toss the salad at table.

RAYMOND THUILIER AND MICHEL LEMONNIER
RECETTES DE BAUMANIÈRE

Marinated Vegetables, Greek-Style

Legumes à la Grecque

Any firm vegetable may be added to or substituted for those in the recipe, such as mushrooms, celery hearts, leeks, cucumbers, red peppers and artichoke hearts.

To serve 8 to 10

24	boiling onions, 1 inch [2½ cm.] in diameter, peeled	24
5 or 6	small zucchini (about 1 lb. [½ kg.]), unpeeled but sliced 1 inch [2½ cm.] thick	5 or 6
5 or 6	small yellow squash (about 1 lb. [½ kg.]), unpeeled but sliced 1 inch [2½ cm.] thick	5 or 6
3	medium-sized green peppers, halved, seeded, deribbed and cut lengthwise into ½-inch [1-cm.] strips	3
½ lb.	whole green beans	¼ kg.
2	lemons, cut into ¼-inch [6-mm.] slices	2

White-wine marinade

1 cup	dry white wine	¼ liter
3 cups	chicken stock (recipe, page 164)	¾ liter
1 cup	olive oil	¼ liter
½ cup	fresh lemon juice	125 ml.
6	sprigs parsley	6
2	large garlic cloves, cut up	2
½ tsp.	dried thyme	1 ml.
10	peppercorns	10
1 tsp.	salt	5 ml.

To make the marinade, stir the ingredients together in a 3- to 4-quart [3- to 4-liter] enameled or stainless-steel saucepan and bring to a boil, partially cover the pan and simmer slowly for 45 minutes. Using a fine sieve, strain the marinade into a large bowl, pressing down hard on the herbs with the back of a spoon to squeeze out their juices before discarding them. Return the marinade to the saucepan.

Bring the marinade to a boil and add the onions; cover and cook over medium heat for 20 to 30 minutes, or until the onions are just tender. With a slotted spoon, remove the onions to a large glass or stainless-steel baking dish.

Add the slices of zucchini and yellow squash to the simmering marinade and cook slowly, uncovered, for 10 to 15 minutes, then put them in the baking dish with the onions. Finally, add the green-pepper strips and string beans to the marinade and cook them slowly, uncovered, for eight to 10 minutes. The vegetables must not be overcooked; they will soften as they cool and marinate. Add the green peppers and string beans to the other vegetables. Taste and season the marinade and pour it over the vegetables, making sure that they are all at least partly covered with the hot liquid.

Cool the vegetables. Then cover the dish tightly with aluminum foil or plastic wrap and let the vegetables marinate in the refrigerator for at least four hours—or overnight if possible—before serving them. To serve, lift the vegetables out of the marinade with a slotted spoon and arrange them attractively on a platter. Moisten the vegetables with a little marinade and garnish them with lemon slices.

FOODS OF THE WORLD
THE COOKING OF PROVINCIAL FRANCE

Garden Vegetables Stewed with Olive Oil

Lahanika Thiafora Me Lathi

To serve 8 to 10

1 lb.	green beans, topped and tailed, and cut into 2-inch [5-cm.] pieces	½ kg.
1	medium-sized eggplant (about 1 lb. [½ kg.]), cut into small pieces	1
1 lb.	zucchini, ends removed, halved lengthwise and cut into 1-inch [2½-cm.] pieces	½ kg.
2	large green peppers, halved, seeded, deribbed and cut into strips	2
3	medium-sized potatoes (about 1 lb. [½ kg.]), peeled and cut into small pieces	3
6	medium-sized tomatoes (about 1½ lb. [¾ kg.]), peeled and sliced	6
2	medium-sized onions, sliced	2
2 tbsp.	salt	30 ml.
½ tsp.	pepper	2 ml.
2 tsp.	sugar	10 ml.
1¼ cups	olive oil	300 ml.
1 handful	chopped fresh parsley	1 handful
1 cup	hot water	¼ liter

Put all of the vegetables together in layers in a large pan. Add the salt, pepper, sugar, olive oil, parsley and hot water. Cover the pan partially and cook over low heat for one and a half hours or bake, covered, in a preheated 325° F. [160° C.] oven for two hours, or until the vegetables are soft and most of the liquid has evaporated. Serve cold.

CHRISSA PARADISSIS
THE BEST BOOK OF GREEK COOKERY

Celery, Artichokes, Onions, Mushrooms and Leeks

Céleri, Artichaut, Oignon, Champignons Sanguins, Poireaux en Hors-d'Oeuvre

This recipe for vegetables *à l'orientale* was popular at the Palace Hotel in Nice between the two wars. The vegetables will keep for over a fortnight in the refrigerator. When they are placed in preserving jars and sterilized by boiling for 60 minutes, the vegetables will keep indefinitely.

To serve 6

50	pickling onions, peeled, or substitute 12 small boiling onions, peeled, plus 12 celery ribs, diced	50
18	small artichokes, with the chokes still unformed, trimmed and quartered	18
30	fresh button mushrooms	30
18	small leeks, cut into 2-inch [5-cm.] lengths	18
½ cup	olive oil	125 ml.
½ cup	raisins (about 2 oz. [75 g.]), soaked in tepid water for 1 hour and drained	125 ml.
10	peppercorns	10
2	large tomatoes, peeled, seeded and chopped	2
1 tsp.	thyme leaves	5 ml.
¾ cup	dry white wine	175 ml.
⅓ cup	strained fresh lemon juice	75 ml.
	salt	

Place 12 of the pickling onions—or all of the boiling onions—in a stainless-steel pan, add a tablespoon [15 ml.] of the olive oil, cover, and cook over a very low heat until the onions are soft. Remove the lid and allow the onions to turn golden brown. Add the raisins, peppercorns and tomatoes and, stirring all the time, reduce to a jamlike consistency.

Add the remainder of the olive oil, up to the level of the vegetables; turn up the heat and, stirring slowly and continuously, mix in the remaining pickling onions or the diced celery, the artichokes, mushrooms, leeks and thyme leaves. Cook for 10 minutes over a fairly high heat, and then add the wine and lemon juice. Bring to a boil and reduce the heat. Cook, uncovered, at a simmer for 30 minutes. Salt to taste when cooked. Remove from the heat. Serve cool or chilled.

JACQUES MÉDECIN
LA CUISINE DU COMTÉ DE NICE

Impromptu Composed Salad

Salade Canaille

As the title suggests, the composition of this type of salad should be inspired by the materials at hand; neither the proportions nor the ingredients need be strictly followed. The technique of peeling peppers is demonstrated on page 42. To prepare the artichokes, see the editor's note for Artichoke Salad with Orange and Celery, page 108.

To serve 6

3	medium-sized firm waxy potatoes, boiled, peeled and sliced while still hot	3
½ cup	dry white wine	125 ml.
3 or 4	large green peppers, broiled, peeled, halved and seeded, flesh torn into strips, juices reserved	3 or 4
3	medium-sized artichokes, turned, rubbed with lemon, parboiled for 6 to 8 minutes, chokes removed and sliced	3
about 1½ cups	leftover cold boiled beef, slivered, cubed or cut roughly into julienne	about 375 ml.
1	small celery heart, thinly sliced	1
2 or 3	scallions, finely slivered, or 1 small onion, thinly sliced	2 or 3
1	small head Boston or romaine lettuce or escarole, separated into leaves	1
1 handful	fresh tender purslane leaves	1 handful
1 handful	fresh rocket leaves	1 handful
1 handful	fresh basil leaves and flowers	1 handful
½ lb.	tender young green beans, parboiled for 4 to 7 minutes and drained	¼ kg.
2 or 3	firm ripe tomatoes, cut into sections	2 or 3
4	eggs, hard-boiled and quartered	4
2 tsp.	finely chopped fresh hyssop leaves	10 ml.
12 to 15	nasturtium blossoms and buds plus small tender leaves	12 to 15

Garlic-flavored vinaigrette

1	small garlic clove	1
	salt and freshly ground pepper	
	red wine vinegar	
	olive oil	

Pour the white wine over the warm potato slices and then set them aside to cool. To prepare the vinaigrette, slice the garlic clove into a salad bowl, add salt and pepper, and work vigorously with a wooden pestle until the garlic is puréed and forms a dry paste with the salt and pepper. Add 1 tablespoon [15 ml.] of vinegar, stir until dissolved, and stir in ½ cup [125 ml.] of olive oil.

Add the peppers with their juices to the vinaigrette and stir vigorously—taking care not to crush the peppers—until the sauce turns cloudy and thickens. Taste for seasoning.

Add the artichokes, then drain the potato slices and add them (the wine may be used for cooking) along with the meat, celery and scallions. Stir everything together well but gently. Taste again; add olive oil or vinegar if necessary.

Place the serving fork and spoon crosswise in the bowl to help protect the salad greens from contact with the dressing, prop a few of the larger leaves on top of the fork and spoon and tumble the rest of the salad greens loosely over them, distributing the green beans over the surface. Decorate with tomato sections and quartered hard-boiled eggs, sprinkle with hyssop, and the nasturtium flowers and leaves. Present the salad, tossing only at the moment of serving.

RICHARD OLNEY
SIMPLE FRENCH FOOD

Mushroom and Potato Salad with Sweetbreads

To prepare sweetbreads, first soak them in lightly salted water for 20 minutes, drain, then poach them in fresh, lightly salted water for 10 minutes. Drain them, peel off their membranes, and cool the sweetbreads under a weighted board.

To serve 8

1 lb.	fresh mushrooms	½ kg.
5	potatoes, boiled and peeled	5
1	pair calf's sweetbreads, cooked and cooled	1
2 tbsp.	butter	30 ml.
1 cup	sour cream	¼ liter
3 to 4 tbsp.	fresh lemon juice	45 to 60 ml.
½ tsp.	salt	2 ml.
¼ tsp.	pepper	1 ml.
2 tbsp.	chopped fresh parsley	30 ml.
10	ripe olives, chopped	10
¼ cup	olive oil	50 ml.
8	crisp cup-shaped lettuce leaves	8

Sauté the mushrooms in butter until tender, about five minutes. Drain and slice them, not too thin. Dice the potatoes. Mince the sweetbreads. Mix the sour cream, lemon juice, seasonings, parsley, olives and olive oil, and pour over the combined mushrooms, potatoes and sweetbreads. Mix lightly, using two spoons. Heap the salad into the lettuce cups.

FLORENCE BROBECK
THE GOOD SALAD BOOK

Sauté or Salad of Bright Winter Vegetable Flowers

All of the vegetables can be prepared ahead of time and kept wrapped tightly with plastic wrap in the refrigerator until they are needed.

To serve 4 to 6

1 cup	small pearl onions, peeled	¼ liter
1	large carrot, scraped	1
2	celery ribs	2
1	large sweet red pepper	1
1	medium-sized zucchini	1
3 tbsp.	olive oil	45 ml.
1	garlic clove, peeled, and flattened with the side of a knife blade	1
1 tbsp.	minced fresh parsley	15 ml.
½ tsp.	finely grated lemon peel	2 ml.
1 tbsp.	fresh lemon juice	15 ml.
	salt and pepper	
	vinegar	

Parboil the onions in boiling salted water. With a vegetable zester or a small knife, make five or six evenly spaced grooves down the length of the carrot. Cut the carrot across in ¼-inch [6-mm.] slices, which will then resemble small flowers. When the onions are just tender—after 10 minutes—add the carrot to the boiling water for two minutes, then drain the vegetables into a colander.

String the celery ribs, then cut them into thin strips 2 inches [5 cm.] long. Halve the red pepper, seed it, cut the flesh into pieces about 1 inch [2½ cm.] square and trim each square into the shape of a tulip flower. Cut the peel off the zucchini lengthwise in thick, wide strips. Cut these strips into squares, then round the corners so each square becomes a circle. Reserve the heart of the zucchini for another use.

Heat the oil and garlic together briefly, then let the oil steep (off the heat) for 10 minutes. Remove the garlic. Reheat the oil and, when it is hot, add the onions, carrot and celery and the red pepper and zucchini circles. Sauté the vegetables over high heat, shaking the pan all the while and letting the vegetables turn and mix in the oil. When the vegetables are hot—the zucchini a vivid green and the celery just at a tender crunch—add the parsley, lemon peel and juice, and seasoning. Give the pan a final shake, and dish the vegetables into a small serving bowl. Let the vegetables cool to room temperature. Add vinegar to taste before serving.

JUDITH OLNEY
COMFORTING FOOD

Mixed Vegetable Stew

Ratatouille Froide

To serve 6 to 8

1 lb.	white onions, cut into quarters or eighths, depending on size	½ kg.
⅔ cup	olive oil	150 ml.
1 lb.	red, yellow and green sweet peppers, halved, seeded, deribbed and cut into 1-inch [2½-cm.] squares	½ kg.
1 lb.	eggplant, cut into ¾-inch [2-cm.] cubes	½ kg.
6	garlic cloves, chopped	6
	salt and cayenne pepper	
4	large firm ripe tomatoes, peeled, halved, seeded and each half cut into sixths or eighths	4
1 tsp.	fresh thyme leaves	5 ml.
3	sprigs parsley	3
1	bay leaf	1
1 lb.	small zucchini, cut into ½- to 1-inch [1½- to 2½-cm.] slices	½ kg.
2 tbsp.	torn up basil, or chopped parsley	30 ml.
	freshly ground pepper	

Heat half of the olive oil in a low, wide, flameproof earthenware casserole or heavy saucepan. Put the onions to cook gently in the oil while preparing the other vegetables. Stir from time to time and do not let them brown.

When the onions are yellowed and soft, add the peppers, eggplant, garlic, salt and a tiny pinch of cayenne pepper. Continue to cook gently for 10 minutes or so, stirring occasionally with a wooden spoon, then add the tomatoes and the thyme, and the parsley sprigs and bay leaf tied together in a bouquet. Bring to a boil and then leave to cook over a very low heat, at a bare simmer, with the lid ajar, for two hours, adding the zucchini after one hour.

Place a colander or sieve over another saucepan, pour in the vegetables and allow them to drain well; then return the vegetables to their casserole or saucepan and continue cooking over a low heat, leaving the lid off. Place the saucepan containing the liquid over a very high heat and, stirring constantly with a wooden spoon, reduce the liquid to a light, syrupy consistency. There should be around ½ to ¾ cup [125 to 175 ml.] of syrupy liquid remaining: Pour it back into the vegetables, remove from the heat and leave to cool. Add the remaining olive oil and half of the basil or chopped parsley. Season with pepper (and more salt, if necessary) and mix together thoroughly, stirring carefully to avoid crushing the vegetables. Pour into a serving dish, chill thoroughly, and sprinkle with the remaining basil or parsley before serving.

RICHARD OLNEY
THE FRENCH MENU COOK BOOK

Malaysian Mixed Salad

Gado Gado

Bean curd, blachan (Malaysian shrimp paste), shrimp chips and dried tamarind are obtainable from Oriental food stores.

To serve 4 to 6

1	small cabbage (about 1 lb. [½ kg.]), quartered, cored and chopped	1
¼ lb.	green beans, cut into 1-inch [2½-cm.] lengths	125 g.
3 or 4	spinach leaves	3 or 4
2 cups	fresh bean sprouts	½ liter
¼ lb.	white bean-curd cake, thinly sliced	125 g.
3 tbsp.	peanut oil	45 ml.
1	small cucumber, peeled and sliced	1
1	egg, hard-boiled and quartered	1
5 or 6	shrimp chips, crumbled	5 or 6

Peppery sauce

2	fresh red hot chilies, finely chopped	2
2	onions, finely chopped	2
2	garlic cloves, finely chopped	2
1 tsp.	*blachan*	5 ml.
2 tbsp.	peanut oil	30 ml.
1 tbsp.	dried tamarind, chopped, soaked in 1 cup [¼ liter] boiling water for 1 hour	15 ml.
¼ lb.	roasted peanuts, ground	125 g.
2 tbsp.	dark soy sauce	30 ml.
1 tbsp.	sugar	15 ml.
	salt	

First prepare the sauce. Fry the chilies, onions, garlic and *blachan* in the oil for two minutes; let the mixture cool and grind it into a paste in a mortar. Squeeze the juice from the tamarind pieces and discard the pieces. Add the peanuts to the tamarind water and boil for 15 minutes. Add the chili paste, soy sauce, sugar and salt to taste, and boil for 10 to 15 minutes until the sauce thickens. Allow to cool.

Parboil the cabbage for a few minutes, then drain it. In another pan, boil the green beans until tender, about five minutes. Drain the beans, but retain the water and parboil the spinach in it for one minute. Then pour the same boiling water over the bean sprouts and let them stand for two minutes. Drain all of the vegetables. Fry the bean-curd slices in the oil until brown on both sides. Arrange the vegetables, bean curd, cucumber and egg quarters on a plate and sprinkle the shrimp chips over them. Serve with the sauce.

KENNETH MITCHELL (EDITOR)
THE FLAVOUR OF MALAYSIA

Raw and Cooked Vegetables with Peanut and Coconut Milk Sauce

Gado Gado

This popular Southeast Asian salad has many variations: The version here is from Java. Trassi (shrimp paste), salam leaves, tamarind water and bean curds are obtainable at Oriental markets. The technique of preparing coconut milk is shown on pages 80-81. For 4 cups [1 liter] of milk, use 4 cups of coarsely chopped coconut meat and 4 cups of hot water.

To serve 6 to 8

2	fresh bean-curd cakes	2
½ tsp.	salt	2 ml.
¼ cup	tamarind water	50 ml.
4	small new potatoes, peeled	4
1 lb.	fresh green beans, trimmed and cut into 3-inch [8-cm.] lengths	½ kg.
1 lb.	fresh bean sprouts	½ kg.
1 lb.	fresh *kang kung* or spinach, coarsely chopped	½ kg.
	vegetable oil for deep frying	
2	hard-boiled eggs, cut crosswise into ¼-inch [6-mm.] slices	2
1 cup	finely shredded iceberg lettuce	¼ liter
1 cup	finely shredded cabbage	¼ liter
2	medium-sized cucumbers, unpeeled but scored lengthwise with a fork and cut into ¼-inch [6-mm.] slices	2

Peanut and coconut milk sauce

1 quart	unsalted peanuts, pulverized in a blender or with a nut grinder	1 liter
4 cups	coconut milk	1 liter
3 tbsp.	vegetable oil	45 ml.
½ cup	finely chopped onions	125 ml.
1 tsp.	finely chopped garlic	5 ml.
1 tsp.	*trassi*	5 ml.
2 cups	hot water	½ liter
3 tbsp.	light brown sugar	45 ml.
1 tbsp.	finely chopped fresh hot chilies	15 ml.
2	*salam* leaves or bay leaves	2
½ tsp.	finely grated fresh ginger root	2 ml.
1 tsp.	salt	5 ml.
¼ cup	tamarind water	50 ml.

To prepare the sauce, heat the oil in a heavy 4- to 6-quart [4- to 6-liter] casserole over moderate heat until a light haze forms above it. Drop in the onions and garlic and, stirring frequently, cook them for about five minutes, or until the onions are soft and transparent but not brown. Watch for any sign of burning and regulate the heat accordingly.

Add the *trassi* and mash it with the back of a spoon until it is well blended with the onions. Pour in the hot water and bring to a boil over high heat. Stir in the peanuts, brown sugar, chilies, *salam* leaves, ginger root and salt.

Then reduce the heat to low and add the coconut milk and the tamarind water. Stirring occasionally, simmer for about 15 minutes, or until the sauce is thick enough to hold its shape lightly in a spoon. Taste for seasoning and set the pan aside off the heat.

To prepare the vegetables, first place the bean-curd cakes and salt in a bowl, pour in the tamarind water, and let the cakes soak for at least 10 minutes, turning them occasionally. Drain the bean-curd cakes and set them aside.

Drop the new potatoes into lightly salted boiling water and boil them until they are almost tender. Drain the potatoes and pat them dry with paper towels. Then cut them crosswise into slices ¼ inch [6 mm.] thick.

Steam the green beans for 10 to 15 minutes; the fresh bean sprouts for three to five minutes; the *kang kung* or spinach for 12 to 15 minutes. When done, the vegetables should be tender but still somewhat crisp to the bite. After they are steamed, set the vegetables aside separately.

While the vegetables are steaming, pour about 3 cups [¾ liter] of vegetable oil into a 12-inch [30-cm.] wok or fill a deep fryer or large, heavy saucepan with oil to a depth of 3 inches [8 cm.]. Heat the oil until it reaches a temperature of 375° F. [190° C.] on a deep-frying thermometer.

Drop in the bean-curd cakes and, turning them gently with a slotted spoon, deep fry for two or three minutes, or until they are golden brown. Drain the bean-curd cakes on paper towels, then cut them crosswise into strips about ¼ inch wide and 1½ inches [4 cm.] long.

Add the potato slices to the hot oil and, stirring them gently about with the slotted spoon, fry them for about four minutes, or until they are crisp and golden brown on both sides. Transfer the potato slices to paper towels to drain.

To serve, mound the *kang kung* or spinach in the center of a large serving plate; arrange the bean-curd strips, potatoes, bean sprouts, green beans, hard-boiled eggs, lettuce and cabbage in rows on each side of the mound. Line the edges of the plate with the cucumber, overlapping the slices slightly.

Serve the sauce at room temperature from a bowl.

FOODS OF THE WORLD
PACIFIC AND SOUTHEAST ASIAN COOKING

Meat and Poultry Salads

Veal with Tuna Sauce

Vitello Tonnato

Instead of braising the meat as called for in this recipe, you may poach it as explained on page 54.

Traditionally in this dish, slices of the delicate veal are coated with a zesty tuna-anchovy paste. That's the way I used to do it. But as pork has become finer and leaner, I now substitute pork loin. It works beautifully. The meat is best roasted the day before, so it can chill thoroughly. The sauce can also be prepared the day before, leaving only the slicing and arranging to do several hours before serving.

To serve 8 to 10		
3 lb.	boned veal roast, or lean, rolled pork loin roast	1½ kg.
2 tbsp.	butter, at room temperature	30 ml.
1 tsp.	rosemary	5 ml.
	salt and pepper	
1	medium-sized onion, quartered	1
1	bay leaf, broken in half	1
½ cup	dry white wine	125 ml.
Tuna sauce		
6½-oz. can	tuna in oil, drained	185-g. can
6 to 8	oil-packed flat anchovy fillets, rinsed and patted dry	6 to 8
2 tbsp.	capers, rinsed and drained	30 ml.
2 cups	mayonnaise *(recipe, page 166)*	½ liter

Preheat the oven to 350° F. [180° C.]. Lay a large piece of heavy aluminum foil in a roasting pan, put the meat on the foil and smear the meat with the butter; sprinkle with the rosemary, salt and pepper. Scatter the onion and bay leaf pieces around the meat. Lift the edges of the foil, pour in the wine and seal the foil over the meat. There should be no open seams through which the juices can escape.

Place the pan in the oven for one and three quarter hours. (If you are not sure about the degree of doneness, carefully open the foil and insert a meat thermometer; it should read 180° F. [85° C.]. You can also test by piercing with a fork—the juices should run clear, with just a touch of pink.) Cool the meat in the sealed foil.

Lift the meat out of the foil, carefully pour off the juices and strain them. Chill the meat and juices separately.

To make the sauce, first remove the congealed fat from the juices by lifting it with a fork; discard it. Pour ½ cup [125 ml.] of the juices into a blender. Add all of the remaining sauce ingredients except the mayonnaise and blend to a smooth purée. Put the mayonnaise in a bowl and beat the purée into it. Chill well.

About three hours before serving, cut the meat into thin slices. If you are using rolled pork, remove all strings and the layer of fat on the outside. One by one, lay the slices of meat on the serving platter, liberally coating one side with the tuna sauce. Stack them together with the uncoated side of the one slice against the sauced surface of the previous slice. Reshape the slices to resemble the original roast and coat the surface with the sauce.

To serve, decorate the *Vitello Tonnato*, if desired, with rolled anchovy fillets, capers and ripe olives. Pass the extra sauce in a sauceboat.

CAROL CUTLER
THE SIX-MINUTE SOUFFLÉ AND OTHER CULINARY DELIGHTS

Salad of Lamb with Olives and Herbs

Gigot en Salade

The following recipe was created by the 18th Century French cookery writer Menon.

To serve 4		
1 lb.	leftover leg of lamb, cut into very fine julienne (about 2 cups [¾ liter])	½ kg.
4	young carrots, thinly sliced	4
4	parsnips, halved, cored and thinly sliced	4
4	onions, thinly sliced and separated into rings	4
1 quart	chicken stock *(recipe, page 164)*	1 liter
1	garlic clove, finely chopped	1
1	sprig fresh tarragon, leaves only	1
1 tbsp.	capers, rinsed and drained	15 ml.
4	sour gherkins, thinly sliced	4
12	ripe olives, pitted	12
6	salt anchovies, filleted, soaked in water for 30 minutes, drained and patted dry	6
	salt and pepper	
⅓ cup	olive oil	75 ml.
2 tbsp.	wine vinegar	30 ml.

Put the carrots, parsnips and onions into a pan with the stock; bring to a boil and simmer, uncovered, for 30 minutes.

Drain, and set the vegetables aside to cool. Mix the lamb with the cold vegetables in a salad bowl; add the garlic, tarragon, capers, gherkins, olives and anchovies. Season with salt and pepper, and sprinkle with the oil and vinegar. Mix well. Serve cool, but not chilled.

CÉLINE VENCE AND ROBERT COURTINE
THE GRAND MASTERS OF FRENCH CUISINE

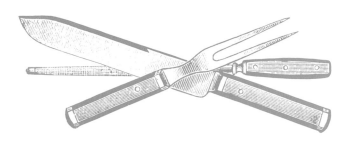

Beef Vinaigrette

Vinaigrette de Boeuf

This 1656 recipe yields a spicy beef that may be presented whole in its jellied coating, or sliced with the jelly diced. While the meat cooks, turn it over once or twice and baste it with the liquids in the dish.

To serve 4

2 lb.	beef bottom round roast, pounded with a meat mallet to flatten it	1 kg.
¼ lb.	fresh pork fat, cut into lardons	125 g.
¾ cup	dry white wine	175 ml.
	salt and pepper	
2 or 3	whole cloves	2 or 3
1	bouquet garni	1
about 1 cup	water	about ¼ liter
1	lemon, sliced	1
2 tbsp.	wine vinegar	30 ml.

Cut slits in the beef—following the grain of the meat—and insert the lardons in the slits. Place the beef in an earthenware dish of a size just large enough to contain it. Add the wine, seasonings and bouquet garni, and enough water to cover the beef. Cover the dish and poach the beef in a 300° F. [150° C.] oven for three to four hours, or until the meat is tender and the cooking liquid is reduced to about ½ cup [125 ml.]. Discard the bouquet, degrease the cooking liquid and cool the beef with its jelly in the dish in which it cooked. Garnish the dish with lemon slices and sprinkle vinegar over the beef before serving it.

PIERRE DE LUNE
LE NOUVEAU CUISINIER

Boiled Beef with Anchovies

Boeuf aux Anchois

To serve 4 to 6

1 lb.	leftover boiled beef, trimmed of fat and sliced	½ kg.
	salt and pepper	
1 tbsp.	vinegar	15 ml.
6	salt anchovies, filleted, soaked in cold water for 30 minutes, drained and patted dry	6
Shallot dressing		
1 or 2	shallots, finely chopped	1 or 2
1 tbsp.	vinegar	15 ml.
	salt and pepper	
2 tbsp.	finely chopped fresh parsley	30 ml.
1	egg, hard-boiled and mashed or chopped	1
¼ cup	oil	50 ml.

Sprinkle the beef with a little salt and pepper and the vinegar. Set the slices aside to marinate for about one hour. Remove the beef slices, arrange them on a serving dish and garnish them with the anchovies.

To make the dressing, blend the vinegar, salt and pepper; add the shallots, parsley and hard-boiled egg and, finally, the oil. Spoon the dressing around the slices of beef without disturbing their arrangement.

LA CUISINE LYONNAISE

Salami and Olive Salad

To serve 4

¼ lb.	salami, thinly sliced	125 ml.
½ cup	ripe olives	125 ml.
1 tbsp.	very finely chopped onion	15 ml.
2 tbsp.	olive oil	30 ml.
2 tbsp.	vinegar	30 ml.
1 tsp.	crushed coriander seeds	5 ml.
1 tsp.	finely chopped fresh basil	5 ml.

Arrange the slices of salami around the outside of a serving plate. Pit the olives and put them into a bowl with the onion, oil, vinegar and coriander seeds. Toss well together and place the mixture in the center of the plate. Sprinkle the salad with the basil just before serving.

JENNIE REEKIE
EVERYTHING RAW: THE NO-COOKING COOKBOOK

Chicken and Raspberry Salad

To serve 4

3 lb.	roasting chicken, cut into 8 serving pieces	1½ kg.
2 cups	fresh raspberries (about ½ lb. [¼ kg.])	½ liter
8	juniper berries	8
8	allspice berries	8
4	whole cloves	4
2 tbsp.	olive oil	30 ml.
1⅓ cups	dry red wine	325 ml.
1 tbsp.	chopped fresh mint	15 ml.

To make the marinade for the chicken, crush the spices together in a mortar, then mix them with the olive oil and ⅔ cup [150 ml.] of the wine in a fairly deep, flat dish. Turn the chicken pieces in this marinade, but leave them cut side down. Cover and refrigerate them for at least eight hours.

At the same time put the raspberries and mint into another bowl; pour in the remaining wine.

When you are ready to cook the chicken, preheat the broiler. Take the chicken pieces from the marinade and shake them gently to remove any excess liquid. Lay them on the cold broiler rack, skin side down, and cook them until they are golden brown. Turn them over and brown the other side. Remove the rack from the broiler pan and place the chicken pieces in the bottom of the pan. Spoon over all of the chicken marinade and continue to cook the chicken, basting and turning it frequently, until the juices run clear when the meat is pierced. Remove the chicken from the broiler and let the pieces cool.

Degrease any juices left in the broiler pan, then mix them into the marinating raspberries. When the chicken is quite cold, arrange it on a serving dish and spoon over the raspberries, together with all of the marinade and pan juices.

GAIL DUFF
FRESH ALL THE YEAR

Leftover-Chicken Salad

To serve 4

1 lb.	cooked chicken, skinned, boned and broken into bite-sized pieces (about 2 cups [½ liter])	½ kg.
1	carrot, thinly sliced	1
3 tbsp.	white wine vinegar	45 ml.
½ tsp.	salt	2 ml.
2	whole cloves	2
	ground mace	
¼ cup	dry white wine	50 ml.
¼ lb.	tender spinach leaves	125 g.
¼ cup	olive oil	50 ml.
	freshly ground black pepper	

Put the chicken and carrot in a small bowl, and add the vinegar, salt, cloves, a pinch of mace and enough wine to form a marinade. Cover and refrigerate overnight.

Drain off any marinade, remove the cloves and arrange the chicken on a bed of spinach leaves. Dress lightly with olive oil and pepper.

JUDITH OLNEY
SUMMER FOOD

Peking Chicken and Cucumber Salad

For this salad, the author suggests cutting the chicken, cucumber and ham julienne 2 inches [5 cm.] long. The sesame paste called for here is made by toasting ½ cup [125 ml.] sesame seeds in a small skillet over low heat for one to two minutes, then grinding them to a paste with a mortar and pestle. The paste also is available ready-made —as tahini— at Middle Eastern food stores.

To serve 6

1 cup	julienned cooked chicken	¼ liter
1⅓ cups	julienned, peeled cucumber	325 ml.
1⅓ cups	Chinese agar-agar strips, cut into pieces 1 inch [2½ cm.] long	325 ml.
¼ cup	julienned cooked ham	50 ml.
2 tbsp.	prepared hot mustard	30 ml.
¼ cup	sesame paste	50 ml.
¼ cup	soy sauce	50 ml.
3 tbsp.	white vinegar	45 ml.
2 tsp.	salt	10 ml.
2 tbsp.	sesame-seed oil	30 ml.

Put the agar-agar in a bowl, cover with tepid water, and let it soak for 15 minutes. Squeeze the agar-agar dry and arrange it on a serving platter. Arrange the cucumber pieces over the agar-agar. Place the chicken over the cucumber and top with the ham strips.

Place the remaining ingredients in a small bowl and mix well. To serve, pour on this sauce and toss the salad well.

RAYMOND SOKOLOV
GREAT RECIPES FROM THE NEW YORK TIMES

Chicken and Avocado Salad

Salade de Poulet aux Avocats

The technique of preparing an avocado is shown on page 31.

To serve 2 to 4

1	cooked whole chicken breast (about ½ lb. [¼ kg.]), skinned, boned and thinly sliced	1
1	ripe avocado, halved, pitted, peeled and thinly sliced	1
1	celery heart, thinly sliced	1
1	bunch watercress, stems removed	1
2	eggs, hard-boiled and sliced	2
1	tomato, sliced	1
Roquefort dressing		
¼ cup	Roquefort cheese, brought to room temperature and crumbled	50 ml.
	salt and pepper	
3 tbsp.	sherry vinegar	45 ml.
2	hard-boiled egg yolks	2
½ cup	olive oil	125 ml.

Arrange the chicken, avocado, celery heart, watercress, hard-boiled eggs and tomato on a serving dish. To prepare the dressing, dissolve the salt and pepper in the sherry vinegar, and mash in the crumbled Roquefort and the hard-boiled egg yolks with a pestle to form a smooth paste. Add the olive oil slowly, stirring with the pestle. Pour the dressing over the salad and serve.

RAYMOND THUILIER AND MICHEL LEMONNIER
RECETTES DE BAUMANIÈRE

Chicken Salad with Cockscomb Pasta

The cockscomb pasta called for in this recipe is obtainable at stores specializing in Italian foods. If not available, use other small pasta shapes such as shells or butterflies.

Creste di gallo, or cockscomb pasta, is a very pretty addition to a salad—and a very substantial addition as well. The curls and crevasses will embrace bits of the salad, so every bite will give a taste of the chicken, dressing and vegetables—a combination of textures: firm and chewy, soft, crisp, oily and altogether delicious.

To serve 4 to 6

1	whole chicken breast, poached in lightly salted water for 4 to 5 minutes, skinned, boned, halved and diced	1
1 lb.	cockscomb pasta, boiled in lightly salted water for 15 to 20 minutes, drained and chilled	½ kg.
⅔ cup	finely diced Gruyère, Emmenthaler, Monterey Jack, Jarlsberg or mozzarella cheese (about ¼ lb. [125 g.])	150 ml.
½ cup	ripe olives, preferably oil-packed Mediterranean olives, pitted and diced	125 ml.
2	celery ribs with leaves, diced	2
1	medium-sized green pepper, seeded, deribbed and diced	1
	romaine lettuce leaves	
2	slices bacon, fried crisp, drained and crumbled	2
Dry-mustard dressing		
1 tsp.	dry mustard	5 ml.
½ tsp.	salt	2 ml.
2 tsp.	red wine vinegar	10 ml.
6 tbsp.	olive oil	90 ml.

To make the dressing, put the mustard, salt and vinegar in the bottom of a large salad bowl and mix with a wooden fork or spoon. Add the oil, stirring vigorously until well blended.

Add the pasta to the dressing and toss well. Then add the cheese, olives, celery, pepper and chicken. Mix thoroughly, and taste and correct the seasoning. Slip the romaine lettuce leaves down under the edges of the salad so that it is surrounded by them. Sprinkle on the bacon and serve.

GERTRUDE HARRIS
PASTA INTERNATIONAL

Turkey Salad with Anchovy

Salade Lyonnaise

To serve 4 to 6

2 cups	diced cooked turkey and crisp skin	½ liter
3	salt anchovies, filleted, soaked in water for 30 minutes, drained and patted dry	3
4	sour gherkins, sliced lengthwise or chopped	4
½ cup	vinaigrette *(recipe, page 167),* made with prepared mustard	125 ml.
3 or 4	medium-sized potatoes, boiled, peeled and sliced while still hot	3 or 4
2 tbsp.	finely chopped fresh parsley	30 ml.
½ cup	dry white wine	125 ml.
	oil	
	vinegar	
1	small beet, cooked, peeled and sliced (optional)	1
1	carrot, sliced (optional)	1

Put the diced turkey pieces into a salad bowl with the anchovy fillets and gherkins. Toss with the vinaigrette, and set aside to steep for about one hour. Add the hot, sliced potatoes. Scatter the parsley over the turkey mixture, sprinkle with the wine, and add oil and vinegar to taste. Mix the salad very gently so as not to crumble the potatoes. If you wish, add a few slices of beet or carrot to this substantial salad.

LA CUISINE LYONNAISE

Brain Salad

Saláta Mialá

The technique of preparing a calf's brain is demonstrated on pages 58-59. If desired, two coarsely chopped, hard-boiled eggs may be mixed with the brain.

To serve 2

1	calf's brain, soaked in cold water for 1 hour and membranes removed	1
1	onion, chopped	1
2 tbsp.	fresh lemon juice	30 ml.
	salt and pepper	
¼ cup	vinaigrette *(recipe, page 167),* made with fresh lemon juice, thyme and finely chopped parsley and chives	50 ml.

Gently simmer the brain in a little water with the onion, lemon juice, salt and pepper for 10 to 15 minutes. When cool,

place the brain with some of the cooking liquid in the refrigerator for two hours; this makes it easier to cut. Cut the brain into small cubes and pour the vinaigrette sauce over the diced brain. Mix, and serve with crusty white bread.

LILO AUREDEN
DAS SCHMECKT SO GUT

Piquant Tongue

The technique of preparing the tongue called for in this recipe is shown on pages 56-57.

To serve 6 to 8

3 lb.	beef tongue	1½ kg.
1 tbsp.	mixed pickling spice	15 ml.
4	garlic cloves, 2 peeled and halved, and 2 cut up	4
4	oil-packed flat anchovy fillets, rinsed and patted dry	4
2 tbsp.	pine nuts	30 ml.
1 tsp.	capers, rinsed and drained	5 ml.
1	slice white bread, soaked in water and squeezed	1
¾ cup	olive oil	175 ml.
¼ cup	red wine vinegar	50 ml.
	freshly ground black pepper	

Cover the tongue with water; add the pickling spices and garlic halves. Cover and simmer gently for two and a half to three hours, until the tongue is tender. Drain.

When the tongue is cool enough to handle, skin it and trim off the gristle and small bones. Chill, then cut the tongue into julienne or dice.

Combine the anchovies, pine nuts, cut-up garlic, capers and bread. Either pound the mixture to a paste in a mortar with a pestle, purée it in a blender or mash it in a bowl with a wooden spoon. Add the oil and vinegar alternately to make a smoothly blended paste. Season with pepper. Combine with the tongue and adjust the seasonings. Serve cold.

MARIAN BURROS
PURE AND SIMPLE

Diced Tongue, Potato, Apple and Red Cabbage

The techniques of cooking, peeling and trimming tongue are explained on pages 56-57.

This salad is especially useful as a means of using up the end of a tongue.

	To serve 4	
1 cup	diced, trimmed, peeled cooked tongue	¼ liter
1 cup	diced, cold boiled potato	¼ liter
1	tart apple, peeled, cored and diced	1
⅔ cup	coarsely chopped, pickled red cabbage	150 ml.
⅓ to ½ cup	vinaigrette *(recipe, page 167)*	75 to 125 ml.
1 tbsp.	finely cut fresh chives	15 ml.
4	small inner cabbage leaves, trimmed into rounds	4

Mix the tongue, potato, apple and pickled cabbage, and season this mixture with the vinaigrette and chives. Dress in small heaps on the cabbage leaves, and serve.

WILLIAM HEPTINSTALL
HORS D'OEUVRE AND COLD TABLE

Spinach and Tongue Salad

The technique of preparing tongue is shown on pages 56-57.

	To serve 4	
1 lb.	spinach, parboiled in salted boiling water for about 2 minutes, drained, squeezed dry and very finely chopped	½ kg.
4	round slices cold boiled or braised beef tongue	4
¼ tsp.	salt	1 ml.
	paprika	
1 tbsp.	oil	15 ml.
1 tbsp.	fresh lemon juice	15 ml.
3 tbsp.	tartar sauce *(recipe, page 167)*	45 ml.
2 tsp.	finely chopped fresh parsley	10 ml.
	lemon slices	

Season the spinach with the salt, a dash of paprika, the oil and the lemon juice. Press the mixture into four oiled molds or cups slightly smaller in diameter than the slices of tongue. Refrigerate.

When the spinach is quite cold, turn it from the molds onto the rounds of tongue, and use a pastry bag to pipe a star of tartar sauce on the top of each mound of spinach. Garnish with the parsley and lemon slices.

JANET MCKENZIE HILL
SALADS, SANDWICHES, AND CHAFING-DISH DAINTIES

Salamongundy

This recipe is from a book published anonymously in 1747, but generally known to have been written by the English cookery writer, Hannah Glasse.

	To serve 8 to 10	
2 or 3	heads romaine or other type of lettuce, cut into fine shreds	2 or 3
2	small chickens, roasted, cooled and skinned, breast and wing meat cut into long thin slices, leg meat diced	2
10	salt anchovies, filleted, soaked in water for 30 minutes, drained, patted dry, 12 fillets cut into narrow strips, the remaining 8 fillets finely chopped	10
1	lemon, finely diced	1
4	hard-boiled egg yolks, finely chopped	4
2 to 3 tbsp.	finely chopped fresh parsley	30 to 45 ml.
about 30	boiling onions, peeled and boiled for 10 to 12 minutes until tender but still firm	about 30
1 cup	vinaigrette *(recipe, page 167)*	¼ liter
	grapes, scalded and peeled, or green beans, blanched and drained, or nasturtium flowers	

With the shredded lettuce make a layer about 1 inch [2½ cm.] thick over the bottom of a large dish. Arrange the slices of breast and wing meat over this and between these lay the strips of anchovy. Mix together the diced chicken-leg meat, lemon, finely chopped anchovies, egg yolks and parsley; place the mixture in a tall heap in the center of the dish.

Put the largest of the onions on top of the salamongundy and the remainder in a border around the edge of the dish. Pour the vinaigrette over and garnish with a few grapes, green beans or nasturtium flowers.

THE ART OF COOKERY MADE PLAIN AND EASY

Siamese Mixed Salad with Rose Petals

The nam pla called for in this recipe is a salty, Siamese, fermented fish sauce obtainable from stores that specialize in Southeast Asian foods. If unavailable, substitute any other Oriental fermented fish sauce, such as Vietnamese nuoc mam. The volatile oils in chili peppers may irritate your skin. Wear rubber gloves when handling them.

To serve 6 to 8

1	whole chicken breast (about ½ lb. [¼ kg.]), poached in lightly salted water for 4 to 5 minutes, drained, skinned, boned and diced	1
1½ lb.	boneless pork, including fat, poached in lightly salted water for about 15 minutes, drained and diced	¾ kg.
½ lb.	fresh shrimp, poached in lightly salted water for about 4 minutes, drained, shelled and diced	¼ kg.
7	shallots, finely chopped	7
10	garlic cloves, finely chopped	10
2 tbsp.	lard	30 ml.
1 tbsp.	*nam pla*	15 ml.
2 tsp.	sugar	10 ml.
3 tbsp.	fresh lime juice	45 ml.
2 tbsp.	finely chopped roasted peanuts	30 ml.
10	roses, petals separated	10
3	sprigs coriander, chopped	3
3	fresh red chilies, seeded and thinly sliced	3

Put the meats and shrimp together in a bowl. Fry the shallots and garlic in hot lard until lightly colored. Drain well. Blend together the *nam pla*, sugar and lime juice. Mix well with the meats and peanuts. Add the rose petals and half of the fried shallots and garlic, and toss lightly. Put the salad on a dish and serve it immediately, sprinkled with the remaining half of the shallots and garlic, the chopped coriander leaves and the sliced chilies.

SIBPAN SONAKUL
EVERYDAY SIAMESE DISHES

Italian Salad

The small salading called for in this 1851 recipe is a mixture of dandelion, corn salad, rocket, hyssop and basil leaves. You may mix different kinds of lettuce —torn into small pieces— and fresh herbs, as available.

Cold fish may be dressed in this way, then hard-boiled eggs may be added; and with either meat or fish, cold boiled vegetables. When nicely garnished, these salads are pretty for supper tables.

To serve 4 to 6

½ lb.	cold cooked meat, poultry, game or lobster, thinly sliced	¼ kg.
2	salt anchovies, filleted, soaked in water for 30 minutes, drained, patted dry and chopped	2
1	shallot, finely chopped	1
½ lb.	small salading (about 1 quart [1 liter])	¼ kg.
2	hard-boiled egg yolks, mashed	2
2 tbsp.	olive oil	30 ml.
1 tbsp.	vinegar	15 ml.
	pepper	
1 tsp.	prepared mustard	5 ml.
	leftover roasting juices, degreased (optional)	
	cold boiled vegetables (optional)	

About three hours before the salad is wanted, chop the anchovies, and mix them in a salad bowl with the shallot and small salading, or lettuce and any herbs fresh gathered. Mix the egg yolks with the oil, vinegar, a little pepper and mustard. To this sauce, put very thin slices of cold roast meat of any kind (and cold roasting juices from the meat), fowl, game or lobster and leave them to soak for about three hours. Mix with the small salading, and cold boiled vegetables if desired, and garnish it prettily.

ANNE COBBETT
THE ENGLISH HOUSEKEEPER

Fish and Shellfish Salads

Herring and Veal Salad

To serve 6

1 lb.	pickled herring	½ kg.
1 lb.	veal stew meat	½ kg.
2 tbsp.	butter	30 ml.
1 tbsp.	water	15 ml.
2	medium-sized beets	2
2	medium-sized potatoes, peeled and diced	2
3	eggs, hard-boiled and the whites and yolks riced separately through a sieve	3
2 tbsp.	capers, rinsed and drained	30 ml.
1½ cups	chopped red onions	375 ml.
1½ cups	chopped dill pickles	375 ml.
½ cup	chopped parsley	125 ml.
10 to 12	oil-packed flat anchovy fillets, rinsed, patted dry and finely chopped	10 to 12
	romaine leaves	
1	lemon, cut into small wedges	1

Sour-cream dressing

4 tbsp.	butter	60 ml.
2 cups	sour cream	½ liter
⅓ cup	vinegar	75 ml.
1 tsp.	paprika	5 ml.
1 tsp.	salt	5 ml.
	freshly ground black pepper	

To prepare the sour-cream dressing, melt the butter in a medium-sized saucepan. Remove it from the heat and stir in the sour cream. Mix in the vinegar, paprika, salt and pepper. Put the dressing into a serving bowl and refrigerate it until you are ready to use it.

To make the salad, lightly brown the veal chunks in the butter, then add the water, cover the pan and braise the veal over low heat for one hour—adding more water if needed. Let it cook, then trim the veal pieces and cut them into cubes about the size of dice. Meanwhile, boil the beets for 30 min-

utes, or until tender; drain, peel them and cut them into julienne. Cook the diced potatoes in boiling salted water for 15 minutes or until tender. Drain and cool them. Drain and trim the herring. Cut the fillets into ½-inch [1-cm.] squares. Mix the capers with the herring pieces.

When everything is cooked and chopped, sliced and diced, refrigerate all of the ingredients, covered, in separate bowls, until you are ready to arrange the salad. Then set out the ingredients, in a bowl or on a platter, as attractively as you can. Garnish the serving dish with romaine leaves and with lemon wedges.

At the table mix the ingredients together with about half of the sour-cream dressing. Pass the rest of the dressing in a sauceboat or small bowl for guests to help themselves.

ELEANOR GRAVES
GREAT DINNERS FROM LIFE

Herrings on Apple Salad

To serve 4

3	salt herrings, rinsed, and heads and tails removed	3
2	apples, peeled, cored and grated coarsely	2
	freshly grated horseradish	
1 cup	sour cream	¼ liter
1 tbsp.	sugar	15 ml.
	lettuce or Savoy cabbage leaves	
2	small tomatoes, sliced, or 1 large carrot, sliced	2
1	leek, green part only, thinly sliced	1

Soak the herrings in water for a few hours, then skin and fillet them. Place the pairs of fillets together again and cut each reassembled herring diagonally in half.

Mix the apples, horseradish, sour cream and sugar. Arrange lettuce or Savoy cabbage leaves on all sides of a square salad dish. Put the apple salad into the dish and pat it out evenly. Place pieces of herring on top and garnish each piece with a tomato or carrot slice, and a round of green leek.

ZOFIA CZERNY
POLISH COOKBOOK

Pickled Salt Herring

Salt herring can be bought from good delicatessens and come in two forms—fillets and whole fish. The most common are the fillets, and the flavor of these will vary slightly according to the method of curing, which is often dependent on the country of origin: Scandinavia, Scotland, etc. To remove the excess salt from the fillets, they should be soaked in cold water or milk for five to six hours before using. Some delicatessens keep barrels of whole salt fish, although this is becoming increasingly rare. These whole herring should be cleaned and boned, then soaked in cold water for 12 hours. Before serving, the fish should be skinned and cut up.

	To serve 4	
6	salt herring fillets, soaked	6
⅓ cup	sugar	75 ml.
1 tbsp.	whole allspice berries	15 ml.
2	bay leaves	2
½ tsp.	black peppercorns	2 ml.
2	small onions, 1 finely chopped and 1 thinly sliced and separated into rings	2
1¼ cups	vinegar, preferably malt vinegar	300 ml.

Lay the herring fillets in a shallow dish. Mix the sugar, allspice, bay leaves, peppercorns and chopped onion with the vinegar, stir until the sugar has dissolved, then pour this marinade over the herring. Cover and refrigerate for at least six hours or overnight. Remove the herring from the marinade. Cut them into narrow strips and place them in a serving dish. Cover the herring with 6 tablespoons [90 ml.] of the strained marinade and garnish with the onion rings.

JENNIE REEKIE
EVERYTHING RAW: THE NO-COOKING COOKBOOK

Smoked Herring Salad

Salade Fécampoise

	To serve 4	
4	smoked herring fillets, cut into 1-inch [2½-cm.] lengths	4
⅓ cup	vinaigrette (recipe, page 167), including 1 tbsp. [15 ml.] prepared mustard	75 ml.
1 lb.	dandelion leaves	½ kg.
	fried bread croutons, rubbed with garlic before frying (recipe, page 167)	

Marinate the herring pieces in the vinaigrette for two hours. Add the dandelion leaves and mix well. Serve the salad with garlic croutons, if desired.

MARIE BISSON
LA CUISINE NORMANDE

Anchovy Salad

Salade d'Anchois

This is how anchovies should be eaten, for they are too strong to eat on their own, and garnishes not only enhance their flavor but also make them look more attractive.

	To serve 4	
12	salt anchovies	12
	wine or vinegar	
2	peeled, cooked beets, 1 cut into julienne, 1 sliced	2
¼ cup	finely chopped fresh parsley	50 ml.
1	lemon, sliced	1
about ¼ cup	chopped salad greens: cress, rocket, purslane or corn salad (optional)	about 50 ml.
1 tbsp.	capers, rinsed and drained (optional)	15 ml.
1 tbsp.	pomegranate seeds	15 ml.
	nasturtiums or other edible flowers (optional)	
¼ cup	olive oil	50 ml.
1 tbsp.	wine vinegar	15 ml.
	white pepper	
	salt	

Remove the heads of the anchovies, if they are still intact, and brush off any salt that clings to their skins. Slit each of them in two lengthwise and remove the spine; this is easily done with the fingers. Let the anchovies soak in water for about seven minutes and then rinse them in wine or vinegar. Drain them and press them slightly (between two towels) to ensure that all of the salty liquid is removed.

Cut the fillets lengthwise into thin slices and lay them out, in a fairly deep dish, in rays projecting from the center. Intersperse the anchovies with beet strips or chopped parsley. In the center of the dish, place two slices of lemon or two slices of beet, or a small mound of salad greens and capers. Decorate the edge of the plate with lemon slices mixed with chopped parsley, pomegranate seeds, flowers or sliced beet. Season the salad with oil, vinegar, white pepper and a tiny pinch of salt.

L. S. ROBERT
L'ART DE BIEN TRAITER

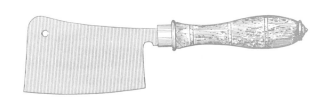

Tunisian Salad with Tuna

Salade Meshouiya

To serve 4

6½-oz. can	tuna, drained and broken into small pieces with a fork	185-g. can
4	green peppers	4
2	tomatoes	2
2	garlic cloves	2
1	onion	1
	salt	
1 tsp.	caraway seeds	5 ml.
2	eggs, hard-boiled	2
	fresh lemon juice	
	olive oil	
	ripe olives	

Over a charcoal fire or under the broiler, grill the peppers, tomatoes, garlic cloves and onion for about 10 minutes, turning them occasionally. Remove the blackened skin of each. Halve and seed the peppers and tomatoes.

In a large mortar, pound some salt with the caraway seeds, then pound in the grilled garlic cloves, peppers, tomatoes and, finally, the onion. Stir in the pieces of tuna.

Put the mixture on a platter and chop the hard-boiled eggs into it. Add some lemon juice and olive oil to make the whole moist, and arrange ripe olives on top.

ALAN DAVIDSON
MEDITERRANEAN SEAFOOD

Fresh Tuna Salad

Salade de Thon Frais

To blanch walnuts, place them in a bowl and pour boiling water over them. Then drain the nuts and rub off their skins.

To serve 6 to 8

1½ lb.	fresh tuna in a single thick slice	¾ kg.
1¼ cups	aromatic court bouillon (recipe, page 165)	300 ml.
3	medium-sized potatoes (about ¾ lb. [350 g.]), boiled and peeled while hot	3
3	tomatoes, thinly sliced	3
6	eggs, hard-boiled and quartered	6
¾ cup	vinaigrette (recipe, page 167) made with walnut oil	175 ml.
6 to 8	walnuts, fresh if possible, blanched	6 to 8

Place the tuna in a pan of a size just large enough to hold it. Pour over the court bouillon. Bring to a boil, reduce the heat

to low, cover and poach the tuna for 15 minutes. Let the tuna cool in its liquid. Drain, and cut the tuna into small pieces. Slice the hot potatoes into the tuna's cooking liquid and let them macerate until cool. Drain.

Place the tuna in a salad bowl with the tomatoes, the potatoes and the eggs. Season with the vinaigrette, garnish with walnuts and serve.

RAYMOND THUILIER AND MICHEL LEMONNIER
RECETTES DE BAUMANIÈRE

Raw Fish Marinated in Lime Juice

Cebiche

The author suggests that shrimp, scallops and crab meat can be used instead of the mackerel in this recipe, which comes from the Mexican state of Guerrero.

To serve 6

1 lb.	skinned mackerel fillets, cut into ½-inch [1-cm.] cubes	½ kg.
1¼ to 1½ cups	strained fresh lime juice (from 6 or 7 large limes)	300 to 375 ml.
2	medium-sized tomatoes (about ¾ lb. [⅓ kg.]), peeled, seeded and chopped	2
3 or 4	canned serrano chilies, chopped with their seeds	3 or 4
¼ cup	olive oil	50 ml.
½ tsp.	oregano	2 ml.
about ½ tsp.	salt	about 2 ml.
	freshly ground pepper	
1	small avocado, halved, pitted, peeled and sliced	1
1	small onion, sliced and separated into rings	1
½ tsp.	finely chopped fresh coriander leaves (optional)	2 ml.

Cover the fish cubes with the lime juice. Cover the bowl and set it in the bottom of the refrigerator for at least five hours, or until the fish loses its transparent look and becomes opaque. Stir the cubes from time to time so that they get evenly "cooked" in the juice.

Add the tomatoes, chilies, oil, oregano, salt and pepper to the fish. Set this mixture aside in the bottom of the refrigerator for at least one hour to season. (You should serve it chilled, but not so cold that the oil congeals.)

Before serving, garnish each portion with the avocado, peeled and sliced at the last moment, and the onion rings, and sprinkle it with a little chopped coriander, if desired.

DIANA KENNEDY
THE CUISINES OF MEXICO

Marinated Raw-Fish Salad

Salade de Poissons Crus Marinés

The American editor of this recipe notes that the salted ginger preserved in vinegar called for has a brilliant red color and is obtainable —as beni shoga —in Japanese grocery stores. The original recipe also calls for fresh bilberries, the equivalent of huckleberries. Small cultivated blueberries can be used as a substitute, but these will be sweeter and less flavorful than the berries intended.

To serve 4

5 to 6 oz.	firm-fleshed fish fillets — one or more kinds, such as salmon and bass	150 to 175 g.
1 tbsp.	olive oil	15 ml.
	salt and pepper	
½	shallot, finely chopped	½
2 tsp.	green peppercorns, drained	10 ml.
1	lemon	1
1	head lettuce, such as Bibb lettuce	1
1½ oz.	salted ginger preserved in vinegar, cut into very fine julienne	65 g.
	a spoonful of fresh huckleberries	

With a sharp knife, cut the fish into slices so thin they are almost transparent. (This is done on the flat of the fillet, at only a slight slant, the way smoked salmon is cut.) Spread the slices on a chilled plate, dribble the oil over them, and sprinkle them evenly with a little salt and pepper, the shallot and green peppercorns.

Cut off the peel of the lemon in thin strips, and cut these into julienne as fine as pine needles. Blanch them in boiling water for one minute, drain in a strainer, and cool them under cold running water. Wash and dry the lettuce and, with scissors, cut the leaves into strips ½ inch [1 cm.] wide (chiffonade). In a bowl, toss the chiffonade with lemon juice, salt, and pepper to taste.

Make a bed of the lettuce on each plate. Scatter over these the lemon-peel julienne and the ginger, berries and green peppercorns. Then arrange the slices of marinated fish on top, radiating from the center like petals of flowers. Refrigerate the salad for at least 15 minutes before serving.

MICHEL GUÉRARD
MICHEL GUÉRARD'S CUISINE MINCEUR

Raw Fish in Lime Juice, Peruvian-Style

Seviche

Among the many fish suitable for this dish are black or sea bass, cod, flounder, halibut, mullet, pickerel, yellow pike, pollack, porgy, red snapper, rockfish and sole.

No one should be put off by the word "raw." The fish is as firmly cooked by the acid of the lime juice as if it had been put under a grill. The strips of fish are white and solid; in fact, the whole dish is solid and should be followed by a fairly light main course.

To serve 4

about 1 lb.	firm white lean-fleshed fish, filleted and skinned	about ½ kg.
½ lb.	small bay scallops, if in season	¼ kg.
2	medium-sized green peppers, halved, seeded, deribbed and cut into narrow bite-sized strips	2
3	medium-sized sweet red onions, or mild Spanish or Bermuda onions; 2 sliced paper-thin, 1 finely chopped	3
8 to 12	fresh limes, or substitute fresh lemons	8 to 12
	freshly ground black pepper	
	cayenne pepper	
	salt	
3	ears fresh corn, boiled in water for 3 to 5 minutes	3
2	medium-sized yams or sweet potatoes, peeled, and boiled in water for 20 to 25 minutes	2
2 tbsp.	olive oil	30 ml.
about 12	ripe olives, pitted	about 12
1	small bunch fresh coriander, chopped, or substitute fresh dill or watercress, chopped	1
	Hungarian sweet paprika	

A day or two ahead, wash the fish and cut it into narrow strips, about ⅜ inch [1 cm.] wide and about 1½ inches [4 cm.] long, then put them into a wide china or glass bowl. If small scallops are used, cut them in half, but slice slightly larger ones; do not use large sea scallops, which may become tough. Add the green-pepper strips to the fish. Then add the onion slices. Blend everything thoroughly with a wooden spoon and then add enough lime juice to barely cover the contents of the bowl. Season with a very little black pepper, just a touch of cayenne, and salt to taste. Cover with a lid or foil, then refrigerate overnight or for up to three days. Stir occasionally. The fish will be magically cooked, firm and opaque.

A few hours before serving, set the corn on a chopping block and, with a sharp and heavy knife, cut each ear of corn crosswise right through the cob into slices ½ inch [1 cm.] thick, so that each is a circle of yellow corn surrounding the cob. Boil the yams or sweet potatoes, then slice them about ⅜ inch thick and trim into decorative triangles.

Delicately stir the olive oil into the fish, then add the finely chopped onion. Taste and add more salt if needed. Decorate with the corn circles, yam triangles, olives, a sprinkling of the chopped green herbs, plus a few dashes here and there of paprika. Keep the bowl in the refrigerator and serve ice-cold with buttered toast triangles.

We usually use a slotted spoon for serving, so as not to include too much juice. Peruvians usually stick a fork into the cob of each corn round, lift it to the mouth and nibble off the corn around the edge.

ROY ANDRIES DE GROOT
FEASTS FOR ALL SEASONS

Fish Salad with Roquefort and Cream Dressing

Salade, Sauce Roquefort

Almost any kind of firm-fleshed white fish—cod or haddock, for example—is suitable for this salad.

To serve 4

½ lb.	cooked fish, boned and cut into strips	¼ kg.
1	head lettuce, the outer leaves removed and left whole and the heart cut into chiffonade	1
	salt and pepper	
	lemon, orange or tomato slices (optional)	
Roquefort and cream dressing		
2 oz.	Roquefort cheese (about ⅓ cup [75 ml.])	75 g.
½ cup	heavy cream	125 ml.
1 tsp.	Cognac	5 ml.
	cayenne pepper	
1 tbsp.	wine vinegar	15 ml.

Cover a round serving platter with the whole lettuce leaves. Mix the rest of the lettuce with the fish, season, and arrange the mixture on top of the leaves. Crush the Roquefort and beat it with the cream, Cognac, a pinch of cayenne pepper and the vinegar. Spoon this dressing over the salad.

A garnish of lemon, orange or tomato slices may be added to the salad, if you wish.

NINETTE LYON
LE GUIDE MARABOUT DU POISSON

Small Fish with Herbs and Tomatoes, Oriental-Style

Poissons de Roche à l'Orientale

To serve 4

2 to 2½ lb.	small mullet, sea bass, mackerel or yellow perch, cleaned	1 kg.
	chopped fresh parsley	
Tomato court bouillon		
1	leek, white part only, finely chopped	1
1	onion, finely chopped	1
1	celery heart, finely chopped	1
3 tbsp.	olive oil	45 ml.
1	garlic clove, finely chopped	1
1	bouquet garni, containing wild fennel	1
3	medium-sized tomatoes, peeled, seeded and chopped	3
¼ tsp.	ground saffron	1 ml.
1 cup	dry white wine	¼ liter
¾ cup	water	175 ml.
	salt and pepper	
	finely chopped parsley	

To make the court bouillon, cook the leek, onion and celery in olive oil in a saucepan without letting them color. Add the garlic, the bouquet garni and the tomatoes and simmer for five minutes. Add a large pinch of saffron, the white wine, water, and salt and pepper to taste. Bring to a boil, then reduce to a simmer and cook for 12 minutes. Take the pan off the heat and let the court bouillon cool.

Arrange the fish in a deep dish and cover them with the court bouillon. Cover the dish with wax paper. Refrigerate overnight to ensure that the fish are thoroughly imbued with the marinade. To cook them, arrange the fish side by side and head to tail in a long heatproof earthenware dish large enough to contain them. Pour in the unstrained marinade and cover the dish with oiled parchment paper. Bring the marinade to a boil, then reduce the heat so that the marinade barely simmers—this is important—for 10 minutes. When the fish are cooked, take the dish off the heat, remove the bouquet garni and dust the fish with a light sprinkling of freshly chopped parsley. Cool, then refrigerate. Serve in the same dish to avoid the possibility of breaking the fish by moving them.

PAUL BOUILLARD
LA CUISINE AU COIN DU FEU

Fish Salad with Mayonnaise

Insalata Maionese

The author suggests using sturgeon, herring, dogfish or peeled shrimp for this recipe.

To serve 4

1 lb.	cold poached fish, cut into small pieces	½ kg.
1	head romaine lettuce, cut into finger-sized strips	1
2	small beets, boiled, peeled and thinly sliced	2
2 or 3	potatoes, boiled, peeled and thinly sliced	2 or 3
4 or 5	salt anchovies, filleted, soaked in water for 30 minutes, drained, patted dry and cut into thin strips	4 or 5
1 tbsp.	capers, rinsed and drained	15 ml.
3 or 4	olives, pitted and sliced	3 or 4
	salt	
½ cup	olive oil	125 ml.
1 tbsp.	wine vinegar	15 ml.
1 cup	mayonnaise *(recipe, page 166)*, made with salt but no pepper, dry mustard, fresh lemon juice and a few drops of vinegar	¼ liter
	butter	

Mix together the lettuce, beets and potatoes, reserving a few slices of beet and potato for decoration. Add the anchovies and the poached fish, together with the capers and olives. Season with salt, olive oil and vinegar, and mix well. Mound the mixture on a serving dish. Spread the surface of the salad with mayonnaise and then decorate it with the remaining slices of beet and potato, finally placing on the very top a flower shape made out of butter.

PELLEGRINO ARTUSI
LA SCIENZA IN CUCINA E L'ARTE DI MANGIAR BENE

Fish Salad with Sweet Pepper and Honey

Salade de Poisson au Citron, Poivron et Miel

Any poached or baked fish is excellent sprinkled with lemon juice and olive oil, or dry white vermouth and peanut oil. Season the fish while still warm and serve it at room temperature. It turns gelatinous when cold.

To serve 2

½ lb.	freshly cooked fish, boned, skinned and cut into small pieces	¼ kg.
1	sweet red pepper, halved, seeded and cut into thin strips	1
4	lemons, plunged into heavily salted boiling water for 3 minutes, drained, peeled, thinly sliced and each slice halved	4
3 tbsp.	olive oil	45 ml.
1 tbsp.	honey	15 ml.
	salt and pepper	
6 to 8	salted almonds, slivered	6 to 8

Arrange the fish, red pepper and lemon slices in a serving dish. Beat the oil, honey and a little seasoning in a bowl. Pour this over the salad and leave to macerate for two hours in a cool place. Sprinkle with the almonds before serving.

NINETTE LYON
LE GUIDE MARABOUT DU POISSON

Smoked Haddock Salad

To serve 6

1½ lb.	smoked haddock	⅔ kg.
1	medium onion, thinly sliced	1
2½ to 3 cups	skim milk	625 ml. to ¾ liter
	pepper	
¾ cup	mayonnaise *(recipe, page 166)*	175 ml.
2 to 3 tbsp.	fresh lemon juice	30 to 45 ml.
¼ cup	bourbon	50 ml.
1½ tsp.	soy sauce	7 ml.
	salt and pepper	
	lettuce leaves	

Spread half of the sliced onions on the bottom of an enameled or copper pot; do not use an aluminum or iron pot. Rinse the haddock and place it on top of the onions, then scatter the remaining onions on top of the fish. Pour in the skim milk; the amount will depend on the size and shape of the pot, but it should almost cover the fish. Add pepper. Cover the pot and put it over a very low heat to slowly warm the milk. Once the milk comes to a simmer, reduce the heat, and poach the haddock slowly for 30 minutes, spooning the milk over it occasionally. Turn off the heat and cool the fish in the milk.

Remove the haddock from the liquid and flake the cooked flesh into a bowl, removing any bones or tough outer skin. Make a dressing by mixing the mayonnaise, 2 tablespoons [30 ml.] of the lemon juice, the bourbon, soy sauce, salt and pepper. Taste. If the dressing seems to lack lemon, add the remaining tablespoon. Pour this dressing over the flaked haddock, mix carefully and well, but do not mash. To serve, line small bowls with crisp lettuce leaves and heap them with the prepared haddock.

CAROL CUTLER
HAUTE CUISINE FOR YOUR HEART'S DELIGHT

Small Octopus, Cuttlefish or Squid in Olive Sauce

Insalata di Moscardini

Moscardini is a type of small octopus common in the Mediterranean; any other small octopus may be substituted.

To serve 6

2½ lb.	small octopus, cuttlefish or squid, cleaned and washed	1¼ kg.
1 quart	water	1 liter
2 tbsp.	vinegar	30 ml.
1	onion	1
1	celery rib	1
2	garlic cloves	2
	salt	
Olive sauce		
¼ cup	ripe olives preserved in brine, pitted and puréed	50 ml.
⅔ cup	oil	150 ml.
3 tbsp.	fresh lemon juice	45 ml.
	salt	
1	pinch finely crumbled, dry bay leaf	1

Put the water and vinegar into a pan and add the onion, celery and garlic. Bring to a boil, then season with salt and

add the octopus, cuttlefish or squid. Cover and simmer for 20 to 25 minutes. Test with a fork to see if the seafood is tender before turning off the heat.

Mix together the ingredients for the sauce. Remove the octopus, cuttlefish or squid from the pan and cut into small pieces. Place the pieces in a serving dish, cover with the sauce, and serve.

LUIGI VOLPICELLI AND SECONDINO FREDA
L'ANTIARTUSI

Crayfish Salad

Écrevisses en Salade

Live crayfish are available commercially in Louisiana —and elsewhere in specialty fish markets —in late winter and spring. For a more flavorful salad, you can pound the shells and heads in a mortar, put the purée through a sieve and mix it with the vinaigrette.

To serve 4

20	large live crayfish	20
about 2 cups	basic court bouillon *(recipe, page 165)*	about ½ liter
about ⅓ cup	vinaigrette *(recipe, page 167)*	about 75 ml.
8	fried croutons, made from thinly sliced small bread rounds *(recipe, page 167)*	8
6	oil-packed, flat anchovy fillets, rinsed and patted dry	6

Bring the court bouillon to a boil, drop in the crayfish, reduce the heat, cover and simmer for seven to eight minutes. Let the crayfish cool in the court bouillon, then shell the crayfish tails. Put the crayfish tails in a dish, and pour over the vinaigrette. Decorate with the croutons and anchovies, and serve.

FRANÇOIS MARIN
LES DONS DE COMUS

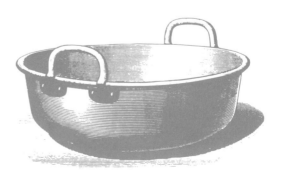

Fisherman's Crab Salad

Esquinado à la Modo di Pescadou

The author recommends using female crabs for this dish because their coral (roe) and tomalley (liver) will improve the sauce. A female crab can be distinguished from a male by the broad, short tail flap on its underside.

To serve 2 to 4

2	medium-sized live female crabs	2
⅓ cup	vinegar	75 ml.
	salt	
4 or 5	peppercorns	4 or 5
1	bay leaf	1

Crab dressing

	reserved crab coral and tomalley	
2	hard-boiled egg yolks	2
1 tsp.	Dijon mustard	5 ml.
3 to 4 tbsp.	fresh lemon juice	45 to 60 ml.
¼ to ⅓ cup	olive oil	50 to 75 ml.

Put enough water to cover the crabs into a pan with the vinegar, salt, peppercorns and bay leaf, and bring to a boil. Plunge the crabs into the boiling water, then simmer for 15 to 20 minutes. Remove the crabs and allow them to cool. When cold, remove the coral and tomalley from the crabs. Remove all of the crab meat, breaking the claw meat into fragments if necessary.

To prepare the dressing, pound the coral and tomalley in a mortar together with the egg yolks and the mustard. Work in the lemon juice, and finally incorporate just enough olive oil to give the sauce a smooth pouring consistency. Toss lightly with the crab meat and serve.

J. B. REBOUL
LA CUISINIÈRE PROVENÇALE

Crab Louis

Crab Louis was created by the chef at the Olympic Club in Seattle, Washington. When the Metropolitan Opera Company played Seattle in 1904, Enrico Caruso kept ordering the salad until none was left in the kitchen.

To serve 4

1½ lb.	cooked lump crab meat	¾ kg.
	shredded lettuce	
	eggs, hard-boiled and quartered	
	tomatoes, peeled and quartered	
	sliced avocado	

Louis dressing

1 cup	mayonnaise *(recipe, page 166)*	¼ liter
½ cup	heavy cream, whipped	125 ml.
¼ cup	chili sauce	50 ml.
2 tbsp.	grated onion	30 ml.
2 tbsp.	finely chopped parsley	30 ml.
	cayenne pepper	

To make the dressing, combine the mayonnaise, cream, chili sauce, onion, parsley and a dash of cayenne, and refrigerate.

Arrange the shredded lettuce on a platter and heap the crab meat on top. Garnish with the hard-boiled eggs, tomatoes, and slices of avocado. Pour the dressing over all.

HELEN MCCULLY (EDITOR)
THE AMERICAN HERITAGE COOKBOOK

Lobster Salad

To serve 6

1 lb.	cooked lobster meat	½ kg.
2 tbsp.	fresh lemon juice	30 ml.
2 tbsp.	dry sherry or white wine	30 ml.
⅔ cup	diced celery	150 ml.
¼ cup	mayonnaise *(recipe, page 166)*	50 ml.
¼ cup	heavy cream, whipped	50 ml.
	salad greens	

Cut the lobster meat into bite-sized pieces and moisten them with the lemon juice and wine. Let them stand for about an hour. Add the celery. Mix the mayonnaise with the cream and fold this dressing into the salad. Blend thoroughly. Serve the salad on a bed of greens.

CAROL TRUAX
THE ART OF SALAD MAKING

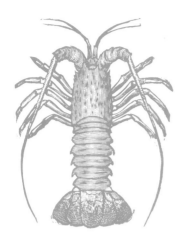

Lobster Constellation

To serve 4

two 1-lb.	rock lobster tails or 4 live 1-lb. [½-kg.] lobsters, boiled in lightly salted water for about 10 minutes, cooled, and cut lengthwise into halves	two ½-kg.
1½ cups	chopped celery	375 ml.
	mayonnaise *(recipe, page 166)*	
½ cup	dry white wine	125 ml.
12	live mussels, scrubbed and bearded	12
12	live clams, scrubbed	12
1½ tbsp.	flour	22 ml.
¼ cup	chopped fresh mushrooms	50 ml.
¼ tsp.	curry powder or a dash of Tabasco sauce	1 ml.
	lemon wedges	

Remove the lobster meat from the shells, and line the shells with the celery mixed with ⅓ cup [75 ml.] of mayonnaise. Cube the lobster meat and pile it on top of the celery. Chill.

To 2 cups [½ liter] of the water in which the lobsters were cooked, add the white wine. Bring to a boil; add the mussels and clams, cover the vessel and simmer until the shells open—about five minutes. Remove the meat and place it on the half shells. Chill.

Strain the broth and boil until it is reduced to 1 cup [¼ liter]. Blend the flour with a little cold water, add it to the broth, and cook, stirring until this mixture is thickened. Add the mushrooms and cook for about one minute. Stir in 2 tablespoons [30 ml.] of mayonnaise. Flavor with curry or Tabasco sauce. Chill.

Arrange the filled lobster shells on a chilled platter and garnish with mayonnaise. Dressing each with mushroom sauce, put the mussels and clams in their half shells around the lobster. Serve with lemon and mayonnaise.

RAYMOND A. SOKOLOV
GREAT RECIPES FROM THE NEW YORK TIMES

Oyster Salad

To serve 4

24	live oysters, shucked	24
5	eggs, hard-boiled, the whites finely chopped and the yolks mashed	5
1	head lettuce	1
2 cups	mayonnaise *(recipe, page 166)*	½ liter

Blanch the oysters in boiling water for about one minute or until plump, then put them immediately into cold water to make them firm. Drain, and put the oysters to one side.

Lay a bed of lettuce on a long dish. Arrange the oysters on the lettuce. Coat them with the mayonnaise. Scatter first the mashed egg yolks over the oysters and then the chopped whites. Do not let the salad stand very long before serving. If you do, the oysters and mayonnaise will become watery.

RECIPES FOR SEA FOOD

Oyster and Celery Salad

Cabbage, sliced as for coleslaw, may be used in this recipe instead of celery.

To serve 4

24	live oysters, shucked and the liquor reserved	24
about ⅓ cup	oil	about 75 ml.
2 tbsp.	fresh lemon juice	30 ml.
	salt and pepper	
1	celery heart, finely chopped	1
1 to 2 tbsp.	pickled nasturtium seeds or capers, rinsed and drained	15 to 30 ml.
about 1 cup	mayonnaise *(recipe, page 166)*	about ¼ liter
	lettuce leaves	
	small sour gherkins	

Poach the oysters by heating them to the boiling point in their own liquor; cool, drain, and, if large, halve each one.

Toss the warm oysters in the oil to coat them nicely, then toss them in the lemon juice, dust with salt and pepper and set them aside to become thoroughly cooled.

When ready to serve, drain the oysters again and add the celery and the nasturtium seeds or capers. Mix with the mayonnaise. Serve on a bed of lettuce and garnish with gherkin fans made by slicing almost through each gherkin lengthwise several times, but with the slices left joined at one end, and then spreading the slices apart.

JANET MCKENZIE HILL
SALADS, SANDWICHES, AND CHAFING-DISH DAINTIES

Poached Oyster Salad

Huitres en Salade

To serve 8

48	live medium-large oysters, shucked and their liquor reserved (about 3 cups [¾ liter] shucked)	48
3	egg yolks	3
1 tsp.	spicy prepared mustard	5 ml.
4 tbsp.	olive oil	60 ml.
1 tsp.	finely grated shallot	5 ml.
2 tbsp.	white wine vinegar	30 ml.
	salt	
	cayenne pepper	
2	heads tender young leaf lettuce	2

Poach the oysters gently in their liquor until they are plump —about five minutes. Set them aside in the liquor to cool.

To prepare the dressing, beat the egg yolks until very thick, then beat in the mustard. Beat in the olive oil, drop by drop. Add the shallot, then the vinegar. (The dressing will be thinner than mayonnaise when finished.) Season to taste with salt and cayenne.

Arrange the tenderest lettuce leaves in a glass bowl to form a nest. When the oysters are quite cold, lift them from their liquor with a slotted spoon and pile them in the center of the lettuce. Pour the dressing over them, coating them all. In the old days this was served with little hot biscuits, lavishly buttered and filled with slivers of country-cured ham.

MORTON G. CLARK
FRENCH-AMERICAN COOKING FROM NEW ORLEANS TO QUEBEC

Oyster and Sweetbread Salad

To prepare the sweetbreads called for in this recipe, see the editor's note for Mushroom and Potato Salad with Sweetbreads, page 127.

To serve 8 to 10

18	live oysters, shucked (about 1 pint [½ liter]), the liquor reserved	18
1	pair calf's sweetbreads, cooked, cooled and cut into small cubes	1
½ cup	vinaigrette (recipe, page 167), made with fresh lemon juice	125 ml.
about 1 cup	mayonnaise (recipe, page 166)	about ¼ liter
	lettuce leaves, watercress or chopped cucumber, seasoned with vinaigrette	

Poach the oysters by heating them to the boiling point in their own liquor; cool, drain, and cut each oyster in half.

Marinate the sweetbreads and the oysters in the vinaigrette, and allow them to stand for at least half an hour. Drain them and mix them with the mayonnaise. Serve on a bed of lettuce leaves or cress, or encircled by chopped cucumber.

JANET MCKENZIE HILL
SALADS, SANDWICHES, AND CHAFING-DISH DAINTIES

Dublin Bay Prawn Salad

Salade de Queues de Langoustines

The original version of this recipe, of course, calls for Dublin Bay prawns, a European crustacean about the size of a large shrimp but with the appearance of a tiny lobster. The tails are sometimes available frozen in the United States.

Sea urchins, which are spine-covered balls 4 to 5 inches [10 to 13 cm.] in diameter, are obtainable on the West Coast. Wearing thick gloves, open sea urchins by first cutting a disk from the orifice side and removing it. The coral roe—the only edible part—is attached in a starlike formation against the walls of the shell and may be removed with a teaspoon.

If fresh white beans are unavailable, substitute ½ cup [125 ml.] of dried white beans: Soak them overnight, then boil them for one and one half to two hours, or until tender.

To serve 4

24	fresh large shrimp, poached in water for 4 to 5 minutes, drained and shelled	24
1 cup	fresh white beans	¼ liter
	watercress	
24	live sea urchins, roe extracted and puréed through a fine sieve	24
about 1 cup	mayonnaise (recipe, page 166), made with peanut oil	about ¼ liter

Boil the beans for 30 to 40 minutes, or until tender, and drain them. Combine the hot beans with the shrimp, and add a few watercress leaves. Add the sea-urchin purée to the mayonnaise. Season the salad with the mayonnaise and serve.

RAYMOND THUILIER AND MICHEL LEMONNIER
RECETTES DE BAUMANIÈRE

Shrimp Salad

To serve 4 to 6

1 lb.	fresh medium-sized shrimp, poached in water for 3 to 4 minutes, drained and shelled	½ kg.
1	large head lettuce, leaves separated and torn into pieces	1
	mustard greens and watercress	
2	eggs, hard-boiled and quartered lengthwise	2
½ cup	red Bordeaux	125 ml.
2 tsp.	wine vinegar	10 ml.
1 tsp.	chutney, chopped	5 ml.

Mix the lettuce, mustard greens and watercress, and heap them up in the middle of a dish. Place the quartered eggs around the edge of the greens, then place the shrimp in a ring around the eggs.

Mix the wine, vinegar and chutney. Pour this dressing over the greens and serve with brown bread and butter.

MRS. C. F. LEYEL
SAVOURY COLD MEALS

Mango Shrimp

The original version of this recipe calls for prawns, an out-sized crustacean resembling a shrimp. The author suggests that crab meat also can be substituted, so long as the amounts of the crustacean and the mango are about equal.

To serve 4

4	mangoes, halved lengthwise, pits removed	4
16	large shrimp, poached in salted water for 5 minutes, peeled and cut into chunks	16
1	sweet red pepper, broiled, peeled, seeded and cut into strips	1
	fresh mint leaves	

Horseradish dressing

2 tbsp.	freshly grated horseradish	30 ml.
1 cup	mayonnaise *(recipe, page 166)*	¼ liter
1 tsp.	fresh lemon or lime juice	5 ml.
1 tsp.	sugar	5 ml.
	freshly ground pepper	
	light cream (optional)	

Remove the flesh from the mangoes in cubes. (One way to do this is to make several lengthwise cuts down to, but not through, the skin, then do the same crosswise; after which the cubes may be removed by running a spoon under the flesh, close to the skin.) Keep the skins.

Mix together the horseradish, mayonnaise, lemon or lime juice, sugar and pepper and a little cream if desired. Now mix the pieces of shrimp and mango with the dressing. There should be enough dressing to cover them well, but without creating a soupy effect. Fill the mango skins with the mixture. Garnish with pepper strips and mint leaves, and serve chilled.

ALAN DAVIDSON
SEAFOOD OF SOUTH-EAST ASIA

Shrimp and Scallop Seviche

To serve 6 to 8

2 lb.	shrimp, boiled in water for 3 to 4 minutes and peeled	1 kg.
1 lb.	scallops, thinly sliced	½ kg.
1 cup	fresh lime juice (about 6 limes)	¼ liter
6 tbsp.	finely chopped red onion	90 ml.
¼ cup	chopped fresh parsley	50 ml.
2 tbsp.	finely chopped green pepper	30 ml.
½ cup	olive oil	125 ml.
½ tsp.	oregano	2 ml.
	dash of Tabasco sauce	
1 tsp.	salt	5 ml.
	freshly ground black pepper	
2	avocados, halved, pitted, peeled and sliced	2

Cut the shrimp into thirds if large and mix with the sliced scallops in a bowl. Add lime juice to marinate the mixture. Cover, let stand at room temperature for one hour, stirring once or twice (marinating should always be done at room temperature for the most flavor). Drain and discard the juice. Add all of the remaining ingredients, except the avocados, to the seafood and toss lightly. Chill for an hour. Arrange the *seviche* on plates with the avocado slices. If you have them, scallop shells make particularly attractive serving dishes for this salad.

ELEANOR GRAVES
GREAT DINNERS FROM LIFE

Japanese Salad with Potatoes and Mussels

Salade Francillon

The techniques of cleaning and bearding mussels are demonstrated on pages 68-69.

Alexandre Dumas the younger, as interested in culinary matters as his father, seized the occasion of his play *Francillon* to bring to the attention of gourmets the unpublished recipe for Japanese Salad, afterward called *Salade Francillon* in honor of the play's success.

	To serve 6	
12	new potatoes, washed but not peeled	12
	salt	
24	live mussels, cleaned and bearded	24
1 cup	dry white wine, preferably Chablis	¼ liter
	pepper	
½ tsp.	thyme	2 ml.
1	bay leaf	1
1	truffle, thinly sliced	1
1	salt herring, filleted, soaked in water overnight, drained, patted dry, skinned and cut into strips	1
1 tbsp.	vinegar	15 ml.
¼ cup	olive oil	50 ml.
	cayenne pepper	
1 tbsp.	coarsely chopped fresh chervil	15 ml.

Cook the potatoes in salted water until just tender.

Meanwhile, place the mussels in a saucepan with ½ cup [125 ml.] of the wine, a pinch of pepper, and the thyme and bay leaf. Cover and cook over high heat for two minutes while shaking the pan. When all of the mussels have opened, take them out of their shells.

Peel and slice the potatoes while still hot. Reserve the 12 most perfect mussels, several slices of potato, and several slices of truffle. Mix all the rest of the mussels, potato slices and truffle slices with the herring. Season the mixture with a little salt and pepper, the vinegar, oil, cayenne pepper and the remaining wine. Allow to macerate for one hour.

Arrange the salad on a serving dish, smoothing the surface with a knife. Decorate with a row of potato slices alternated with truffle slices, the reserved mussels and, in the center, the chervil.

PHILÉAS GILBERT
LA CUISINE DE TOUS LES MOIS

Seafood Salad

Insalata di Frutti di Mare

The techniques of cleaning and bearding mussels are demonstrated on pages 68-69.

	To serve 6	
3 lb.	live mussels, washed in salted water, scrubbed and beards removed	1½ kg.
12	live hard-shell clams (about 1½ lb. [¾ kg.]), washed in salted water and scrubbed	12
	salt	
about ⅔ cup	olive oil	about 150 ml.
1½ lb.	octopus, cleaned, rinsed and beaten with a mallet to tenderize it	¾ kg.
1½ lb.	shrimp	¾ kg.
about ⅓ cup	strained fresh lemon juice	about 75 ml.
1 tsp.	prepared French mustard	5 ml.
2 or 3	sprigs parsley, finely chopped	2 or 3
	salt and freshly ground pepper	

Pour 2 to 3 tablespoons [30 to 45 ml.] of the olive oil into a large pan, add the mussels and clams, cover, and cook over high heat for five to 10 minutes, shaking the pan from time to time. When the shells open, take out the shellfish, reserving the liquid. Strain the liquid and put it aside.

Put the octopus into a large pan, add the strained liquid from the mussels and clams, and cook gently for about two hours. Add the shrimp and continue cooking for 10 minutes.

Take the octopus and shrimp from the pan. Shell the shrimp and cut the octopus into small pieces. Put all of the shellfish together attractively in a salad bowl.

Mix plenty of olive oil (here the quantity is to taste, but use at least twice as much oil as lemon juice) with the lemon juice, mustard, parsley, a little salt and a good sprinkling of freshly ground pepper. Pour this dressing over the seafood, mix lightly, and leave for about two hours before serving.

ADA BONI
ITALIAN REGIONAL COOKING

Mussel Salad with Saffron and Hearts of Lettuce

Salade de Moules au Safran et aux Coeurs de Laitue

The techniques of cleaning and bearding mussels are shown on pages 68-69.

	To serve 4	
32	live mussels	32
2	Bibb lettuce hearts, cut in half, plus a few perfect extra leaves	2
¼ cup	fish stock *(recipe, page 164)*	50 ml.
2 tbsp.	dry white wine	30 ml.
½	leek, white part only, cut into fine julienne	½
1	shallot, finely chopped	1
3 to 4 tbsp.	fresh lemon juice	45 to 60 ml.
2	celery ribs, cut into thin julienne 2 inches [5 cm.] long	2
½	small tomato, peeled, seeded, diced and drained	½
½ tsp.	coarsely chopped fresh tarragon leaves	2 ml.
	Saffron sauce	
	ground saffron or crumbled saffron threads	
1 tsp.	olive oil	5 ml.
½	shallot, finely minced	½
1 tsp.	tart cream dressing *(recipe, page 166)*	5 ml.

In a large saucepan, bring to a boil the fish stock, white wine, leek and shallot. Add the mussels, cover and cook for six minutes, or just until all of the shells are open. Remove the mussels from the pan; strain the cooking liquid and reserve it. Remove all the mussels from their shells except the four that will be used for decoration.

In a small saucepan, heat the olive oil and add the chopped half shallot, the tart cream dressing, a pinch of saffron and about 6 tablespoons [90 ml.] of the reserved cooking liquid. Boil for one minute, then stir in the mussels. Take the pan off the heat and let the mussels cool in the sauce.

Arrange the lettuce leaves and hearts on chilled plates, and season with a squeeze of lemon. Arrange the mussels on the lettuce, and spoon just a little of their sauce over each one. Decorate the salads with the celery julienne, diced tomatoes, the four mussels in their shells, and the tarragon.

MICHEL GUÉRARD
MICHEL GUÉRARD'S CUISINE MINCEUR

Egg and Cheese Salads

Hard-boiled Egg Halves Filled with Tapenade

Demis Oeufs Durs Garnis de Tapénade

According to the author, tapenade was created by M. Meynier, chef of the Maison Dorée restaurant in Marseilles during the mid-19th Century. The name of the purée derives from ta-péno, the Provençal word for capers. If desired, the tapenade can be made in a food processor. Packed into a jar, covered with a film of olive oil and refrigerated, the prepared tapenade will keep for many months.

	To serve 8	
12	hard-boiled eggs, halved lengthwise	12
1½ cups	ripe olives, preferably oil-packed Mediterranean olives, pitted	375 ml.
15	salt anchovies, filleted, soaked in water for 30 minutes, drained, patted dry and coarsely chopped (about ¾ cup [175 ml.] chopped)	15
¼ lb.	tuna, poached in aromatic court bouillon *(recipe, page 165)* for 15 minutes, drained, boned and skinned	125 g.
1 tbsp.	English dry mustard	15 ml.
1½ cups	capers, rinsed and drained	375 ml.
about 1 cup	olive oil	about ¼ liter
	quatre épices	
	pepper	
about ½ cup	Cognac	about 125 ml.

Pound the olives in a mortar together with the anchovy fillets, tuna, mustard and capers. When well pounded, pass the mixture through a sieve into a bowl. Using a whisk, gradually incorporate ¾ cup [175 ml.] of the olive oil, the *quatre épices*, a generous amount of pepper and the Cognac.

Remove the egg yolks from the hard-boiled eggs and crush them in a mortar with about ½ cup [125 ml.] of the *tapenade*, adding a little olive oil if necessary to make the mixture smooth. Fill each egg half with some of the mixture, shaping it into a dome with the blade of a small knife.

J. B. REBOUL
LA CUISINIÈRE PROVENÇALE

Tomatoes Shaped Like Mushrooms

Tomates en Forme de Champignons

To serve 6

3	small tomatoes, cut in half and hollowed out	3
6	eggs, hard-boiled	6
	romaine lettuce leaves, shredded	
	chopped hard-boiled egg white	

Trim the white at the large end of each egg to form a flat base so that the egg will stand upright. Chop the trimmed whites and reserve. Arrange the eggs on a platter and surround them with the shredded lettuce leaves. Turn the hollowed-out tomato halves upside down and cap each standing egg with a tomato half. To complete the resemblance to mushrooms, sprinkle a bit of chopped hard-boiled egg white on the tomato caps. Serve with mayonnaise in a separate dish.

ÉDOUARD DE POMIANE
LE CARNET D'ANNA

Cheese Salad Italienne

To serve 4 to 6

3 cups	mozzarella cheese, cut into matchsticks 2 inches [5 cm.] long (about 1 lb. [½ kg.])	¾ liter
1	small white onion, thinly sliced	1
½ cup	thinly sliced pitted green olives	125 ml.
1	green Italian pepper, halved, seeded, deribbed and thinly sliced	1
2 tbsp.	tiny capers, rinsed and drained	30 ml.
1 cup	finely cubed celery	¼ liter
2 or 3	oil-packed flat anchovy fillets, rinsed, patted dry and finely mashed	2 or 3
1	garlic clove, mashed to a paste	1
1½ tbsp.	white wine vinegar	22 ml.
½ cup	olive oil	125 ml.
	salt and freshly ground black pepper	
1 tbsp.	finely chopped fresh parsley	15 ml.
8	slices Italian salami	8

In a mixing bowl, combine the cheese, onion, olives, green pepper, capers and celery. In a small jar, combine the anchovies, garlic, vinegar and olive oil. Close the jar tight and shake to blend this dressing, then pour it over the cheese mixture and toss lightly. Season with salt and a generous grinding of black pepper, and chill for two to three hours.

Thirty minutes before serving, bring the salad to room temperature, correct the seasoning, and place the salad in a rectangular serving dish. Sprinkle with the parsley and arrange the salami slices in an overlapping line down the center of the salad.

PERLA MEYERS
THE PEASANT KITCHEN

Herbed Cottage Cheese and Asparagus Salad

To serve 6

1 lb.	creamed cottage cheese	½ kg.
1½ lb.	asparagus, trimmed but left whole, boiled in lightly salted water for 5 to 8 minutes, drained and cooled	¾ kg.
2 tsp.	finely chopped fresh basil or ½ tsp. [2 ml.] dried basil	10 ml.
¼ cup	olive or salad oil	50 ml.
1½ tbsp.	wine vinegar	22 ml.
¾ tsp.	salt	4 ml.
¼ tsp.	cracked black pepper	1 ml.
	finely cut fresh chives or scallion tops	
	pimiento, cut into thin strips	

Combine the basil, oil, vinegar, ½ teaspoon [2 ml.] of the salt, and the pepper. Lay the asparagus in a deep platter or plate; spoon over the dressing. Let stand for at least 30 minutes at room temperature. Combine the cottage cheese, 1 tablespoon [15 ml.] of chives or scallion tops, and the remaining ¼ teaspoon [1 ml.] of salt. Mix well. Place the cheese mixture in the center of a platter; surround it with the marinated asparagus. Garnish the cheese with additional chives; garnish the asparagus with strips of pimiento.

JEAN H. SHEPARD
THE FRESH FRUITS AND VEGETABLES COOKBOOK

Danish Cheese Salad

Danish Samsoe cheese is a semihard, pale yellow cheese with cherry-sized holes. You can substitute Swiss cheese.

To serve 2 or 3

½ cup	diced Samsoe cheese (about 3½ oz. [125 g.])	125 ml.
¼ cup	crumbled Danish blue cheese (about 1 oz. [50 g.])	50 ml.
1	sweet red pepper	1
1	green pepper	1
¼ cup	corn oil	50 ml.
1 tbsp.	fresh lemon juice	15 ml.
	dry mustard	
	salt and freshly ground black pepper	
1	sweet onion, finely chopped	1

Slice the peppers fine into rings, discarding the cores and seeds, and place the rings in a serving bowl. Put the oil, lemon juice, a pinch of mustard, and salt and pepper to taste into a screw-top jar and shake until the mixture is well blended, then pour it over the peppers and let them marinate for four hours. Add the cheeses and onion to the peppers and toss all of the ingredients together.

JENNIE REEKIE
EVERYTHING RAW: THE NO-COOKING COOKBOOK

Flossy Cottage Cheese

The cheese can be drained, as shown on pages 82-83, in a clay pot and it may be kept draining for up to 24 hours, if desired.

To serve 6

1 lb.	small-curd creamed cottage cheese	½ kg.
1 cup	heavy cream	¼ liter
1 tsp.	salt	5 ml.
½ tsp.	freshly ground pepper	2 ml.
1 tbsp.	finely chopped fresh tarragon	15 ml.
1 tbsp.	finely chopped fresh parsley	15 ml.
1 tbsp.	finely cut fresh chives	15 ml.
1	shallot, finely chopped (or 1 tbsp. [15 ml.] finely chopped scallion)	1
3 tbsp.	oil	45 ml.
3 to 4 tbsp.	white wine vinegar	45 to 60 ml.
	lettuce leaves, tomato wedges or cherry tomatoes	

With a wire whisk or electric beater, beat the cream until very stiff, adding the salt once the cream is thick. Beat one third of the cottage cheese at a time into the whipped cream. Beat in the remaining ingredients, adding only 3 tablespoons [45 ml.] of the vinegar at first; then taste and, if you prefer a sharper flavor, add the other tablespoon.

Line a strainer or colander with cheesecloth and place it over a deep bowl. Scoop the seasoned cottage cheese into the cheesecloth, then press it down lightly. Fold the corners of the cheesecloth over the cottage cheese and refrigerate the cheese, still in the bowl. Allow at least two hours for the excess liquid to drip out. Drain off the liquid if a lot collects.

To serve, unfold the top layer of cheesecloth, and reverse the dome of seasoned cottage cheese onto a serving dish lined with lettuce leaves, or spoon individual portions onto lettuce leaves arranged on salad plates. Garnish the salad with tomato wedges or cherry tomatoes.

CAROL CUTLER
THE SIX-MINUTE SOUFFLÉ AND OTHER CULINARY DELIGHTS

Bread, Grain and Pasta Salads

Panzanella

To serve 4

8	slices stale firm-textured white bread	8
1	large white onion, thinly sliced	1
1	cucumber, peeled and sliced	1
4	ripe tomatoes, thinly sliced	4
10	fresh basil leaves, cut up with scissors, or 1 tsp. [5 ml.] dried basil	10
⅓ cup	olive oil	75 ml.
2 tbsp.	wine vinegar	30 ml.
	salt and pepper	
1	salt anchovy, filleted, soaked in water for 30 minutes, drained, patted dry and cut into pieces	1
2 tbsp.	capers, rinsed and drained	30 ml.

Soak the bread in cold water for a few minutes, then squeeze out the excess water and put the bread in a salad bowl. Add the onion, cucumber, tomato slices and basil leaves. Season with the olive oil and vinegar, and salt and pepper to taste; toss well. Sprinkle with the capers and anchovy, and serve.

WILMA PEZZINI
THE TUSCAN COOKBOOK

Wild-Rice Salad

To serve 4 to 6

½ lb.	wild rice	¼ kg.
4 cups	boiling water	1 liter
½ lb.	fresh mushrooms, coarsely chopped (about 2½ cups [625 ml.] when chopped)	¼ kg.
3 tbsp.	oil	45 ml.
2 tbsp.	fresh lemon juice	30 ml.
2	eggs, hard-boiled and coarsely chopped	2
1	green pepper, halved, seeded, deribbed and finely chopped	1
½ lb.	fresh medium-sized shrimp, poached in water for 3 to 4 minutes, drained, shelled and cooled (about 1½ cups [375 ml.] when shelled)	¼ kg.
Aioli sauce		
4	garlic cloves	4
	salt and white pepper	
2	egg yolks	2
2¼ cups	olive oil	½ liter
3 tbsp.	fresh lemon juice	45 ml.
2 tbsp.	tepid water	30 ml.

First prepare the aioli sauce. With a garlic press, squeeze the garlic into a mortar. Add a pinch of salt and of white pepper and the yolk of an egg. With the pestle, reduce these ingredients to a paste. Add the second egg yolk. Begin to incorporate the olive oil, drop by drop. When the egg has absorbed about 3 tablespoons [45 ml.] of oil, add ½ tablespoon [7 ml.] of lemon juice. Continuing to stir, now add oil more briskly. When the sauce soon becomes firm again, add ½ tablespoon of tepid water. Continue to add oil, lemon juice and water.

Put the wild rice in a pan with the water, cover and cook over low heat for 45 minutes to one hour, or until tender. Drain the rice, let it cool and place it in a salad bowl. Cook the mushrooms for 10 minutes in the oil and lemon juice. Add the mushrooms, hard-boiled eggs, pepper and shrimp to the rice and mix lightly. Serve with the aioli sauce.

ALICE B. TOKLAS
THE ALICE B. TOKLAS COOK BOOK

Tomato, Rice and Mushroom Salad

La Salade Poitevine

To serve 4

2	small firm ripe tomatoes, halved, seeded and sliced	2
1 cup	raw unprocessed rice	¼ liter
1½ cups	fresh mushrooms	375 ml.
	salt	
about ⅓ cup	vinaigrette *(recipe, page 167)*	about 75 ml.
1	onion, chopped	1
2 tsp.	chopped fresh tarragon	10 ml.

Boil the rice in a large pot of salted water for about 20 minutes, until tender, then strain it and dry it on a cloth. Cook the mushrooms slightly in a little simmering salted water, then strain and dry them. Cool the rice and mushrooms.

Prepare the vinaigrette in a salad bowl. Add all of the elements of the salad and mix well. Then sprinkle with the tarragon and serve.

J. BERJANE
FRENCH DISHES FOR ENGLISH TABLES

Spiced Rice Salad

To serve 4 to 6

1 cup	raw unprocessed rice	¼ liter
1	piece fresh ginger root	1
	salt	
	freshly ground black pepper	
	grated nutmeg	
½ tsp.	pounded coriander seeds	2 ml.
1 tbsp.	fresh lemon juice	15 ml.
1	shallot, thinly sliced	1
about ¼ cup	olive oil	about 50 ml.
½ cup	raisins and dried currants, simmered in water for a few minutes until plump	125 ml.
4	fresh apricots, or dried apricots soaked in water overnight and poached for a few minutes	4
about ¼ cup	roasted almonds or pine nuts	about 50 ml.

Boil the rice with the ginger in salted water for 14 to 15 minutes, drain very carefully; remove the ginger; while the rice is still warm, season it with the black pepper, grated nutmeg, coriander, lemon juice and sliced shallot. Stir in enough olive oil to make the rice moist but not mushy, then add the raisins and currants and the apricots. Garnish with roasted almonds or pine nuts.

ELIZABETH DAVID
SUMMER COOKING

Creole Salad

The original version of this 1897 recipe calls for canned mushrooms and shrimp—an unnecessary compromise today, when fresh products are readily available.

To serve 4

1 cup	raw unprocessed rice	¼ liter
	crisp lettuce leaves	
½ cup	finely chopped fresh mushrooms	125 ml.
¼ lb.	fresh shrimp, poached for 3 to 5 minutes, shelled and deveined	125 g.
1	egg, hard-boiled, the yolk pressed through a sieve and the white finely chopped	1
	salt and pepper	
½ tsp.	paprika	2 ml.
1 tsp.	curry powder	5 ml.
½ cup	olive oil	125 ml.
¼ cup	dry sherry	50 ml.
3 to 4 tbsp.	fresh lemon juice	45 to 60 ml.
1	sweet red pepper, halved, seeded, deribbed and finely chopped	1
2 tbsp.	finely chopped fresh parsley	30 ml.

Boil the rice for 20 minutes, throw it into cold water, drain and dry it. Line the salad bowl with lettuce leaves, put in a layer of rice, then shrimp, then a dusting of mushrooms, the finely chopped white of the egg, a dusting of the yolk of the egg, salt and pepper, and so continue until you have used all of the ingredients, having the last layer shrimp.

Put 1 teaspoon [5 ml.] of salt, the paprika, curry and oil in a bowl, add a piece of ice, and stir until the salt is dissolved; remove the ice, and add the sherry and lemon juice. Beat thoroughly; add the red pepper and parsley. Baste this over the salad, toss carefully and serve at once.

MRS. S. T. RORER
NEW SALADS

Cracked Wheat Salad

Tabbouleh

The technique of preparing bulgur (cracked wheat) is demonstrated on pages 76-77.

Tabbouleh is the unquestioned star of Lebanese salads and a national passion. Some finely chopped tomato, cucumber and green pepper may be added if desired.

To serve 4

1 cup	fine bulgur, soaked in cold water to cover for about 20 minutes	¼ liter
1	medium-sized mild onion, finely chopped or 4 scallions, including 2 inches [5 cm.] of the green tops, finely chopped	1
1½ cups	finely chopped, fresh flat-leafed parsley (about 2½ oz. [80 g.])	375 ml.
¼ cup	finely chopped fresh mint	50 ml.
¼ cup	olive oil	50 ml.
¼ cup	strained fresh lemon juice	50 ml.
	salt	
2	romaine lettuce hearts, separated into leaves	2
2	medium-sized tomatoes, cut into wedges or sliced	2
1	small green pepper, seeded and sliced into rings (optional)	1

Drain the bulgur and squeeze out as much moisture as possible with your hands. Combine the bulgur, onion or scallions, parsley and mint in a bowl. Sprinkle with the oil, lemon juice and a little salt, and mix thoroughly. Taste and adjust the seasoning. Cover, and chill in the refrigerator.

To serve, mound the salad in the center of a serving platter. Decorate with the lettuce leaves, tomatoes and green pepper rings, if desired. The lettuce leaves may be used to scoop up the salad.

SONIA UVEZIAN
THE BOOK OF SALADS

Bulgur-Basil Stuffing

To make enough stuffing for 6 medium-sized peppers or 8 to 10 tomatoes

1 cup	bulgur, soaked in 3 cups [¾ liter] of water for 2 hours	¼ liter
½ cup	finely chopped fresh basil	125 ml.
1	garlic clove, crushed to a paste	1
3 tbsp.	olive oil	45 ml.
	salt and freshly ground pepper	

Drain the bulgur well and pat it dry with paper towels. Stir in the basil, garlic, oil, salt and pepper and be sure they are well combined. Taste and adjust the seasoning—you may want to add a good bit more basil.

MOLLY FINN
SUMMER FEASTS

Tossed Shredded Chicken Salad Jade West

The technique of frying rice noodles is shown on page 78.

To serve 4

1 lb.	boneless chicken white meat, skinned and cut into chunks	½ kg.
2 oz.	rice noodles	75 g.
	oil for deep frying	
1 tsp.	dry mustard	5 ml.
1 cup	*hoisin* sauce	¼ liter
5 tsp.	finely crushed almonds	25 ml.
	salt	
1 tbsp.	sesame seeds	15 ml.
½	head iceberg lettuce, sliced into strips	½
4	sprigs fresh coriander, chopped	4
6	scallions, white parts only, chopped	6

Heat the oil in a large pot to about 375° F. [190° C.]. Add the chicken, a few chunks at a time, and deep fry for five minutes. Drain the cooked chicken on paper towels. Then cut the chicken into strips 2 inches [5 cm.] long. Add the noodles, a handful at a time, to the hot oil. When they are golden and puffed, remove the noodles and drain them on paper towels.

Place the chicken strips in a large salad bowl. In a separate bowl, mix the mustard, *hoisin* sauce, almonds, a pinch of salt and the sesame seeds. Add this dressing to the chicken, mix well, then add the lettuce, coriander, scallions and the fried noodles. Toss thoroughly, but take care not to overtoss, lest the salad become soggy.

KAREN GREEN
THE GREAT INTERNATIONAL NOODLE EXPERIENCE

Raw Fish and Noodle Salad

The rice-stick noodles (py mei fun), pickled scallions and tea melons called for in this recipe are obtainable from Chinese grocers. To toast sesame seeds, cook them in a dry skillet over low heat for one or two minutes, shaking the pan frequently.

To serve 4 to 6

1 lb.	skinned white fish fillets, cut into thin strips	½ kg.
4 oz.	rice-stick noodles	125 g.
	peanut oil	
1 tbsp.	sesame-seed oil	15 ml.
½ tsp.	white pepper	2 ml.
¼ tsp.	ground cinnamon	1 ml.
6	pickled scallions, slivered	6
2	fresh scallions, cut into thin julienne	2
1	cucumber, peeled, halved, seeded and cut into thin julienne	1
1	carrot, cut into thin julienne	1
6	sprigs coriander, cut into 2-inch [5-cm.] lengths	6
½ cup	preserved tea melons, cut into julienne	125 ml.
¼ cup	preserved ginger, cut into julienne	50 ml.
	iceberg lettuce, shredded	
2 tbsp.	sesame seeds, toasted	30 ml.
3 tbsp.	fresh lemon juice	45 ml.

In a wok or skillet, heat a layer of peanut oil at least ½ inch [1 cm.] deep. When the oil is very hot, drop a small handful of noodles into it. They will expand many times their original size in a few seconds. If the noodles are not completely immersed in the oil, turn them over. When the fried noodles are lightly golden, remove them with a slotted spoon and set them on a rack to drain. Repeat with the remaining noodles.

Combine the fish, sesame-seed oil, 1 tablespoon [15 ml.] of peanut oil, the white pepper and cinnamon. Marinate the fish for 15 minutes. Just before serving, toss the fish with the pickled and fresh scallions, the cucumber, carrot, coriander, tea melons, ginger and two thirds of the rice-stick noodles.

Place the mixture on a bed of iceberg lettuce and garnish with the remaining rice-stick noodles and the sesame seeds. Sprinkle with lemon juice and serve immediately.

MARGARET GIN AND ALFRED E. CASTLE
REGIONAL COOKING OF CHINA

Macaroni, Tomato, Pineapple and Mint Salad

To prepare the fresh pineapple and juice called for in this recipe, place peeled fresh pineapple in a shallow bowl to reserve the juices as you dice it, or set a hand grater in a bowl and shred the pineapple against the medium-sized holes.

To serve 4

1½ cups	elbow macaroni (about ½ lb. [¼ kg.]), boiled about 8 minutes until tender, drained, cooled under cold running water and drained again	375 ml.
2	medium-sized tomatoes (about ½ lb. [¼ kg.]), peeled, seeded and diced	2
about ½ cup	diced or coarsely shredded fresh pineapple	about 125 ml.
½ cup	vinaigrette (recipe, page 167), made with Dijon mustard	125 ml.
¼ cup	fresh pineapple juice (optional)	50 ml.
2 tsp.	finely chopped fresh mint	10 ml.

Mix the macaroni, tomatoes and pineapple. Season with the French-mustard vinaigrette, combined with the pineapple juice if desired. Sprinkle with the mint, and serve.

WILLIAM HEPTINSTALL
HORS D'OEUVRE AND COLD TABLE

Green Pasta Salad

To serve 6

12 oz.	small shell or elbow macaroni, boiled in lightly salted water for 8 to 10 minutes, drained and cooled	⅓ kg.
¼ cup	olive oil	50 ml.
½ cup	fresh parsley leaves	125 ml.
½ cup	fresh basil leaves	125 ml.
1	large garlic clove, crushed	1
½ cup	plain yogurt	125 ml.
½ cup	mayonnaise (recipe, page 166)	125 ml.
1 tbsp.	fresh lemon juice	15 ml.
3	scallions, sliced, including 2 inches [5 cm.] of the green tops	3
	salt and freshly ground black pepper	
2	eggs, hard-boiled and quartered	2
1 tbsp.	finely cut fresh chives	15 ml.

Put the oil, parsley, basil and garlic in the container of an electric blender. Cover and blend to a paste. Add the yogurt, mayonnaise, lemon juice, scallions, and salt and pepper. Cover and blend to a pale green creamy dressing.

Place the cooled pasta in a salad bowl. Add the green dressing and toss gently but thoroughly. Adjust the seasoning. Cover and refrigerate for several hours, or overnight. Serve garnished with eggs and sprinkled with chives.

SONIA UVEZIAN
THE BOOK OF YOGURT

Feta and Spinach Salad with Butterfly Pasta

Farfallette, or butterfly pasta, is obtainable where Italian foods are sold. To toast the pine nuts, brown them lightly in a heavy skillet with a little vegetable or olive oil.

To serve 8 to 10

⅔ cup	feta cheese (about ¼ lb. [125 g.]), diced or crumbled	150 ml.
2 lb.	spinach, stems removed and the leaves torn into 1-inch [2½-cm.] pieces	1 kg.
1 lb.	butterfly pasta, boiled in lightly salted water for 7 to 8 minutes, drained and chilled	½ kg.
½ cup	olive oil	125 ml.
2 tbsp.	fresh lemon juice	30 ml.
2 tbsp.	white wine vinegar	30 ml.
½ tsp.	salt	2 ml.
¼ tsp.	ground cinnamon	1 ml.
¼ tsp.	dry mustard	1 ml.
⅛ tsp.	freshly ground black pepper	½ ml.
2 tbsp.	toasted pine nuts	30 ml.
2	cucumbers, peeled and sliced	2
5	eggs, hard-boiled, and sliced or cut into wedges	5
4	scallions, finely chopped	4

Put the spinach leaves in a very large salad bowl. In a jar with a tight-fitting lid combine the oil, lemon juice, vinegar, salt, cinnamon, mustard and pepper. Shake well, pour half of this dressing over the spinach leaves and toss well. Sprinkle on the pine nuts and pasta. Arrange on top, in concentric circles or layers, the slices of cucumber, the egg slices and the feta cheese. Sprinkle on the scallions and pour on the last of the dressing.

GERTRUDE HARRIS
PASTA INTERNATIONAL

Molded Salads

Mrs. Stephenson's Cucumber Mousse

This recipe came from Mrs. Victoria Stephenson, who makes a variety of mousses and salads for Justin de Blanks provision shops in London. Always provide whole-wheat or rye bread with cucumber mousse; the rich, cool mixture needs that kind of flavor to set it off.

To serve 6

½	large cucumber, peeled, halved, seeded and finely diced	½
1½ tbsp.	salt	22 ml.
3 tbsp.	tarragon or wine vinegar	45 ml.
1 cup	heavy cream, or ½ cup [125 ml.] each light and heavy cream	¼ liter
2 tbsp.	unflavored powdered gelatin, softened in ⅓ cup [75 ml.] cold water for a few minutes and then heated until dissolved	30 ml.
1 lb.	pot cheese, broken up, or ½ lb. [¼ kg.] each sieved cottage cheese and cream cheese	½ kg.
	superfine sugar (optional)	
	freshly ground black pepper	
1 tbsp.	chopped fresh chives	15 ml.
1 tbsp.	chopped fresh parsley	15 ml.
¼ cup	finely chopped scallions	50 ml.

Mix the cucumber, salt and vinegar in a bowl thoroughly. Then turn it into a colander, put a heavy plate on top and leave for an hour at least. Remove the plate and press the cucumber with a clean cloth to get the last of the liquid away.

Gradually whisk the cream into the dissolved gelatin until the mixture is smooth and very thick, but not stiff. Add the cheese to the cream and mix in the cucumber.

Taste and add a little more vinegar and salt if necessary, but be careful to overdo neither. Sometimes a couple of pinches of superfine sugar will help to bring out the flavor; this depends on how good the cucumber was to start with. Grind in plenty of black pepper and add an abundance of chopped chives, parsley and scallion—enough to make a strongly speckled effect. Tip the mixture into a 1-quart [1-liter] oiled decorative mold and leave overnight in the refrigerator to set. Turn out onto a serving dish.

JANE GRIGSON
JANE GRIGSON'S VEGETABLE BOOK

Cucumber Mousse

To produce a green mousse as shown on pages 86-87, substitute 2 pounds [1 kg.] of fresh spinach or watercress for the two cucumbers used to flavor this mousse. Blanch the trimmed spinach or watercress leaves for three minutes in boiling water, rinse them under cold water to stop the cooking, drain them, squeeze the leaves completely dry and chop them fine. To flavor this green version, eliminate the Worcestershire sauce listed below and increase the dill to 1 teaspoon [5 ml.].

To serve 6

3	cucumbers	3
2 tsp.	fresh lemon juice	10 ml.
1 tbsp.	unflavored powdered gelatin	15 ml.
2 tbsp.	hot water	30 ml.
¾ tsp.	salt	4 ml.
½ tsp.	pepper	2 ml.
½ tsp.	Worcestershire sauce	2 ml.
½ tsp.	dill	2 ml.
	Tabasco sauce	
¼ cup	mayonnaise (recipe, page 166)	50 ml.
½ cup	heavy cream	125 ml.
2 tsp.	oil	10 ml.
½ cup	vinaigrette (recipe, page 167)	125 ml.

Bring about a quart [1 liter] of water to a boil while peeling two cucumbers. Cut them in quarters lengthwise, remove the seeds, and cut the slices in half crosswise. Add the cucumbers to the water with 1 teaspoon [5 ml.] of the lemon juice and boil for five or six minutes, or until they just turn transparent. Drain at once, and cool the cucumbers under cold running water. Drain again.

Soften the gelatin in the 2 tablespoons [30 ml.] of hot water. Put the cucumbers in the blender and purée them. Add the gelatin to the purée. Add the remaining lemon juice, the salt, pepper, Worcestershire sauce, dill and a dash of Tabasco. Blend, scrape the mixture into a bowl, and cool.

Fold the mayonnaise into the cooled purée. Whip the cream until stiff and fold it into the purée. Lightly oil a 3-cup [¾-liter] ring mold (or other form) and spoon in the mousse. Tap the mold on the counter to settle the mousse in the container. Chill for at least two hours. Score the peel of the remaining cucumber lengthwise with the tines of a fork, and slice it thin. Marinate the slices in the vinaigrette.

To serve, run a hot knife around the edge of the mousse, then dip the bottom of the mold into hot water. Place a chilled serving dish over the top of the mold and reverse the two together. The mousse will ease onto the platter. Drain the marinating cucumber slices and use them as garnish—piled in the center of the mold if it is ring-shaped.

CAROL CUTLER
THE SIX-MINUTE SOUFFLÉ AND OTHER CULINARY DELIGHTS

Molded Spring Vegetables in Herbed Jelly

If the chicken stock called for here has been made with enough gelatinous elements to set naturally into a firm jelly, you can make this mold without adding gelatin. Similarly, if the stock is naturally clear and limpid, you do not need to clarify it with egg whites and shells.

To serve 8 to 10

2 lb.	asparagus	1 kg.
1 lb.	small, tender carrots	½ kg.
2 cups	sliced scallions, white parts only	½ liter
2	egg whites	2
2	eggshells, crumbled	2
2 tbsp.	unflavored powdered gelatin, softened in ¼ cup [50 ml.] cold water	30 ml.
	flat-leafed parsley or burnet leaves	
	herb mayonnaise *(recipe, page 166)*	
Herbed jelly		
6 cups	chicken stock *(recipe, page 164)*	1½ liters
1	bay leaf	1
	several sprigs of parsley, thyme and savory	
1	lovage stalk or celery rib, sliced	1
	several green scallion tops	

Place the stock, herbs and scallion tops in a saucepan and boil to reduce the stock to 4 cups [1 liter]. Cool the stock to room temperature.

Break each asparagus stalk off at its tender point and cut it into ¼-inch [6-mm.] slices. Wash and scrape the carrots, and slice them thin.

Boil the carrot slices in well-salted water until perfectly tender but not overcooked—about 10 minutes. Strain out the slices with a wire skimmer. Boil the scallion slices in the same water. When cooked, strain them out into a second bowl. Add the asparagus slices last and cook them at a rolling boil until tender but still bright green. Put all of the vegetables aside to cool in separate containers.

Whisk the egg whites and crumbled shells together until light. Combine the egg-white mixture, softened gelatin and stock in a saucepan and heat gently. Whisk continuously until the mixture comes to a boil and forms the thick matting of egg-white albumin and herb stalks, which will draw off all impurities. Stop stirring and let the broth maintain a slow boil for 15 minutes. Cover the pan, remove it from the heat, and let the broth sit for 10 minutes.

Rinse a clean dish towel with cold water, wring it out, and use it to line a large strainer. Place the strainer over a deep bowl and carefully pour in the broth. Allow the broth to drip undisturbed. If the resulting jelly is not perfectly clear,

let it filter through the frothy debris again. (The strainer bottom must not touch and defile the clear liquid beneath.)

Pour a layer of jelly ¼ inch [6 mm.] thick into an 8- or 9-cup [2- or 2¼-liter] soufflé dish. Place leaves of parsley or burnet in the dish to decorate the top when the dish is unmolded, and refrigerate until the jelly sets. Cool the remaining jelly. When the jelly in the mold is firm, add the carrots in a smooth layer, then the onions, then the asparagus. Pour the cooled jelly over all and return the salad to the refrigerator until set. Unmold and serve with herb mayonnaise.

JUDITH OLNEY
SUMMER FOOD

Wine Jelly

Weingelee

To serve 4 to 6

1 cup	dry white wine	¼ liter
1 tbsp.	unflavored powdered gelatin	15 ml.
1 cup	water	¼ liter
1 tbsp.	fresh lemon juice	15 ml.
¼ cup	sugar	50 ml.
½ cup	sliced strawberries	125 ml.
½ cup	sliced peaches	125 ml.
½ cup	pitted cherries	125 ml.

Put ½ cup [125 ml.] of the water into a small saucepan, and add the gelatin. Soak for a few minutes, then set over a low heat and stir until the gelatin dissolves. Stir in the lemon juice and sugar. Continue stirring until the sugar dissolves. Remove the pan from the heat. Add the remaining ½ cup [125 ml.] of water and the wine. Chill the mixture until syrupy, then add the fruits and spoon the jelly into a 1-quart [1-liter] mold. Chill thoroughly until set. Unmold and serve.

MICHELE EVANS
THE SALAD BOOK

Rose-Champagne Mold

To serve 12

8 or more	rosebuds	8 or more
3¼ cups	Champagne, at room temperature	800 ml.
2 tbsp.	unflavored powdered gelatin	30 ml.
½ cup	water	125 ml.
½ cup	sugar	125 ml.
3 to 4 cups	seedless white grapes	¾ to 1 liter
	mint leaves	

For easy unmolding, rinse a 2-quart [2-liter] ring mold with cold water, shake out the droplets, and refrigerate the mold until ready to fill it.

Sprinkle the gelatin over the water in a saucepan to soften. Place over low heat and stir until dissolved. Add the sugar and stir until dissolved. Remove from the heat and combine with the Champagne; refrigerate until slightly thickened (like egg white).

Pour about ½ cup [125 ml.] of the gelatin mixture into the mold and arrange four rosebuds in inverted positions so they will be upright when unmolded. Chill until firm. Combine 3 cups [¾ liter] of the grapes and the remaining rosebuds with the remaining gelatin mixture. Pour ½ cup of the grape-and-gelatin mixture into the mold, being careful not to disturb the roses. Let it set and then add the remainder.

This can be unmolded on mint leaves, or mint leaves can be placed around the outside. Fill the center with grapes.

LEONA WOODRING SMITH
THE FORGOTTEN ART OF FLOWER COOKERY

Russian Salad Mold

Salade Moulée à la Russe

This formal presentation is essentially an elegant way of using leftover meats. Not all of the following ingredients need be used; the choice depends on the cook's discretion. In the 19th Century, truffle was added to this kind of mold for the beauty of the décor, but not for the truffle's flavor. The ravigote sauce for this recipe is vinaigrette (recipe, page 167) to which chopped sour gherkins, capers, scallions, chervil and tarragon are added. The piccalilli called for is a kind of pickle relish, originally East Indian, made with chopped vegetables, vinegar, mustard and spices.

To serve 6 to 8

½ cup	diced cooked chicken breast meat	125 ml.
½ cup	diced cooked partridge or grouse breast meat	125 ml.
½ cup	diced cooked ham	125 ml.
½ cup	diced cold roast beef	125 ml.
1	medium-sized fresh truffle, diced (optional)	1
3	salt anchovies, filleted, soaked in water for 30 minutes, drained, patted dry and diced	3
½ cup	diced smoked salmon	125 ml.
	pepper and salt	
	fresh lemon juice	
1 tbsp.	finely chopped fresh chervil	15 ml.
1 tsp.	finely chopped fresh tarragon	5 ml.
1	carrot, trimmed or diced, and parboiled for 3 minutes	1
1 or 2	celeriac, trimmed into balls or dice, and parboiled for 4 to 5 minutes	1 or 2
1	waxy potato, trimmed into balls or dice, and parboiled for 4 to 5 minutes	1
½ cup	asparagus tips, parboiled for 1 minute	125 ml.
½ cup	green beans (about 2 oz. [75 g.]), cut diagonally into ¼-inch [6-mm.] pieces and parboiled for about 1 minute	125 ml.
½ cup	freshly shelled young peas, parboiled for 30 seconds	125 ml.
½	cucumber, peeled, seeded and trimmed into balls or dice	½
30	dried cepes, soaked in water until soft, then rapidly parboiled in heavily salted water and diced	30
1	small cooked beet, peeled and trimmed into balls or dice	1
1 cup	ravigote sauce	¼ liter
1 tbsp.	piccalilli	15 ml.
about 2 cups	aspic jelly (basic meat stock, made with gelatinous cuts; recipe, page 164)	about ½ liter
4	eggs, hard-boiled	4
	caviar	

Season the chicken, partridge, ham, beef, truffle, anchovy fillets and smoked salmon with pepper, salt and lemon juice, then sprinkle with the finely chopped chervil and tarragon. Meanwhile, prepare the vegetables; season them with pepper, salt, a little ravigote sauce and piccalilli. Drain the meats in a strainer and mix with the vegetables. Add a little melted aspic jelly and correct the seasoning. Set a 2-quart [2-liter] dome mold over crushed ice and coat the inside surfaces with aspic; decorate with the vegetables, sticking them in place with the aspic, and chill until set. Fill the mold with the rest of the salad, adding more aspic to cover the surface, and chill over crushed ice for two hours or place in the refrigerator for three to four hours or overnight.

Turn the mold out onto a round serving plate. Decorate the plate with the eggs, halved lengthwise and their yolks replaced by caviar, and fill the spaces between the eggs with chopped aspic jelly.

JOSEPH FAVRE
DICTIONNAIRE UNIVERSEL DE CUISINE PRATIQUE

Poached Salmon in Aspic

Other large fish such as bass or red snapper may be prepared in the same manner.

	To serve 10 to 12	
1	whole salmon (about 6 lb. [3 kg.])	1
2½ quarts	water	2½ liters
	lemons	
	several fresh dill stalks	
	several parsley sprigs	
	several celery tops	
1	carrot	1
1	onion, stuck with a whole clove	1
1	bay leaf	1
¼ cup	salt	50 ml.
3 cups	dry white wine	¾ liter
3 tbsp.	unflavored powdered gelatin	45 ml.
1	egg white and crushed shell	1
1	cucumber, peeled and sliced (optional)	1
	mayonnaise *(recipe, page 166)*, made with fresh dill or grated horseradish	

Wash the salmon, rub it inside with lemon and keep it refrigerated. For the poaching broth combine the water, dill, parsley, celery, carrot, onion, bay leaf and salt in a large pot and simmer for one to two hours. Strain the liquid. This court bouillon can be prepared the day before.

Line a roasting pan with a double thickness of cheesecloth. Allow generous flaps of cloth to overhang at both ends.

Place the salmon on top of the cloth. Pour the white wine over it, then fill up the pan with enough of the strained poaching broth to cover the fish completely.

Place the pan over two burners, bring it to the boiling point, then immediately turn down the heat to a simmer. Cover. Watch carefully so that the cooking liquid does not boil, but stays at a simmer. Simmer for 45 minutes at the most. To test whether the salmon is done, scrape off a small piece of the skin and lift the flesh with a fork. The flesh should flake easily and look opaque.

Use potholders to grasp the ends of the cheesecloth. Gently lift the fish from the pan to a serving platter. Wipe off any remaining liquid with paper towels. While the salmon is still on the cheesecloth, remove loose bits of the peeled-off skin with paper towels. Turn the platter so that the belly side of the fish is nearest you. Pulling the fish toward you, lift the belly side and turn the fish over, using the heavier back side as a pivot. Scrape off the skin from the second side; wipe the platter clean; discard the cheesecloth. Chill the salmon.

Pour 5 cups [1¼ liters] of the poaching liquid into a saucepan to cool. Sprinkle the liquid with the gelatin. Beat the egg white and add it along with the shell. Slowly bring the liquid to the boiling point, stirring often. Remove the pan from the heat and let the liquid aspic settle. Strain it through a double thickness of kitchen toweling. Let it cool and chill, but do not allow the aspic to jell. When it begins to thicken, coat the chilled fish all over with the aspic. Repeat until a good, shiny coat has been built up. Chill.

The classic decoration is peeled cucumber slices arranged to resemble fish scales. Dip the slices in the aspic and arrange them over and around the fish while you are coating it. If the cucumbers slide off, secure them with toothpicks; remove the toothpicks after the aspic has set. Serve with dill or horseradish mayonnaise.

IRMA RHODE
COOL ENTERTAINING

Molded Avocado Cream

To serve 6

2	large avocados, peeled, pitted and mashed	2
1 tbsp.	unflavored powdered gelatin	15 ml.
¼ cup	cold water	50 ml.
1 cup	unflavored yogurt	¼ liter
1	large tomato, peeled, seeded and finely chopped	1
¼ cup	finely chopped, mild white onion	50 ml.
1	very small garlic clove, crushed to a smooth purée	1
2 tsp.	olive oil	10 ml.
2 tbsp.	strained fresh lemon or lime juice	30 ml.
1 tsp.	chili powder	5 ml.
	salt	
1 lb.	shrimp, cooked in boiling water for 3 to 5 minutes, shelled and deveined	½ kg.
	salad greens	
	cherry tomatoes	
	pitted ripe olives	
	lime or lemon slices	

In a saucepan, soften the gelatin in the water. Stir over low heat until the gelatin is dissolved. Remove from the heat. Add the yogurt, avocados, tomato, onion, garlic, oil, lemon or lime juice, chili powder and salt. Mix thoroughly. Taste and adjust the seasoning. Turn the mixture into a rinsed and chilled 3½-cup [875-ml.] ring mold. Cover with aluminum foil and chill for at least four hours, or until set.

To unmold, have ready a chilled round platter large enough to allow for the garnish. Run the pointed tip of a knife around the edges of the mold to release it. Dip the mold up to the rim into a basin of hot water for just a few seconds. Place the platter upside down over the mold. Hold the platter and mold together and invert. Shake gently to release the avocado cream. If it does not release, repeat the process. Lift off the mold, then refrigerate the avocado cream.

Shortly before serving, fill the center of the ring with the shrimp. Garnish the outside of the ring with the salad greens, cherry tomatoes, olives and lime or lemon slices.

SONIA UVEZIAN
THE BOOK OF YOGURT

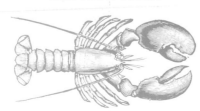

Lobster Medallions in Aspic

To serve 4

1	large live spiny or rock lobster, or 2 large lobster tails	1
1½ quarts	basic court bouillon, made with white wine *(recipe, page 165)*	1½ liters
4 to 6	large pitted ripe olives	4 to 6
1	pimiento	1
2 cups	shredded lettuce	½ liter
	fresh parsley, dill, mint or coriander sprigs	
	hard-boiled eggs or cherry tomatoes	
Fish aspic		
3 cups	reduced court bouillon, made by boiling down the lobster cooking liquid	¾ liter
1 cup	tomato juice	¼ liter
2 tbsp.	unflavored powdered gelatin	30 ml.
2	egg whites	2
1 tsp.	onion juice	5 ml.
1	bay leaf, broken	1
	salt and freshly ground black pepper	
2 tbsp.	Cognac	30 ml.

Boil the whole lobster or lobster tails in the court bouillon. Remove the tail meat in one piece by cutting along the outer edges of the shell and running the knife under the meat to loosen it from the shell. Slice the tail meat into circles, or medallions, about ¼ inch [6 mm.] thick. Refrigerate.

To make the aspic, combine the reduced court bouillon, tomato juice and gelatin in a saucepan. Stir until the gelatin softens, then add the egg whites, onion juice, bay leaf, salt and pepper. Cook slowly, stirring, until the mixture comes to a boil. Remove from the heat and strain through a colander lined with dampened cheesecloth. Stir in the Cognac and refrigerate until the aspic is thick enough to coat a spoon, but still liquid. If the aspic begins to harden while you are using it, melt it over a low heat, then cool it until slightly thickened again.

Set the medallions on a wire rack and coat them with the still-liquid aspic. Chill. When the aspic is set, remove the medallions from the refrigerator and top them with decoratively cut slices of olives or pimiento, which have been dipped in aspic and chilled. Coat the medallions with more aspic and chill them until ready to serve.

Place a bed of shredded lettuce down the center of a large well-chilled platter and top with an overlapping row of medallions. Chop the remaining aspic on a wooden board and arrange it in a ring around the lettuce. Edge the platter with sprigs of fresh herbs, stuffed or garnished hard-boiled eggs, or cherry tomatoes. Serve with mayonnaise.

JANE CHEKENIAN AND MONICA MEYER
SHELLFISH COOKERY

Molded Cottage Cheese and Apple Salad

To serve 6 to 8

1 cup	cottage cheese, sieved	¼ liter
1½ cups	diced unpeeled apples	375 ml.
2 tbsp.	unflavored powdered gelatin	30 ml.
½ cup	cold water	125 ml.
½ tsp.	salt	2 ml.
⅛ tsp.	white pepper	½ ml.
½ cup	milk	125 ml.
⅓ cup	mayonnaise *(recipe, page 166)*	75 ml.
1 tsp.	grated lemon peel	5 ml.
1½ cups	hot water	375 ml.
⅓ cup	fresh lemon juice	75 ml.
⅔ cup	sugar	150 ml.
	diced unpeeled apples and unpeeled apple slices	

Soften 1 tablespoon [15 ml.] of the gelatin in ¼ cup [50 ml.] of the cold water. Dissolve it in the top of a double boiler over hot water. Combine the dissolved gelatin with the cottage cheese, salt, white pepper, milk, mayonnaise and grated lemon peel. Mix well. Turn into a 5-cup [1¼-liter] ring mold that has been rinsed in cold water. Chill the mixture until it is firm—about two hours.

In the meantime, soften the remaining tablespoon of gelatin in the remaining ¼ cup [50 ml.] of cold water. Add the hot water, lemon juice and sugar and stir until dissolved. Chill until the mixture is about as thick as unbeaten egg whites. Fold in 1½ cups [375 ml.] of diced apples. Pour the apple mixture into the mold over the cottage cheese layer. Chill for at least two hours, or until ready to serve.

Unmold the salad and fill the ring's center with extra diced apples and arrange apple slices around the outside.

JEAN H. SHEPARD
THE FRESH FRUITS AND VEGETABLES COOKBOOK

Dressings

Other recipes for dressings appear in Standard Preparations, pages 164-167.

Almond Dressing

The author recommends this dressing for fruit salad.

To make 1 ½ cups [375 ml.] dressing

½ cup	ground blanched almonds	125 ml.
1 to 2 tbsp.	sherry	15 to 30 ml.
½ cup	heavy cream, whipped	125 ml.

Mix the almonds and sherry into a paste. Carefully fold in the whipped cream.

BERYL M. MARTON
THE COMPLETE BOOK OF SALADS

Farm Folk Salad Dressing

This recipe produces a tangy dressing that keeps well in a tightly covered jar.

To make about 2 cups [½ liter] dressing

3 tbsp.	sugar	45 ml.
3 tbsp.	flour	45 ml.
1 tsp.	salt	5 ml.
1 tsp.	dry mustard	5 ml.
½ tsp.	black pepper	2 ml.
2 cups	vinegar, boiled for 5 minutes	½ liter
3 tbsp.	butter	45 ml.
1	egg, beaten	1
½ cup	cream	125 ml.

Mix together the sugar, flour, salt, dry mustard and black pepper. Stirring constantly, add the mixture to the boiling vinegar, then add the butter and cook over medium heat, still stirring constantly, until smooth—about five minutes.

Now add the well-beaten egg and the cream and cook, stirring, for two minutes longer.

MARIAN HARRIS NEIL (EDITOR)
FAVORITE RECIPES COOK BOOK

Turkish Salad Dressing

This sauce is very good with salads of white beans and chickpeas. Sprinkle the salad with fresh herbs before serving.

To make about 2 cups [½ liter] dressing

1 cup	walnuts (about 3 oz. [100 g.])	¼ liter
1	garlic clove	1
¼ cup	dry bread crumbs	50 ml.
1 cup	chicken or meat stock *(recipe, page 164),* or milk	¼ liter
	salt	
	fresh lemon juice	
	cayenne pepper	
	chopped fresh parsley or mint	

Pound the walnuts and garlic to a paste; stir in the bread crumbs, then the stock or milk, and season with salt, lemon juice and cayenne pepper. The dressing should be about the consistency of cream.

ELIZABETH DAVID
A BOOK OF MEDITERRANEAN FOOD

Cucumber Sauce

The author recommends this dressing for fish or egg salads.

To make 2 cups [½ liter] dressing

1	small cucumber, peeled, halved, seeded, finely chopped and drained in a strainer	1
½ cup	heavy cream	125 ml.
2 tbsp.	cider vinegar	30 ml.
¼ tsp.	salt	1 ml.
¹⁄₁₆ tsp.	white pepper	¼ ml.
½ tsp.	paprika	2 ml.

Beat the cream until thick but not stiff. Gradually beat in the vinegar until the cream stands in soft peaks. Fold in the drained cucumber, salt, pepper and paprika.

JEAN H. SHEPARD
THE FRESH FRUITS AND VEGETABLES COOKBOOK

Boiled Dressing

To make 2 cups [½ liter] dressing

3	eggs, the yolks beaten lightly and the whites beaten stiff	3
1 tsp.	dry mustard	5 ml.
2 tsp.	salt	10 ml.
¼ tsp.	cayenne pepper	1 ml.
2 tbsp.	sugar	30 ml.
2 tbsp.	melted butter or oil	30 ml.
1 cup	cream or milk	¼ liter
½ cup	vinegar, heated	125 ml.

Combine all of the ingredients in the top of a double boiler and cook, stirring, until the mixture thickens like soft custard. This dressing will keep in a cool place for two weeks, and is an excellent accompaniment for lettuce, celery, asparagus, string beans and cauliflower.

MRS. MARY J. LINCOLN
MRS. LINCOLN'S BOSTON COOK BOOK

Low-Fat Lemon-Yogurt Sauce

The author recommends this dressing for use with both cold meat and fish salads.

This recipe came from the brilliant chef Jacques Maniere at his Le Pactole in Paris, in answer to my challenge whether he could prepare satisfactory cold savory sauces entirely without oil. I have translated and adapted it to our American ingredients.

To make about ½ cup [125 ml.] sauce

1 to 2 tbsp.	fresh lemon juice	15 to 30 ml.
½ cup	plain low-fat yogurt	125 ml.
1 or 2	hard-boiled egg yolks	1 or 2
3	shallots	3
2 tbsp.	chopped fresh parsley	30 ml.
	coarse salt	
	freshly ground black pepper	

In a food processor or electric blender, combine 1 tablespoon [15 ml.] of the lemon juice, one hard-boiled egg yolk, the yogurt, shallots and parsley with salt and pepper to taste. Run the machine until the ingredients are thoroughly mixed and smooth, but not a pasty mush—usually in no more than four seconds. This sauce should have body, but should be just thin enough to pour. Obviously, more hard-boiled egg yolk would thicken it; more lemon juice, or a dash of dry white wine, would thin it. It keeps perfectly for several days refrigerated in a tightly lidded jar. Taste it occasionally and adjust, as needed, any or all of the aromatic ingredients.

ROY ANDRIES DE GROOT
REVOLUTIONIZING FRENCH COOKING

French Dressing with Herbs

Sauce Vinaigrette Minceur

To serve 4

1 tbsp.	olive oil	15 ml.
⅓ cup	chicken stock *(recipe, page 164)*	75 ml.
1	garlic clove	1
½ tsp.	finely chopped fresh tarragon	2 ml.
½ tsp.	finely chopped fresh chervil or parsley	2 ml.
2	leaves fresh basil, finely chopped	2
1 tbsp.	sherry vinegar	15 ml.
1 tbsp.	fresh lemon juice	15 ml.
	salt and pepper	

Combine the olive oil, stock, garlic and herbs in a small bowl, and let them marinate together for two hours. Add the vinegar, lemon juice, and salt and pepper, and mix well with a fork. Discard the garlic.

MICHEL GUÉRARD
MICHEL GUÉRARD'S CUISINE MINCEUR

Olive, Caper and Anchovy Purée

Tapenade

This purée is delicious spread on slices of meat (pages 50 and 52-53), and makes an excellent accompaniment to crudités (raw vegetables). It also can be used as a stuffing for tomatoes (page 88) or hard-boiled eggs (page 75). If you like, the purée can be prepared in a food processor.

To make about 1 cup [¼ liter] purée

1 cup	small ripe oil-packed Mediterranean olives, pitted and roughly chopped (about 5 oz. [150 g.])	¼ liter
4	salt anchovies, filleted, soaked in water for 30 minutes, drained and patted dry	4
2 tbsp.	capers, rinsed and drained	30 ml.
1 tbsp.	fresh lemon juice	15 ml.
½ tsp.	Dijon mustard	2 ml.
	freshly ground black pepper	
2 tbsp.	Cognac	30 ml.
¼ to ½ cup	fruity olive oil	50 to 125 ml.

In an electric blender, blend the olives, anchovy fillets, capers, lemon juice, mustard, pepper to taste, and the Co-

gnac until the mixture is pasty. Still blending, pour in just enough olive oil in a steady stream to obtain a smooth, thick sauce. Scoop into a pretty pottery bowl; chill well and serve.

PAULA WOLFERT
MEDITERRANEAN COOKING

Sweet Basil Sauce, Genoa-Style

Pesto

The authors suggest that Tuscan pecorino cheese, if obtainable, yields a finer pesto than the more readily available Romano pecorino. Because the Tuscan variety is less salty, the amount of pecorino used should be increased to ¾ ounce [37 g.] or 3 tablespoons [45 ml.].

To serve 6 or 7

3 cups	fresh basil leaves	¾ liter
1	garlic clove	1
3 tbsp.	pine nuts	45 ml.
2 oz.	Parmesan cheese (about ½ cup [125 ml.] grated)	75 g.
½ oz.	pecorino cheese (about 2 tbsp. [30 ml.] grated)	25 g.
¾ cup	olive oil	175 ml.
	salt	

To make the pesto by hand, first chop the basil leaves and place them in a mortar (earthenware is preferred to wooden). Chop the garlic and add it, then add the pine nuts. Work the mixture with a pestle until you have obtained a coarse paste. Grate the two cheeses.

Place the basil mixture in a bowl, and use the pestle to work in some of the cheeses. When the mixture becomes too solid to handle, start adding the oil a little at a time. Continue adding cheese, alternating it with the oil. Taste, and add salt if needed. Keep mixing until all of the oil has been used.

If you have a food processor, place the basil leaves, garlic and pine nuts in the processor. Using the sharp blade, run the motor for three seconds. Put the mixture into a mixing bowl and set aside.

Place the chunks of Parmesan and pecorino in the processor bowl and run the motor for five seconds, according to the age of the cheese. If the Parmesan is very hard, you might need a couple of seconds longer. Add the basil mixture to the cheeses. Keeping the processor running, pour the oil into the bowl in a steady thin stream as you would for a mayonnaise. Pesto, however, should be thicker than a mayonnaise.

HEDY GIUSTI-LANHAM AND ANDREA DODI
THE CUISINE OF VENICE

Mint Dressing

To make about 1 ¼ cups [300 ml.] dressing

1 tbsp.	coarsely chopped fresh mint	15 ml.
1 cup	plain yogurt	¼ liter
3 tbsp.	fresh lemon juice	45 ml.
	salt, preferably sea salt	
1	small garlic clove, finely chopped or put through a press (optional)	1

Combine all of the ingredients in a blender and blend until smooth. Or chop the mint into fine bits and stir it into the other ingredients.

MARTHA ROSE SHULMAN
THE VEGETARIAN FEAST

Standard Preparations

Fish Stock

If this stock—or fumet—is to be used as a jelly, choose gelatinous fish such as turbot, halibut or monkfish. You may substitute less gelatinous fish, but 3 tablespoons [45 ml.] of powdered gelatin, softened in a little water, should be dissolved in the stock after it has been strained. The prepared stock will keep for several days in the refrigerator.

To make about 2 quarts [2 liters] stock

2 to 2½ lb.	fish heads, carcasses and trimmings, rinsed and broken into pieces	1 kg.
1	onion, sliced	1
1	carrot, sliced	1
1	celery rib, sliced	1
2 or 3	garlic cloves, crushed	2 or 3
1 or 2	fresh fennel stalks, or ½ tsp. [2 ml.] dry fennel seeds	1 or 2
1	bouquet garni	1
1½ quarts	water	1½ liters
	salt	
2 cups	dry white wine	½ liter

Place the fish, vegetables and herbs in a large pan. Add the water and season lightly with salt. Bring to a boil slowly, over low heat. With a large, shallow spoon, skim off the scum that rises to the surface as the liquid reaches a simmer. Keep skimming until no more scum rises, then cover the pan and simmer the mixture very gently for 15 minutes. Add the wine and continue to simmer for a further 15 minutes.

Strain the stock into a bowl through a colander lined with dampened muslin or a double thickness of dampened cheesecloth. Cool the stock to room temperature, then cover with foil or plastic wrap and refrigerate overnight, or until the stock has set to a jelly. With a spoon, carefully remove any fat from the surface of the jellied stock.

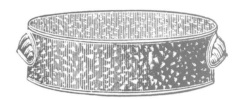

Basic Meat Stock

This stock may be made, according to your taste and recipe needs, from beef, veal, pork or chicken—or a combination of these meats. For the beef, use such cuts as shank, short ribs, chuck and oxtail; for the veal, use neck, shank and rib tips; for the pork, use hocks, Boston shoulder and back ribs; for the chicken, use backs, necks, wings and carcasses. Adding gelatinous elements such as pig's feet or pork rind will make the finished stock set to a clear, firm jelly that can serve as an aspic if prepared carefully enough.

To make about 2 quarts [2 liters] stock

4 to 5 lb.	meat, bones and trimmings of beef, veal, pork or chicken	2 to 2½ kg.
1 lb.	pig's, calf's or chicken feet, pig's ears or fresh pork rind (optional)	½ kg.
3 to 4 quarts	water	3 to 4 liters
4	carrots	4
2	large onions, 1 stuck with 2 or 3 whole cloves	2
1	celery rib	1
1	leek, split and washed	1
1	large bouquet garni	1

Put the pieces of bone on a rack in the bottom of a heavy stockpot, and place the meat and trimmings on top of them. Add cold water to cover by 2 inches [5 cm.]. Bring to a boil over low heat, starting to skim before the liquid reaches the boil. Keep skimming, occasionally adding a glass of cold water, until no scum rises. Do not stir, lest you cloud the stock.

Add the vegetables and bouquet garni to the pot, pushing them down into the liquid so that everything is submerged. Continue skimming until a boil is reached again. Reduce the heat to very low, partially cover the pan, and cook at a bare simmer for two hours if you are using only chicken trimmings, otherwise for five hours—skimming off the surface fat three or four times during the cooking period.

Strain the stock by pouring the contents of the pot through a colander into a large bowl or clean pot. Discard the bones and meat trimmings, vegetables and bouquet garni. Cool the strained stock and skim the last traces of fat from the surface. If there is any residue at the bottom of the container after the stock cools, decant the clear liquid carefully and discard the sediment.

Refrigerate the stock if you do not plan to use it immediately; it will keep safely for three to four days. To preserve the stock longer, refrigerate it for only 12 hours—or until the last bits of fat solidify on the top—then scrape off the fat and warm the stock enough so that it may be poured into four or five pint-sized freezer containers. Be sure to leave room in the containers to allow for expansion, and cover the containers tightly. The freezer stock will keep for six months while you draw on the supply as necessary.

───────────◆───────────

Basic Court Bouillon

This court bouillon is a general-purpose poaching liquid. The amount of wine may be varied according to taste. In place of the wine, you can use ¾ cup [175 ml.] of red or white wine vinegar, but add it to the pan with the vegetables, herbs and water. If desired, an unpeeled garlic clove may also be included.

To make about 2 quarts [2 liters] court bouillon

1	large onion, sliced	1
1	large carrot, sliced	1
1	large leek, sliced	1
1	celery rib, diced	1
12	sprigs parsley	12
2	sprigs thyme	2
2	sprigs dill (optional)	2
1	bay leaf	1
6 cups	water	1½ liters
	salt	
2 cups	dry white or red wine	½ liter
5 or 6	peppercorns	5 or 6

Put the vegetables, herbs and water into a large pan, and season with a pinch of salt. Bring to a boil, then reduce the heat, cover and simmer for approximately 15 minutes. Pour in the wine and simmer for an additional 15 minutes, adding the peppercorns during the last few minutes of cooking. Strain the court bouillon through a sieve into a bowl or a clean pan before using it.

Aromatic Court Bouillon

This wine court bouillon is suitable for poaching fish that will be served with their cooking liquid *(pages 64-65)*. If the court bouillon is to be used for vegetables *à la grecque (pages 46-47)*, substitute water for half of the wine, add about ½ cup [125 ml.] of olive oil and the juice of a lemon, and bring the mixture to a boil before adding vegetables and seasonings.

To make about 1 ½ quarts [1 ½ liters] court bouillon

1½ quarts	dry white wine	1½ liters
2	carrots, sliced	2
2	onions, sliced	2
2	garlic cloves, crushed	2
1 or 2	bay leaves	1 or 2
1	sprig fresh coriander or ½ tsp. [2 ml.] coriander seeds	1
1	sprig thyme	1
1 or 2	fresh fennel stalks, or 1 tsp. [5 ml.] dry fennel seeds	1 or 2
	salt	
5 or 6	peppercorns	5 or 6

Bring the wine to a boil in a stainless-steel or enameled saucepan. Add all of the remaining ingredients except the peppercorns. Reduce the heat, cover, and simmer for about 15 minutes, adding the peppercorns for the last few minutes of cooking. Strain before using.

───────────◆───────────

Lemon and Cream Dressing

For fruit or cucumber salads, six to eight fresh mint leaves may be crushed in the lemon juice, left to macerate for 15 to 20 minutes, and removed before the lemon juice and cream are combined. For fish or cucumber salads, dill may be added to the lemon juice. For chicken or ham salads, 1 or 2 teaspoons [5 or 10 ml.] of Dijon mustard may be stirred into the seasoned lemon juice before adding the cream.

To make about 1 ½ cups [375 ml.] dressing

¼ cup	strained fresh lemon juice	50 ml.
1 cup	heavy cream, chilled	¼ liter
1 tsp.	salt	5 ml.
¼ tsp.	white pepper	1 ml.

Put the salt and pepper into a chilled bowl. Add the lemon juice and stir until the salt dissolves. Whisking constantly, gradually pour in the cream. Continue whisking until the dressing is thick enough to form a ribbon when the whisk is lifted from the bowl. Taste for seasoning, and use at once.

Tart Cream Dressing

For this dressing, based on an American version of France's *crème fraîche,* use the pasteurized—but not ultrapasteurized—heavy cream obtainable at health-food stores and specialty dairy markets.

To make about 2 cups [½ liter] dressing		
2 cups	heavy cream	½ liter
1 tbsp.	cultured buttermilk	15 ml.
¼ cup	strained fresh lime or lemon juice	50 ml.
	salt and pepper	

In a small, heavy enameled saucepan, stir the cream and buttermilk together until well blended. Set the pan over low heat and insert a meat-and-yeast thermometer into the cream mixture. Stirring gently but constantly, warm the mixture until the thermometer registers 85° F. [30° C.].

Immediately remove the pan from the heat and pour the cream mixture into a 1-quart [1-liter] jar—preferably a Mason jar that has been scalded by filling it with boiling water, then pouring out the water. Cover the jar loosely with foil or wax paper. Set the cream mixture aside at a room temperature of 60° F. to 85° F. [15° C. to 30° C.] for eight to 24 hours, or until it reaches the consistency of lightly beaten cream. The heavy cream has now become a *crème fraîche.*

Cover the jar tightly and refrigerate the cream until you are ready to use it. It will keep refrigerated for about a week. Before serving, whisk in the lime or lemon juice, and season to taste with salt and pepper.

Blender or Processor Mayonnaise

To form an emulsion with the oil and the egg, both should be at room temperature. The basic mayonnaise may be turned into a green mayonnaise or flavored with garlic, mustard or herbs as described for Handmade Mayonnaise *(right).*

To make about 1 ½ cups [375 ml.] mayonnaise		
1	egg	1
2 tsp.	vinegar or fresh lemon juice	10 ml.
	salt and white pepper	
1 to 1½ cups	oil	250 to 375 ml.

Combine the egg, vinegar or lemon juice, and salt and pepper in the jar of an electric blender or the bowl of a food processor equipped with a steel blade. Cover and blend for a few seconds to mix the ingredients thoroughly. Without stopping the machine, pour in the oil in a slow stream through the hole in the cover of the blender or through the tube of the processor. Add 1 cup [¼ liter] of oil for a soft mayonnaise, but up to 1½ cups [375 ml.] for a firm one.

Turn off the machine and use a rubber spatula to transfer the mayonnaise to a bowl. Taste and add more seasonings, vinegar or lemon juice if desired.

Handmade Mayonnaise

To prevent curdling, the egg yolks, oil, and vinegar or lemon juice should be at room temperature and the oil should be added very gradually at first. The ratio of egg yolks to oil can be varied according to taste. The prepared mayonnaise will keep for several days in a covered container in the refrigerator. Stir it well before use.

To make about 1 ½ cups [375 ml.] mayonnaise		
2	egg yolks	2
	salt and white pepper	
2 tsp.	vinegar or fresh lemon juice	10 ml.
1 to 1 ½ cups	olive oil	250 to 375 ml.

Put the egg yolks in a warmed dry bowl. Season with a little salt and pepper and whisk for about a minute, or until the yolks become slightly paler in color. Add the vinegar or lemon juice and whisk until thoroughly mixed.

Whisking constantly, add the oil, drop by drop to begin with. When the sauce starts to thicken, pour the remaining oil in a thin, steady stream, whisking rhythmically. Add only enough oil to give the mayonnaise a firm but pourable consistency. It should just hold its shape when lifted in a spoon. If the mayonnaise is too thick, add 1 to 2 teaspoons [5 to 10 ml.] more vinegar or lemon juice or warm water.

Green mayonnaise. Parboil ¼ pound [125 g.] of spinach leaves for one to two minutes; drain the spinach in a strainer, plunge it into cold water to stop the cooking, and squeeze the spinach dry with your hands. Chop the spinach fine, then purée it through a food mill or in a food processor. Stir the purée into the prepared mayonnaise, along with 1 tablespoon [15 ml.] of fines herbes.

Garlic mayonnaise. In a mortar, pound one or two garlic cloves to a paste with coarse salt. Mix thoroughly with the egg yolks and vinegar or lemon juice before adding the oil.

Mustard mayonnaise. Add 1 teaspoon [5 ml.] of Dijon mustard or ¼ teaspoon [1 ml.] of dry mustard to the egg yolks, along with the vinegar or lemon juice.

Herb mayonnaise. Stir about 1 teaspoon [5 ml.] each of finely chopped fresh chives, chervil, tarragon, and parsley into the prepared mayonnaise.

Tartar Sauce

Add 1 tablespoon [15 ml.] each (or more according to taste) of finely chopped sour gherkins, capers and fines herbes to 1½ cups [375 ml.] of prepared mayonnaise.

Vinaigrette

The proportion of vinegar to oil may be varied according to the acidity of the vinegar used and the tartness of the food to be dressed; but one part of vinegar to four or five parts of oil is a good mean ratio. Despite its name, this dressing may be made, if desired, with lemon juice instead of vinegar.

To make about ½ cup [125 ml.] vinaigrette

1 tsp.	salt	5 ml.
¼ tsp.	freshly ground pepper	1 ml.
2 tbsp.	wine vinegar	30 ml.
½ cup	oil	125 ml.

Put the salt and pepper into a small bowl. Add the vinegar, and stir until the salt dissolves. Finally, stir in the oil.

Garlic vinaigrette. In a mortar or small bowl, pound half of a garlic clove to a purée with the salt and pepper before adding the vinegar.

Mustard vinaigrette. Mix about 1 teaspoon [5 ml.] of Dijon mustard or ¼ teaspoon [1 ml.] dry mustard with the salt and pepper. Add the vinegar and stir until the mustard dissolves before adding the oil.

Tomato vinaigrette. Add 2 tablespoons [30 ml.] of cooked, reduced puréed tomato to the prepared vinaigrette.

Green vinaigrette. After adding the vinegar, stir in 2 tablespoons of puréed spinach, made by parboiling ¼ pound [125 g.] for two minutes, draining it, squeezing it dry, chopping it and then puréeing it through a food mill or in a processor. Then stir in 1 tablespoon [15 ml.] of fines herbes and finely chopped fresh cress. Finally, add the oil.

Vinaigrette with egg. Before adding the oil, stir in the yolk of a soft-boiled egg. The egg white may be chopped and added to the prepared vinaigrette.

Other variations. Any prepared vinaigrette may be flavored with chopped fresh herbs (such as parsley, fines herbes, basil, mint, marjoram or hyssop), capers, chopped shallots or finely sliced sour gherkins. Alternatively, the juices from roasted peppers or, if the dressing is to be used for a meat salad, 1 to 2 tablespoons [15 to 30 ml.] of degreased roasting juices may be stirred into the vinegar mixture.

Flavored Vinegar

To make about 1 quart [1 liter] vinegar

2 handfuls	fresh tarragon, basil, mint, dill or rosemary sprigs	2 handfuls
1 quart	white wine vinegar or rice vinegar	1 liter

Remove any wilted leaves from the sprigs. Then wash the sprigs briefly in a bowl of cold water and roll them gently in a cloth towel to dry them thoroughly. Pack the sprigs into a 1-quart [1-liter] jar—preferably a Mason jar that has been scalded by filling it with boiling water, then pouring out the water. In an enameled or stainless-steel saucepan, heat the vinegar to the simmering point (about 130° F. [60° C.] on a meat-and-yeast thermometer). Immediately pour the vinegar over the sprigs, filling the jar to the rim. Cover the jar tightly and set the vinegar mixture aside at room temperature to develop its flavor for 10 to 20 days.

Strain the vinegar into a clean jar through a sieve lined with a double thickness of dampened cheesecloth. Discard the herb sprigs.

Garlic vinegar. Substitute about 12 peeled garlic cloves for the herb sprigs.

Berry vinegar. Substitute 2 cups [½ liter] fresh raspberries, blueberries or hulled strawberries for the herb sprigs. You may also substitute red wine vinegar for the white wine vinegar or rice vinegar.

Croutons

To prepare croutons as a garnish for delicate-tasting salads, you can substitute clarified butter for the combination of butter and oil specified in this recipe. If the croutons are to accompany strong-flavored salads, you may prefer to sauté the bread cubes in olive oil. If you want to toast the croutons instead of sautéing them, spread the cubes on an ungreased baking sheet and toast them for two to three minutes on each side in a preheated 400° F. [200° C.] oven.

To make about 1 cup [¼ liter] croutons

2	bread slices, ½ inch [1 cm.] thick, cut from a day-old, firm-textured white loaf	2
4 tbsp.	butter	60 ml.
¼ to ½ cup	oil	50 to 125 ml.

Remove the crusts from the bread and cut the slices into cubes. Combine the butter and ¼ cup [50 ml.] of the oil in a large skillet. Melt the butter over medium heat and, as soon as the butter-and-oil mixture is hot, add the bread cubes and increase the heat to high. Turn the cubes frequently with a broad metal spatula so that they brown evenly on all sides, and add more oil as necessary to keep the cubes from burning. Before serving, drain the croutons on paper towels.

Recipe Index

All recipes in the index that follows are listed by their English titles except in cases where a food of foreign origin, such as aioli, is universally recognized by its source name. Entries also are organized by the major ingredients specified in the recipe titles. Foreign recipes are listed by country or region of origin. Recipe credits appear on pages 174-176.

General Index/ Glossary

Included in this index to the cooking demonstrations are definitions, in italics, of special culinary terms not explained elsewhere in this volume. The Recipe Index begins on page 168.

Recipe Credits

The sources for the recipes in this volume are shown below. Page references in parentheses indicate where the recipes appear in the anthology.

Adams, Charlotte, *The Four Seasons Cookbook.* Copyright 1971 in all countries of the International Copyright Union by The Ridge Press, Inc. Reprinted by permission of The Ridge Press, Inc. and Crown Publishers, Inc.(107, 122).

Adamson, Helen Lyon, *Grandmother in the Kitchen.* © 1965 by Helen Lyon Adamson. Used by permission of Crown Publishers, Inc.(121).

Alston, Elizabeth, *The Best of Natural Eating Around the World.* Copyright © 1973 by Elizabeth Alston. Reprinted by permission of the David McKay Company, Inc.(106, 108).

Androuet, Pierre, *La Cuisine au Fromage.* Published by Éditions Stock, Paris, 1978. Translated by permission of Éditions Stock(93, 104).

The Art of Cookery, Made Plain and Easy. By a Lady. Published by James Donaldson, Edinburgh 1747(135).

Artusi, Pellegrino, *La Scienza in Cucina e l'Arte di Mangiar Bene.* Copyright © 1970 Giulio Einaudi Editore S.p.A., Torino. Published by Giulio Einaudi Editore S.p.A., Torino(142).

Aureden, Lilo, *Das Schmeckt so Gut.* © 1965 by Lichtenberg Verlag, München. Published by Lichtenberg Verlag, Munich, 1973. Translated by permission of Kindler Verlag, GmbH, Munich(134).

Beard, James, *James Beard's American Cookery.* Copyright © 1972 by James A. Beard. Reprinted by permission of Little, Brown and Company(95).

Beauvilliers, A., *L'Art du Cuisinier.* First Edition, published in 1814(109).

Berjane, J., *French Dishes for English Tables.* Copyright Frederick Warne & Co., Ltd., London, 1931. Published by Frederick Warne & Co., Ltd., London. By permission of Frederick Warne & Co., Ltd., London(118, 122, 152).

Berto, Hazel, *Cooking with Honey.* Copyright © 1972 by Hazel Berto. Used by permission of Crown Publishers, Inc.(105).

Bisson, Marie, *La Cuisine Normande.* © Solar, 1978. Published by Solar, Paris. Translated by permission of Solar(138).

Blanch, Lesley, *Around the World in Eighty Dishes.* Copyright © 1955 by Lesley Blanch Gary. Reprinted by permission of Harper and Row, Publishers, Inc.(103).

Bocuse, Paul, *Paul Bocuse's French Cooking.* Copyright © 1977 by Random House, Inc. Published by Pantheon

Books Inc., New York. Reprinted by permission of Pantheon Books, a Division of Random House, Inc.(119).

Boni, Ada, *Italian Regional Cooking.* Copyright © 1969 s.c. by Arnoldo Mondadori. English translation, copyright © 1969 s.c. by Thomas Nelson & Sons Ltd. and E. P. Dutton and Co., Inc. Published by Bonanza Books, a Division of Crown Publishers, Inc., New York. By permission of Arnoldo Mondadori(116, 148).

Bouillard, Paul, *La Cuisine au Coin du Feu.* Copyright 1928 by Albin Michel. Published by Éditions Albin Michel, Paris. Translated by permission of Éditions Albin Michel(141).

Brand, Margery, *Fifty Ways of Cooking Vegetables in India.* Published by Thacker, Spink and Co. (1933) Ltd., Calcutta(109).

Břízová, Joza and Maryna Klimentová, *Tschechische Küche.* Published by Verlag Práce, Prague and Verlag für die Frau, Leipzig. Translated by permission of Práce(90, 113).

Brobeck, Florence, *The Good Salad Book.* Copyright © 1952 by Florence Brobeck. Published by M. Barrows & Company, Inc., New York(127).

Brown, Helen Evans, *Helen Brown's West Coast Cook Book.* Copyright 1952 by Helen Evans Brown. Published by Little, Brown and Company, Boston. By permission of Little, Brown and Company(93).

Burros, Marian, *Pure and Simple.* Copyright © 1978 by Marian Fox Burros. By permission of William Morrow and Company(134).

Cadwallader, Sharon, *Sharon Cadwallader's Complete Cookbook.* Copyright © 1977 by Sharon Cadwallader. Reprinted by permission of San Francisco Book Co., Inc.(117).

California Bicentennial Celebration Committee, *Official California Bicentennial Cookbook.* © Copyright 1968 by the California Bicentennial Celebration Committee. © Copyright 1969 Curtin Productions, Inc., New York City(105).

Caruana Galizia, Anne and Helen, *Recipes from Malta.* Copyright © Anne and Helen Caruana Galizia 1972. Published by Progress Press Co. Ltd., Valetta. By permission of the authors(117).

Chantiles, Vilma Liacouras, *The Food of Greece.* Copyright © 1975 by Vilma Liacouras Chantiles. Published by Atheneum Publishers, New York. By permission of Vilma Liacouras Chantiles(112).

Chekenian, Jane and Monica Meyer, *Shellfish Cookery.* Copyright © 1971 by Jane Chekenian and Monica Meyer. Reprinted with permission of Macmillan Publishing Co., Inc.(160).

Clark, Morton G., *French-American Cooking from New Orleans to Quebec.* Copyright © 1967 by Morton Clark (Funk & Wagnalls). Reprinted by permission of Harper & Row, Publishers, Inc., New York(146).

Cobbett, Anne, *The English Housekeeper.* Published by A. Cobbett, Strand 1851(136).

Coelho, Isidore, *The Chef.* Published by C. Coelho, Bombay 1974(91).

La Cuisine Lyonnaise. Published by Éditions Gutenberg, 1947(94, 131, 134).

Cutler, Carol, *Haute Cuisine for Your Heart's Delight.* Copyright © 1973 by Carol Cutler. Used by permission of Clarkson N. Potter, Inc.(142).

Cutler, Carol, *The Six-Minute Soufflé and Other Culinary Delights.* Copyright © 1976 by Carol Cutler. Used by permission of Clarkson N. Potter, Inc.(130, 151, 156).

Czerny, Zofia, *Polish Cookbook.* Copyright © 1961, 1975 Państwowe Wydawnictwo Ekonomiczne. Published by Państwowe Wydawnictwo Ekonomiczne, Warsaw. By permission of Agenja Autorska, Warsaw, for the author(137).

Dannenbaum, Julie, *Menus for All Occasions.* Copyright © 1974 by Julie Dannenbaum. Published by Saturday Review Press/E. P. Dutton & Co., Inc., New York. By permission of Edward J. Acton, Inc., New York(101).

David, Elizabeth, *A Book of Mediterranean Food.* (Penguin Handbooks, Second revised edition, 1975.) Copyright © Elizabeth David, 1958, 1965. Reprinted by permission of Penguin Books Ltd.(162).

David, Elizabeth, *Summer Cooking.* Copyright © Elizabeth David, 1955, 1965. Published by Penguin Books Ltd., London. By permission of Penguin Books Ltd.(119, 120, 152).

Davidson, Alan, *Mediterranean Seafood.* Copyright © Alan Davidson, 1972. Published by Penguin Books Ltd., London. By permission of Penguin Books Ltd.(139).

Davidson, Alan, *Seafood of South-East Asia.* Copyright © Alan Davidson, 1977. Published by Federal Publications Singapore. By permission of Alan Davidson(147).

De Bonnefons, Nicolas, *Les Délices de la Campagne.* 1655(93).

De Crémonne, Baptiste Platine, *Le Livre de l'Honneste Volupté.* Published in 1539(95, 118).

de Croze, Austin, *Les Plats Régionaux de France.* Published by Éditions Daniel Morcrette, B.P. 26, 95270-Luzarches, France. Translated by permission of Éditions Daniel Morcrette(99, 124).

De Groot, Roy Andries, *Feasts For All Seasons.* Copyright © 1976 by Roy Andries de Groot. Published by McGraw-Hill Book Company, New York. By permission of McGraw-Hill Book Company(140).

De Groot, Roy Andries, *Revolutionizing French Cooking.* Copyright © 1976 by Roy Andries de Groot. Used with permission of McGraw-Hill Book Company(162).

De la Chapelle, Vincent, *The Modern Cook.* London 1733(108).

De Loup, Maximilian, *The American Salad Book.* Copyright by Geo. R. Knapp 1899. Copyright by Double-

...y, Page & Company 1900. Published by Doubleday, ...ge & Company, Garden City, New York, 1926(121).

...e Lune, Pierre, *Le Nouveau Cuisinier*. Paris, ...56(131).

...e Pomiane, Edouard, *Le Carnet D'Anna*. Published ...y Éditions Paul-Martial, Paris, 1938. Copyright © 1967 by ...ditions Calmann-Lévy. Reprinted by permission of Edi- ...ns Calmann-Lévy, Paris(150).

...uff, Gail, *Fresh All the Year*. © Gail Duff 1976. First pub- ...hed by Macmillan London Ltd., 1976. Also published by ...n Books Ltd., 1977. By permission of Macmillan London ...d. and Basingstoke(107, 132).

...ton, Mrs. Mary, *The Cook and Housekeeper's Com- ...ete and Universal Dictionary*. Bungay, 1822(96).

...fendi, Turabi, *Turkish Cookery Book*. Published by ...H. Allen and Co., London, 1884(92, 96).

...vans, Michele, *The Salad Book*. Copyright © 1975 by ...ichele Evans. Reprinted with the permission of Contem- ...orary Books, Inc., Chicago(105, 157).

...amularo, Joe and Louise Imperiale, *The Festive Famularo ...tchen*. Copyright © 1977 by Joe Famularo and ...ouise Imperiale. Published in 1977 by Atheneum Publish- ...s, New York. Reprinted by permission of Atheneum ...ublishers(94).

...avre, Joseph, *Dictionnaire Universel de Cuisine Pra- ...ue*. Published by Laffitte Reprints, Marseilles 1978. Trans- ...ted by permission of Laffitte Reprints(96, 159).

...nn, Molly, *Summer Feasts*. Copyright © 1979 by Molly ...nn. Reprinted by permission of Simon & Schuster, a Divi- ...on of Gulf & Western Corporation(154).

...oods of the World, *The Cooking of Provincial France; ...acific and Southeast Asian Cooking*. © 1968 Time Inc.; ...opyright © 1970 by Time Inc. Published by Time-Life ...ooks, Alexandria(125, 129).

...ilbert, Philéas, *La Cuisine de tous les Mois*. Published ...y Abel Goubaud, Éditeur, Paris 1893(101, 148).

...illiers, *Le Cannameliste Français*. 1768(113).

...in, Margaret and Alfred E. Castle, *Regional Cook- ...g of China*. Copyright 1975 Margaret Gin and Alfred E. ...astle. Published by 101 Productions, San Francisco. By ...ermission of 101 Productions(99, 154).

...iusti-Lanham, Hedy and Andrea Dodi, *The Cui- ...ne of Venice & Surrounding Northern Regions*. © 1978 by ...arron's Educational Series, Inc. Reprinted with permission ...f Barron's Educational Series, Inc., Woodbury, New ...ork(163).

...raves, Eleanor, *Great Dinners from Life*. Copyright © ...969 Time Inc. Published by Time-Life Books, Alexan- ...ria(115, 137, 147).

...he Great Cooks' Guide to Salads. Copyright © ...977 by Morris Propp. Published by Random House, Inc., ...ew York. By permission of Michael Batterberry, Editor-in- ...hief of the *International Review of Food & Wine*(112 — ...ichael Batterberry); by permission of Florence Fabri- ...ant(90 — Florence Fabricant); by permission of Raymond ...Sokolov(103 — Raymond A. Sokolov).

...reen, Karen, *The Great International Noodle Experi- ...nce*. Copyright © 1977 by Karen Green. Reprinted by per- ...ission of Atheneum Publishers(154).

...rigson, Jane, *Jane Grigson's Vegetable Book*. Copy- ...ght © 1968 by Jane Grigson. Published by Atheneum ...ublishers, New York. By permission of Atheneum Publish- ...rs(123, 156).

...uérard, Michel, *Michel Guérard's Cuisine Minceur*. ...ranslated by Narcisse Chamberlain with Fanny Brennan. ...nglish translation Copyright © 1976 by William Morrow ...nd Company, Inc. Originally published in French under ...e title *La Grande Cuisine Minceur*. Copyright © 1976 by ...ditions Robert Laffont, S.A. By permission of William Mor- ...ow and Company(140, 149, 163).

...uinaudeau-Franc, Zette, *Les Secrets des Fermes en ...érigord Noir*. © 1978, Éditions Serg, Paris. Published by ...ditions Serg, Paris. Translated by permission of Madame ...uinaudeau-Franc(120).

...arris, Gertrude, *Pasta International*. Copyright 1978 ...ertrude Harris. Published by 101 Productions, San Fran- ...sco. By permission of 101 Productions(133, 155).

...azelton, Nika, *The Regional Italian Kitchen*. Copyright ...) 1978 by Nika Standen Hazelton. Published by M. Evans

and Company, Inc., New York. Translated by permission of M. Evans and Company, Inc., New York(110).

Heptinstall, William, *Hors d'Oeuvre and Cold Table*. © William Heptinstall 1959. First published in 1959 by Faber and Faber Ltd., London. By permission of Beatrice M. Low-rance(135, 155).

Heyraud, H., *La Cuisine à Nice*. Published by Imprimerie-Librairie-Papeterie, Nice 1922(97, 110).

Hill, Janet McKenzie, *Salads, Sandwiches, and Chafing-Dish Dainties*. Copyright 1899, 1903, 1914 by Ja-net M. Hill. Published by Little, Brown and Company, Bos-ton, 1920(108, 135, 145, 146).

Hodgson, Moira, *Cooking With Fruits and Nuts*. Copy-right © 1973 by Moira Hodgson. Reprinted by permission of the publisher, The Bobbs-Merrill Company, Inc.(106).

Isnard, Léon, *La Cuisine Française et Africaine*. Copy-right 1949 by Éditions Albin Michel. Published by Éditions Albin Michel, Paris. Translated by permission of Éditions Albin Michel(111).

Jolly, Martine, *Réussir Votre Cuisine*. © 1979 Éditions Robert Laffont S.A. Published by Éditions Robert Laffont S.A., Paris. Translated by permission of Éditions Robert Laf-font S.A.(98).

Kahn, Odette, *La Petite et la Grande Cuisine*. © Calmann-Lévy 1977. Published by Éditions Calmann-Lévy, Paris. Translated by permission of Éditions Calmann-Lévy(91).

Kamman, Madeleine, *When French Women Cook*. Copyright © 1976 by Madeleine M. Kamman. Reprinted by permission of Atheneum Publishers(110).

Kennedy, Diana, *The Cuisines of Mexico*. Copyright © 1972 by Diana Kennedy. Published by Harper & Row, Pub-lishers, Inc., New York. Reprinted by permission of Harper & Row, Publishers, Inc.(139).

Khawam, René R., *La Cuisine Arabe*. © Éditions Albin Michel, 1970. Published by Éditions Albin Michel, Paris. Translated by permission of Éditions Albin Michel(119).

Kiehnle, Hermine and Maria Hädecke, *Das Neue Kiehnle Kochbuch*. © Walter Hädecke Verlag. Published by Walter Hädecke Verlag (D-7252 Weil der Stadt). Translat-ed by permission of Walter Hädecke Verlag(111, 121).

Kuper, Jessica (Editor), *The Anthropologists' Cookbook*. Published by Universe Books, New York, 1978. Copyright The Royal Anthropological Institute 1977. By permission of Universe Books(115 — Elaine Baldwin).

Lagattolla, Franco, *The Recipes that Made a Million*. © Franco Lagattolla 1978. Published by Orbis Publishing Limited, London. By permission of Orbis Publishing Limited(122).

Langseth-Christensen, Lillian, *How to Present and Serve Food Attractively*. Copyright © 1976 by Lillian Langseth-Christensen. Reprinted by permission of Double-day & Company, Inc.(100).

Leyel, Mrs. C. F., *Savoury Cold Meals*. Published by George Routledge and Sons, Ltd., London. By permission of Routledge and Kegan Paul Limited(147).

Leyel, Mrs. C. F. and Miss Olga Hartley, *The Gentle Art of Cookery*. © The Executors of the estate of Mrs. C. F. Leyel 1925. Published by Chatto & Windus Ltd., London. By permission of Chatto & Windus Ltd.(106, 108).

Lin, Florence, *Florence Lin's Chinese Regional Cookbook*. Copyright © 1975 by Florence Lin. Reprinted by permission of Hawthorn Books, A Division of Elsevier-Dutton Publish-ing Co., Inc.(111).

Lincoln, Mrs. Mary J., *Mrs. Lincoln's Boston Cook Book*. Published by Little, Brown and Company, Boston, 1904(162).

Lyon, Ninette, *Le Guide Marabout du Poisson*. © 1967 by Éditions Gerard & Co., Verviers (Belgique). Published by Éditions Gerard & Co., Verviers. Translated by permis-sion of Les Nouvelles Éditions Marabout S.A., Brus-sels(141, 142).

McCully, Helen (Editor), *The American Heritage Cook-book*. Copyright © 1964 by American Heritage Publishing Co., Inc. Published by American Heritage Publishing Co., Inc., New York. By permission of American Heritage Pub-lishing Co., Inc.(144).

Marin, François, *Les Dons de Comus*. Paris, 1739(109, 143).

Marton, Beryl M., *The Complete Book of Salads*. Copy-right © 1969 by Beryl M. Marton. Published by Random House, Inc., New York. Reprinted by permission of Ran-dom House, Inc.(161).

Médecin, Jacques, *La Cuisine de Comté de Nice*. Copy-right © 1972. Published by Éditions René Julliard, Paris. Translated by permission of Penguin Books Ltd., Lon-don(100, 126).

Meyers, Perla, *The Peasant Kitchen*. Copyright © 1975 by Perla Meyers. Reprinted by permission of Harper & Row, Publishers, Inc.(98, 123, 150).

Miller, Gloria Bley, *The Thousand Recipe Chinese Cook-book*. Copyright © by Gloria Bley Miller. Published by Grosset & Dunlap, Inc. Reprinted by permission of the author(97).

Miller, Jill Nhu Huong, *Vietnamese Cookery*. Copy-right in Japan, 1968, by The Charles E. Tuttle Company, Inc., Tokyo and Rutland, Vermont. First published in 1968 by The Charles E. Tuttle Company, Inc. By permission of The Charles E. Tuttle Company, Inc.(90, 99).

Mitchell, Kenneth (Editor), *The Flavour of Malaysia*. Published by Four Corners Publishing Co. (Far East) Ltd., Hong Kong. By permission of Four Corners Publishing Co. (Far East) Ltd.(128).

Neil, Marian Harris (Editor), *Favorite Recipes Cook Book*. Published by Willey Book Company, New York, 1931(161).

Norberg, Inga, *Good Food from Sweden*. First pub-lished by Chatto & Windus, London 1935. By permission of Curtis Brown Ltd., London(95, 120).

Olney, Judith, *Comforting Food*. Copyright © 1979 by Judith Olney. Used by permission of Atheneum Publishers(127).

Olney, Judith, *Summer Food*. Copyright © 1978 by Ju-dith Olney. Reprinted by permission of Atheneum Publish-ers(132, 152).

Olney, Richard, *The French Menu Cook Book*. Copyright © 1970 by Richard Olney. Published by Simon & Schuster, New York. By permission of John Schaffner, Literary Agent, New York(128).

Olney, Richard, *Simple French Food*. Copyright © 1974 by Richard Olney. Published by Atheneum Publishers, New York. By permission of Atheneum Publishers(104, 126).

Ortiz, Elisabeth Lambert, *The Complete Book of Car-ibbean Cooking*. Copyright © Elisabeth Lambert Ortiz, 1973, 1975. Published by M. Evans and Company, Inc., New York. By permission of John Farquharson Ltd., literary agents(104).

Owen, Sri, *The Home Book of Indonesian Cookery*. © Sri Owen, 1976. Published by Faber & Faber Ltd., London. By permission of Faber & Faber Ltd.(102).

Paradissis, Chrissa, *The Best Book of Greek Cookery*. Copyright © 1976 P. Efstathiadis & Sons. Published by P. Efstathiadis & Sons, Athens. By permission of P. Efstathia-dis & Sons(116, 118, 125).

Petrov, Dr. L., Dr. N. Djelepov, Dr. E. Iordanov and S. Uzunova, *Bulgarska Nazionalna Kuchniya*. Copyright © by the authors, 1978, c/o Jusautor, Sofia. Published by Zemizdat, Sofia 1978. Translated by permis-sion of Jusautor Copyright Agency, Sofia(117).

Pezzini, Wilma, *The Tuscan Cookbook*. Copyright © 1978 by Wilma Pezzini. Used by permission of Atheneum Publishers(151).

Raris, F. and T., *Les Champignons, Connaissance et Gas-tronomie*. © Librairie Larousse, 1974 pour les droits de la langue Française. Published by Librairie Larousse, Paris. Originally published by Fratelli Fabbri Editori, Milan as *I Funghi, Cercarli, Conoscerli, Cucinarli*. © 1973 Fratelli Fabbri Editori, Milano. Translated by permission of Fratelli Fabbri Editori(101).

Rayes, Georges N., *L'Art Culinaire Libanais*. Published by Librairie du Liban, Beirut(116).

Reboul, J. B., *La Cuisinière Provençale*. First published by Tacussel Éditeur, Marseilles, 1895. Translated by permis-sion of Tacussel, Éditeur(144, 149).

Recipes for Sea Food. Copyrighted, 1913, by J. H. Griffin. Privately published for the Boston Fish Market Corporation(145).

Reekie, Jennie, *Everything Raw: The No-Cooking Cookbook.* (New York: Penguin Books, 1977.) Copyright © 1977 by Jennie Reekie. Reprinted by permission of Penguin Books(131, 138, 151).

Rhode, Irma, *Cool Entertaining.* Copyright © 1976 by Irma Rhode. Reprinted by permission of Atheneum Publishers(159).

Robert, L. S., *L'Art de Bien Traiter.* Paris, 1674(138).

Romagnoli, Margaret and G. Franco, *The Romagnolis' Meatless Cookbook.* Copyright © 1976 by Margaret and G. Franco Romagnoli. Reprinted by permission of Little, Brown and Company(97).

Rorer, Mrs. S. T., *New Salads.* Published by Arnold and Company, Philadelphia 1897(107, 153).

Ross, Janet and Michael Waterfield, *Leaves from our Tuscan Kitchen.* Copyright © 1974 by Janet Ross and Michael Waterfield. Used by permission of Atheneum Publishers(97).

Saint-Ange, Madame, *La Cuisine de Madame Saint-Ange.* © Éditions Chaix. Published by Éditions Chaix, Grenoble. Translated by permission of Éditions Chaix(91).

St. Paul's Greek Orthodox Church, The Women of, *The Art of Greek Cookery.* Copyright © 1961, 1963 by St. Paul's Greek Orthodox Church, Hempstead, Long Island, New York. Reprinted by permission of Doubleday & Company, Inc.(102).

Salles, Prosper and Prosper Montagné, *La Grande Cuisine.* Published by Imp. A. Chène, Monaco, 1900(114).

Sarvis, Shirley, *Women's Day Home Cooking Around the World.* © Copyright 1978 by Fawcett Publications, Inc. Published by Simon & Schuster, a Division of Gulf & Western Corporation, New York. By permission of C.B.S. Publications, Inc., New York(92).

Schultz, Sigrid (Editor), *Overseas Press Club Cookbook.* Copyright © 1962 by Overseas Press Club of America, Inc. Published by Doubleday & Company, Inc., Garden City, New York, 1962. By permission of Doubleday & Company, Inc.(98).

Shepard, Jean H., *The Fresh Fruits and Vegetables Cookbook.* Copyright © 1975 by Jean H. Shepard. By permission of Little, Brown and Company(150, 161, 162).

Shulman, Martha Rose, *The Vegetarian Feast.* Copyright © 1979 by Martha Rose Shulman. Reprinted by permission of Harper & Row, Publishers, Inc.(164).

Sitas, Amaranth, *Kopiaste.* Published by Amaranth Sitas, Limassol, 1974. By permission of Amaranth Sitas(93).

Smith, Leona Woodring, *The Forgotten Art of Flower Cookery.* Copyright © 1973 by Leona Woodring Smith. Published by Harper & Row, Publishers, Inc., New York. Reprinted by permission of Harper & Row, Publishers, Inc.(158).

Sokolov, Raymond A., *Great Recipes from The New York Times.* Copyright © 1973 by Raymond A. Sokolov. Published by Quadrangle/The New York Times Book Company. By permission of Times Books, a Division of Quadrangle/The New York Times Book Company(132, 145).

Sonakul, Princess Sibpan, *Everyday Siamese Dishes.* Published by Pracandra Press, Bangkok, 1952. By permission of Mrs. Nivatvar Na Pombejra, for Princess Sibpan(136).

Suzanne, Alfred, and C. Herman Senn, O.B.E., F.R.H.S., *A Book of Salads.* Published by Ward, Lock and Co., Limited, London(92, 113).

Thiébault, Sylvie, *Salades et Assiettes Froides.* © Solar 1978. Published by Solar, Paris. Translated by permission of Solar(94, 114).

Thuilier, Raymond and Michel Lemonnier, *Recettes de Baumanière.* Published by Éditions Stock, Paris. Translated by permission of Éditions Stock(124, 133, 139, 146).

Toklas, Alice B., *The Alice B. Toklas Cook Book.* Copyright 1954 by Alice B. Toklas. Published by Harper & Row, Publishers, Inc., New York. By permission of Harper & Row, Publishers, Inc.(152).

Toulouse-Lautrec and Maurice Joyant, *L'Art de la Cuisine.* Copyright © 1966 by Edita Lausanne. Published by Edita S.A., Lausanne, 1966. Translated by permission of Edita S.A.(114).

Troisgros, Jean and Pierre, *The Nouvelle Cuisine of Jean & Pierre Troisgros.* English translation Copyright © 1978 by William Morrow and Company, Inc. Originally published under the title *Cuisiniers à Roanne.* Copyright 1977 by Éditions Robert Laffont, S.A. By permission of William Morrow and Company(121).

Truax, Carol, *The Art of Salad Making.* Copyright © 1968 by Carol Truax. Reprinted by permission of Doubleday & Company, Inc.(144).

Tschirky, Oscar, *Oscar of the Waldorf's Cook Book.* Copyright © 1973 by Oscar Tschirky. Reprinted by permission of Dover Publications, Inc.(103).

Uvezian, Sonia, *The Book of Salads.* Copyright © 1977 Sonia Uvezian. Published by 101 Productions, San Francisco. By permission of 101 Productions(153).

Uvezian, Sonia, *The Book of Yogurt.* Copyright © 1978 Sonia Uvezian. Published by 101 Productions, San Francisco. By permission of 101 Productions(124, 155, 160).

Vence, Céline and Robert Courtine, *The Grand Masters of French Cuisine.* Copyright © 1978 by G. P. Putnam's Sons, New York. Originally published in France as "Les Grands Maîtres de la Cuisine Française." Copyright © 1972 Éditions Bordas. Published by G. P. Putnam's Sons, New York. By permission of G. P. Putnam's Sons(130).

Volpicelli, Luigi and Secondino Freda, *L'Antiartusi.* © 1978 Pan Editrice, Milano. Published by Pan Editrice, Milan. Translated by permission of Pan Editrice(143).

White, Merry, *Cooking For Crowds.* Copyright © 1974 by Basic Books, Inc., Publishers, New York. Reprinted by permission of Basic Books, Inc.(90).

Wolfert, Paula, *Couscous and Other Good Food from Morocco.* Copyright © 1973 by Paula Wolfert. Reprinted by permission of Harper & Row, Publishers, Inc.(106, 112, 116).

Wolfert, Paula, *Mediterranean Cooking.* Copyright © 1977 by Paula Wolfert. Published by Quadrangle/The New York Times Book Co., Inc., New York. By permission of Times Books, a Division of Quadrangle/The New York Times Book Co.(163).

Woolfolk, Margaret, *Cooking With Berries.* © 1979 by Margaret Woolfolk. Used by permission of Clarkson N. Potter, Inc.(105).

Wright, Jeni, *The All Colour Cookery Book.* © Hennerwood Publications Ltd., 1977. Published by Sundial Books Limited, London. By permission of Sundial Books Limited(91).

Acknowledgments

The indexes for this book were prepared by Louise W. Hedberg. The editors are particularly indebted to Pat Alburey, Hertfordshire, England; Dr. F. William Cooler, Dr. George Flick, Charles Wood, Dept. of Food Science and Technology, Virginia Polytechnic Institute and State University, Blacksburg; Gene Cope, Seafood Research, Information and Consumer Division, Dept. of Commerce, Washington, D.C.; Elisabeth Lambert Ortiz, London; Marie Powell, Arlington, Va.; and Dr. Allan K. Stoner, Research Horticulturist, U.S. Dept. of Agriculture.

The editors also wish to thank: Richard Brassette, Louisiana Department of Wildlife and Fisheries, Baton Rouge, La.; Sarah Bunney, London; Chris Calomiris, Washington, D.C.; Cannon Seafood, Washington, D.C.; Josephine Christian, Somerset, England; Jennie Choy, New York; Claire Clifton, London; Tony Craze, London; Diane Creedon, Mary Lyons, Food and Wines from France, Inc., New York; Jennifer Davidson, London; The J. A. Demonchaux Company, Topeka, Kans.; Lindsay Duguid, London; Fiona Duncan, London; Dr. Miklos Faust, Fruit Laboratory, Agriculture Research Center, U.S. Dept. of Agriculture, Beltsville, Md.; Mrs. Max Fehr, German Deli, Washington, D.C.; Carmel Friedlander, London; Ramona-Ann Gale, Surrey, England; Fayal Greene, London; Gillian Gutman, Surrey, England; Maggie Heinz, London; Christie Horn, London; Randy Houk, Washington, D.C.; Hudson Brothers, Washington, D.C.; Marion Hunter, Surrey, England; Brenda Jayes, London; Ati Kadarmanto, Indonesian Embassy, Washington, D.C.; Rosemary Klein, London; Mary Jane Laws, United Dairy Industry Association, Rosemont, Ill.; John Leslie, London; Vivian McCorry, London; Maria Mosby, London; Michael Moulds, London; Dilys Naylor, Surrey, England; Jo Oxley, Surrey, England; Dr. Louis Rockland, Professor of Nutrition and Food Science, Chapman College, Orange, Calif.; Joanna Roberts, London; Manuel Rodríguez, José Sanchez, Ivano Greengrocers, London; Nick Sciabica & Sons, Modesto, Calif.; Michael Schwab, London; Cynthia A. Sheppard, Washington, D.C.; Adelma G. Simmons, Caprilands Herb Farm, North Coventry, Conn.; Stephanie Thompson, Surrey, England; Georges Vivier, Yzeure, France; Jane Walker, Madrid; Charles B. Wilson, Harris Seed Company, Rochester, N.Y.; Dr. R. Wooten, Dept. of Agriculture and Fisheries for Scotland, Aberdeen.

Picture Credits

Library of Congress Cataloguing in Publication Data
Time-Life Books.
    Salads.
    (The good cook, techniques and recipes)
    Includes index.
    1. Salads.   I. Title.   II. Series: Good cook, techniques and recipes.
TX740.T46 1980   641.8'3   79-27419
ISBN 0-8094-2881-4
ISBN 0-8094-2880-6 lib. bdg.
ISBN 0-8094-2879-2 retail ed.